Dear Reader:

The book you are about to read is the latest bestseller from the St. Martin's True Crime Library, the imprint the New York Times calls "the leader in true crime!" Each month, we offer you a fascinating account of the latest, most sensational crime that has captured the national attention. St. Martin's is the publisher of bestselling true crime author and crime journalist Kieran Crowley, who explores the dark, deadly links between a prominent Manhattan surgeon and the disappearance of his wife fifteen years earlier in THE SURGEON'S WIFE. Suzy Spencer's BREAKING POINT guides readers through the tortuous twists and turns in the case of Andrea Yates, the Houston mother who drowned her five young children in the family's bathtub. In Edgar Award-nominated DARK DREAMS, legendary FBI profiler Roy Hazelwood and bestselling crime author Stephen G. Michaud shine light on the inner workings of America's most violent and depraved murderers. In the book you now hold, TAKEN FROM HOME, acclaimed author Eric Francis takes a closer look at the mysterious disappearance of a mother and daughter.

St. Martin's True Crime Library gives you the stories behind the headlines. Our authors take you right to the scene of the crime and into the minds of the most notorious murderers to show you what really makes them tick. St. Martin's True Crime Library paperbacks are better than the most terrifying thriller, because it's all true! The next time you~~~~ ~~~~~ good read, make sure it'~~~~~~~~~~~~~~~~~~~~~brary logo on the spine—~

Charles E. Spicer, Jr.
Executive Editor, St. Martin's True Crime Library

**Also by Eric Francis**

*The Dartmouth Murders*

*A Wife's Revenge*

*Broken Vows*

**Available from
St. Martin's True Crime Library**

# Taken From
# HOME

*A Family, a Dark Secret,
and a Brutal Murder*

# ERIC FRANCIS

St. Martin's Paperbacks

TAKEN FROM HOME

Copyright © 2008 by Eric Francis.

Cover photo of door © Owaki-Kulla/Corbis. Cover photo of Blagg family © Mesa County Sheriff's Department.

For information address St. Martin's Press, 175 Fifth Avenue, New York, NY 10010.

ISBN: 0-312-93679-6
EAN: 978-0-312-93679-2

Printed in the United States of America

St. Martin's Paperbacks edition / July 2008

St. Martin's Paperbacks are published by St. Martin's Press, 175 Fifth Avenue, New York, NY 10010.

10  9  8  7  6  5  4  3  2  1

The material in this book derives from public records and the author's own personal interviews and visits to Grand Junction, as well as news reports from the Grand Junction *Daily Sentinel*, *Grand Junction Free Press*, *Rocky Mountain News*, *The Denver Post*, *The Greenville News*, Cox News Service, *The Oklahoman*, *The Atlanta Journal-Constitution*, *Fort Worth Star-Telegram*, *The Macon Times*, Associated Press, *People* magazine, CBS News *48 Hours*, and ABC News *Good Morning America*, among others.

"Love is caring for someone."
—Abby Blagg 1995–2001

# 1

IT had just been one of those days.

The boss was out of town, so responsibility for overseeing the entire 180-person AMETEK Dixson manufacturing plant in the Orchard Mesa district on the southern industrial fringe of Grand Junction, Colorado, had been passed along to Michael Blagg, the factory's director of operations.

Mike Blagg was the kind of capable, detail-oriented manager who would handle anything you asked him to do, so the small executive cadre at the plant didn't question whether he could cope with a few days' worth of extra duties, but at the same time there were some lingering doubts about whether Mike really had what it took in the long run to make it in the corporate world.

It seemed like an odd issue to be dogging a man who, at 38 years of age, had already been around the world, with an impressive record of accomplishments. Mike had graduated from Georgia Tech with a degree in nuclear engineering, and joined the Navy in 1985. During Desert Storm, he'd done two tours of duty as a pilot on Seahawk antisubmarine helicopters in the Persian Gulf and risen to the rank of lieutenant commander. He'd spent the last years of his naval career on the aircraft carrier U.S.S. *Kitty Hawk* as a flight deck officer, where he'd supervised over 20,000 launches and landings of multi-million-dollar military aircraft without a single incident.

Mike's decision in 1995 to leave the Navy and switch

to civilian life had come as a surprise to his comrades on the "Battle Cat," as the sailors liked to call the *Kitty Hawk*. They felt confident that he had the dedication and leadership qualities that could have eventually made him a flag officer in the fleet if he'd stayed in the military.

Leaving the Navy after a decade of service had required some soul-searching on Mike's part, but he was in his early 30s, and Jennifer, his wife of four years, was having some difficulties with her first pregnancy. Mike knew that he'd been changing, maybe even evolving, largely thanks to Jennifer, who had lured him away from his younger, hard-partying Navy days. He'd been drawn further into Jennifer's world of evangelical Christianity, with its emphasis on family values, and he knew that the skill sets he'd picked up in his fast-paced, life-and-death naval aviation career should be saleable ones in the business world.

Mike took to studying the principles of "lean manufacturing"—originally a Japanese concept pioneered at Toyota, where workers zealously sought to reduce waste and defects in order to maximize product "flow" and, of course, profits—and he worked at it with the same dedication and attention to detail that he used looking for anti-ship mines and enemy submarines in his helicopter out in the middle of the Persian Gulf at night.

When friends asked him what he did now, he would say he was a trouble-shooter, a problem-solver with "a black belt in lean manufacturing."

Yet even way out here, in his new job amongst the remote high desert plateaus on the Western Slope of the Rocky Mountains, working for a company that was making over a billion dollars a year selling gauges and instrument clusters that were installed in the dashboards of large trucks and heavy machinery all over the globe, Mike still couldn't shake the impression among some of his colleagues that his heart just wasn't in it.

For all of the business world's alleged enlightenment

about "work–life balance" and the host of other buzzword-heavy concepts whose time had supposedly come, there was still a view that Mike was really more of a family man than a company man. His last job performance rating had just been "acceptable," and it was little things that were contributing to the impression of Mike as an executive who somehow was less than committed. Little things like what he was doing on the afternoon of November 13, 2001, as he strolled out the front doors of the factory clutching his car keys before most of his line workers had even punched out.

It wasn't as if Mike was scooting out early on just any old routine day at the plant. AMETEK Dixson was in the midst of merging some of the Colorado location's operations with a newly acquired factory down in Mexico, and several pieces of the Grand Junction facility's assembly line were about to be shipped south of the border. Tractor-trailers were scheduled to pick up the equipment later in the week, and numerous items needed to be inspected, packed, and recorded in order to ensure their smooth passage through Mexican customs.

While the rest of the merger process was underway, Mike and other members of the Colorado staff were also taking a crash course in the new software system that the Mexican factory used to manage their workflow. And though he was in charge of the factory and its special projects in the midst of this particularly busy week, Mike did what he did most afternoons right after four o'clock—he grabbed his coat and headed for home.

Any number of hard-charging business people might have debated Blagg's priorities that afternoon, but on one level, Mike really didn't care. If he'd wanted to prove to other people that above all else, he was a loyal team player, he could have kept right on signing up for tours in the US Navy. Mike had long since decided that, because he arrived early and took his lunch at his desk most days, he'd earned the right to leave mid-afternoon in order to be back home in plenty of time for dinner and a reasonable evening spent with Jennifer and their 6-year-old daughter Abby.

Besides, at that moment on this particular Tuesday afternoon, Mike was actually more distracted by a nagging concern over Jennifer and Abby than anything that was going on at work.

On most days, Mike had time to squeeze in two or three phone calls to Jennifer: first as a gentle double-check to see that she and Abby had actually gotten out of bed on time, so Abby wouldn't be late to her Christian school across town; then maybe a quick hello around noon; and sometimes a brief check-in right before Mike left for the day, so Jennifer could firm up plans for the family dinner. But today had been different. Despite six or seven tries, Mike couldn't get Jennifer on the phone. He'd ended up getting the answering machine and he left messages, but still she hadn't called him back.

During the morning, Mike hadn't been overly concerned. By the time the afternoon rolled around, things at the busy plant had been sufficiently distracting that he hadn't had time to be much more than puzzled by the lack of response to his calls. But now, driving home, he had time to wonder. Mike couldn't recall a previous workday ever going by without his being able to connect with Jennifer.

As the years passed, Mike had become more and more of a worrier, and the terrorist attacks at the World Trade Center and the Pentagon just two months earlier certainly hadn't helped calm him any. The general sense of anxiety that had rippled across the United States in the wake of September 11 was still being felt—even clear out here in just about the last place Al-Qaeda would ever get around to attacking.

After 9/11, Mike had starting putting together a disaster plan for Jennifer. His job regularly required him to fly, so he thought it was the prudent thing to do. He typed up all of their emergency phone numbers, banking data, and insurance plans, and when he'd completed the fourth and final draft, he signed the document cover with the words, "I love you Jennifer. This should be all the information you need in case of a disaster."

Mike took a deep breath and decided to put all the missed calls out of his mind. Things were fine. If he hadn't been caught up in an especially hectic day at work, he would have had time to make even more calls and then he would probably have gotten through. He would be home soon enough and Jennifer would probably have some funny anecdote that would explain what had come up to detain her and Abby . . . perhaps an unplanned lunch with friends that evolved into a shopping trip downtown. Mike knew there'd be an explanation. He would just have to wait and hear it.

# 2

**MIKE'S** drive home from work each day took only eleven minutes, but his route wound right past the heart and soul of Grand Junction—where the mighty Colorado River is joined by the Gunnison, its fifth-largest tributary. The juncture of those two rivers, which Mike could see just over the edge as he crossed the Fifth Street Bridge, was *the* "grand junction" for which the town is named.

Ironically, the actual junction is one of the least grand vistas in an area that is so thoroughly surrounded by spectacular mountains, cliffs, and mesas that guidebooks quickly run out of adjectives ("majestic," "awe-inspiring," "jaw-dropping") to describe them all.

The town's name actually made more sense a century-and-a-half ago, when the early settlers referred to the upper reaches of the Colorado as "the Grand River."

In the 1800s, the river called the Colorado actually

began in Moab, Utah, where the Grand River joined with the Green River and continued westward toward the Grand Canyon. After Colorado became a state, it was noted that the river bearing its name did not run within its boundaries so in 1921, acting at the request of Colorado's governor, Congress corrected that indignity and renamed the entire length of the Grand River the Colorado as well. Overnight Grand Junction and the Grand Valley had the distinction of being named for something that no longer existed.

The mighty Colorado roars down through the Rockies confined by the breathtaking scenery of Glenwood Canyon's steep and towering pink-, orange-, salmon-, and red-tinged cliffs before twisting out from the mountains and snaking its way into a ten-mile-wide valley that it literally took millennia to carve for itself.

The Grand Valley stretches over 30 miles from the base of the Rockies downward and westward clear to the Utah border. Because of the valley's extremely arid high desert climate, it's impossible to overstate the significance of the river that created it, and which to this day allows it to support any life at all from a jackrabbit on up to the 42,000 people who live in the eleven-mile-long, nine-mile-wide oval-shaped area of the valley floor that is the city of Grand Junction.

No matter where you stand within the Grand Valley, no matter what direction you face, there is always something large and amazing looming on the horizon. The majestic peaks of the Rockies might be just a few minutes to the east, but you can't see them from Grand Junction, because rising nearly 12,000 feet up into the foreground is the world's largest flat-topped mountain—the Grand Mesa— which covers fifty square miles of western Colorado. To the north of town, the Bookcliffs rise abruptly, the regular undulating vertical channels worn down their sandstone faces giving them their name, since they resemble a library shelf full of leather-bound books. The bookend at the easternmost limit of the Bookcliffs is the distinctively dome-shaped Mount Garfield, which serves as the main landmark on Grand Junction's northeastern skyline. If you followed the Bookcliffs west as they march along the northern edge of the Grand Valley looking for their end, you would have to run clear out to Price, Utah, more than 180 miles away.

The southern boundary of Grand Junction's downtown is formed by one of the gentle curves in the Colorado River, and just beyond it, the rolling hills again begin to climb rapidly westward from the Gunnison River Valley until they reach the upthrust cliff walls of the 20-million-year-old Uncompahgre Plateau. When the light hits them, the deep pink striated cliffs glow with just a hint of red.

Mike's brief commute took him through a small corner of downtown Grand Junction that was nonetheless the historic city center, passing near the abandoned railroad station—a lonely masterpiece of Renaissance Revival architecture, where so much of the town's history had come and gone for over a century, and skirting the end of Main Street, where wide and winding pedestrian-friendly sidewalks that meandered among eccentric sculpture gardens had helped revitalize and restore hundred-year-old buildings that once supplied the boom-and-bust farming and mining economies by turning them into shops, restaurants, and sidewalk cafes.

Time and time again over the decades, Grand Junction has been forced to reinvent its very reason to exist as the main economic focus has shifted from cattle to peaches to uranium and a host of other minerals, to experiments with shale oil and natural gas drilling, and most recently to wineries and tourism.

Mike skimmed right along the edge of the downtown and turned back to the southwest across another unremarkable highway-style bridge spanning the river, this time ending up on the far side of both the Colorado and the Gunnison, headed straight up a road named Broadway into the hilly country known as the Redlands.

The Redlands were a new part of the Grand Junction scene, running along for several miles in between the Colorado and the remaining massive landmark on the Grand Junction skyline—the otherworldly rock formation of cliffs, canyons, arches, and spires known as the Colorado Monument.

In the Redlands, new homes were appearing year after year in what had once been, at best, horse country or cattle pasture. For the most part, it was an upper-middle-class area of Grand Junction, and with his executive job at one of the town's larger companies, Mike certainly fit into that bracket. He was pulling down an annual salary of $110,000, which put him in the upper echelons of a city where many of the younger guys were making $22 an hour to work on natural gas drilling rigs, and thinking they were rich.

As he drove along Broadway past all the recently added lanes, drives, courts, and cul-de-sacs branching off into dozens of small subdivisions, Mike thought that on any other day, the drive up into these hills would have been relaxing. But he still couldn't shake his sense of unease.

Mike was a minute out from home as he turned right onto 22 1/2 Road—one of the many numbered north–south roads throughout the Grand Valley that were named by their exact mileage in from the Utah border. He passed quickly by the Broadway Elementary School and its playground and then made another right downhill onto Greenbelt Drive, a short, steep but busy little connector that led to Redlands Parkway.

Halfway down Greenbelt, Mike slowed to make the turn into his cul-de-sac, Pine Terrace Court, pausing for just a moment to let his next-door neighbor Tammy Eret, a Mesa County deputy district attorney who'd driven up Greenbelt just ahead of him, go first.

Although he'd driven northward up a brief ramp to get to the T-intersection at the center of it, the short span of Pine Terrace Court actually ran east-to-west, with a circular turnaround at each end. Of the fourteen houses in the little development, Mike's was the second on the left, facing directly onto the west turnaround.

Mike was planning to stay home for the rest of the evening, so he swung his white Dodge Stratus around the circle and pulled to a stop right in front of his two-story contemporary-style house, parking on the street and facing his car toward the lone exit to Greenbelt so he'd be ready to go again early the next morning.

Hopping out of his car, Mike spotted Tammy Eret walking to her residence next door. The Blaggs hadn't really gotten to know Eret in the ten months they'd lived on Pine Terrace, but he gave her a friendly wave before turning his attention to gathering up a bag full of CDs and other Christmas presents that he'd been keeping hidden in his car. From experience he knew that in all likelihood, Jennifer would be cooking dinner by now, which meant Abby would be busy watching television, so he'd have a moment or two to stash the gifts in the hall closet before Abby heard him arrive and whirled herself clear to the front of the house to greet him.

As he turned to walk up the driveway, Mike checked the mailbox on its post out by the street. Jennifer usually remembered to collect the mail by mid-afternoon, but sometimes she forgot, and clearly this had been one of those days.

Mike scooped up the mail, strode past his garage with its fluttering American flag, and stopped again on the front porch to pick up a small package that UPS had delivered. With a turn of his key in the front door, Mike stepped inside, reflexively locking the handle and the deadbolt behind him as he primed himself for what was usually the best part of his day.

"I'm home!" Mike called out expectantly.

No one answered.

The house wasn't large, and it had the high-ceilinged, open-plan layout popular in homes in the high desert West, where keeping cool was usually more of an issue than staying warm, so Mike was immediately struck by the oppressive vacant silence.

"Jennifer? . . . Abby? . . . Peanut? . . . Where are you?" Mike called out again.

Nothing stirred.

Instinctively Mike set the mail and the gifts down on the tile floor of the foyer as he cautiously took another step deeper into his home. A wave of anxiety began to rise; within seconds he knew that things didn't look right. The living room on his right was empty, as was the kitchen in front of him, but straight back through, in the small dining nook that looked out into the tiny fenced-in back yard, the only other door that led outside was standing wide open.

Suddenly the fact that Jennifer hadn't picked up the phone all day long had gone from being a curious quirk to a source of real concern. Mike glanced to his left down a short hallway between the kitchen and the staircase to the second floor, past the laundry room, to where the door to the master bedroom was slightly ajar. Even from here he could see something was definitely amiss. There was a pile of stuff on the bedroom floor.

Mike strode swiftly into the bedroom for a closer look. Jennifer's purse had been dumped out on the dresser and most of the contents—change, keys, pill bottles—had been scattered out onto the carpet, along with her overturned jewelry box, some clothing, and a handful of other items that would normally have been on top of the dresser. Mike stepped over the pile of debris and glanced at their bed. It hadn't been made and there was something else—something far more significant—which instantly dispelled any notion that not having heard from Jennifer was just some sort of misunderstanding in an otherwise normal day.

There was blood. Lots of it. Mike had been across the Pacific and Indian Oceans on ships where, over the years, there'd been a number of serious injuries. But this was definitely the most blood he'd ever seen in his life. The covers were ripped partially back and a large red circle of blood was on the mattress up near the wall where Jennifer's pillows would normally be.

Thinking Jennifer might have rolled off and be on the floor, Mike walked around the far side of the bed, only to discover that there was even more blood over there.

The blood on the bed had dripped like paint down the side, splattered onto the nightstand, and pooled on the pink carpet, coagulating into a deep red, almost black, crust that had gotten so thick it had cracked in several places as it had dried, revealing more angry red bloodstains beneath. Mike's pillow was still over on his side of the bed, but both of Jennifer's were missing.

Mike had seen enough. For a half-second he started toward the phone on the nightstand, but the proximity to the gore repelled him, and instead he turned and ran for the kitchen.

Mike grabbed the portable phone off the counter and, hands trembling, forced himself to focus as he carefully punched in the numbers 9-1-1.

# 3

IT was 4:20 P.M. when Mike's call rang into the Grand Junction Regional Communication Center.

"911. Where's your emergency?" the female dispatcher wondered.

"Oh my God! It's in my house," Mike wailed.

"Okay. What's going on?"

"I just got home from work and there's blood all over the bed, and there's stuff all over the floor. My family's gone. My daughter and my wife aren't here."

"Okay, calm down. You're at twenty-two fifty-three Pine Terrace Court?"

"Yeah," Mike sobbed.

"Okay, hold on," the dispatcher replied as she began typing the information into her computer. "And the blood's on the bed?"

"Yes, and the back door's open," Mike replied.

"Things are messed up in your house?"

"Um, just in the master bedroom, it looks like . . ."

"How old is your wife?"

"She's thirty-four. She'll be thirty-five this January."

"And how old is your child?"

"Six. Oh God . . ."

"Is your wife's car out front? . . . Mike?"

"Let me look at the garage," Mike replied as his voice began to crack from emotion.

"Yes, in the garage," he croaked out.

"Is your wife's purse or anything there? Does it look like she had time to grab her purse?" the dispatcher asked.

"It's all spread out on the floor."

"Her purse?" the dispatcher clarified.

"Yes."

"Okay, hold on . . ." Mike could hear the dispatcher typing on her computer terminal. "Have you touched anything, Mike?"

"The front door. I came through the front door, and now I touched the garage door to look into the garage."

"And the phone, correct?"

"Uh, yes," Mike agreed.

"Okay, don't touch anything else, okay? Can you tell me about the blood? What does it look like? Does it look

like somebody laid there and bled? Does it look like it
was splattered?"

"Um ... Oh ... Her pillows are gone ... Um ..."
Mike answered distractedly.

"Her pillows?"

"Yeah, she sleeps with two pillows, and they're gone,
and there's a big, big pool of blood about where they
would be, and then it's dripped all down the side of the
bed onto the floor . . ." Mike's voice trailed away as he described it.

"Okay, hold on. So the blood's dripping off the bed
onto the floor?"

"Yes," Mike choked out in a grief-stricken voice.

"Okay, Mike, do you have a cordless phone?"

"Yes."

"Can I get you to go outside and talk to me, please?"

"Yes."

"Okay, let me know when you are outside."

"Okay."

"Okay, you're outside?" the dispatcher clarified.

"Yes," Mike affirmed.

"Okay, what I want you do, Mike, can you sit on your
stairs? Do you have a porch or something you can sit on?"

"I'm on the back porch."

"I want you to sit down and I want you to breathe real
deep and real slow for just a minute, okay?"

Mike took a series of deep breaths that rattled down
the phone line.

"Okay, Mike, how old are you?"

"Thirty-eight."

"Have you and your wife been having problems?"

"No," Mike whispered.

"No?" the dispatcher clarified.

"No."

"Okay, and when was the last time you talked to your
wife?"

"Last night before we went to bed."

"And everything was okay?"

"Yes," Mike replied with a distraught croak.

"Does your daughter go to school?"

"Yes. She goes to the Bookcliff Christian School."

"Did she go to school today?"

"Nobody's called. I don't know," Mike sniffled.

"When did you leave this morning?"

"I always leave at six o'clock in the morning. I'm going back inside. I'm going to go up and look in my daughter's room."

"You are going to go look in the daughter's room?"

"Yes," Mike insisted.

"Okay, you need to tell me what you are seeing."

The stairway leading up to the smaller second floor was directly between the front door and the master bedroom, so it only took Mike a few moments to reach it. The door to Abby's little bedroom was closed and Mike hesitated as he reached for the doorknob, afraid he might mess up any fingerprints that could have been left by an intruder.

"I pushed open the door without touching anything, turned on the light switch, her school clothes are still laid out waiting for her. Her bed is messed up," Mike began to narrate as he took a look around.

"Her bed is messed up as if she slept in it?" the dispatcher asked.

The covers had been pulled about two-thirds of the way down, and Abby's favorite baby doll, Claire, was sitting on the pillow. But Mike was more interested in what he wasn't seeing.

"The covers are pulled all back and . . . and . . . There's no blood though," Mike noted.

"And her school clothes are still laid out, so she never put them on?"

"No, she never put them on," Mike confirmed, adding,

"Her fan is still on too, so she didn't turn off her fan this morning."

"So she never got dressed?"

"No," Mike said.

"Okay, Mike, I need you to go back outside, okay?"

"Okay, do you want me to go in the front or the back?"

"Let's go out back, that way we are not going to cause a scene. Okay, let me know when you are back outside."

"Okay, I'm back outside," Mike announced. "I'm sitting on my porch again. I'm sitting down on the step again."

"Okay, take some deep breaths and let them out real slow. I don't want you to go into shock or anything. Mike, do you want me to send an ambulance to check you out?"

"I don't know. I don't know what to do," Mike sighed.

"Okay, we have officers en route, and I'm going to keep you on the phone until they get there, okay?"

"Okay," Mike replied, starting to rack with sobs.

"Okay, Mike, let's take some deep breaths and let 'em out real slow.

"Okay?" the dispatcher wondered when she didn't get a reply.

"Okay," Mike whispered back.

"Mike, just continue breathing for me, okay?"

"Okay."

"And as soon as we get some deputies there, hopefully we can piece all this together."

"Okay, I can't see the front from where I am."

"That's okay. They know that you're sitting in the back. Can they walk around the side of your house to where you're at?"

"Yes."

"Okay, keep breathing for me, okay? Okay, you're doing good, Mike. Okay, I know it's really hard, and not knowing is really hard, but you are really doing a good job . . ."

"Where can they be?" Mike, his voice now a distraught howl, cut her off.

"Mike, I don't know. And you said you and your wife were getting along . . ."

"Yes."

"And everything was okay?"

"Yes."

"And when you left this morning, was she up?"

"No. She stays asleep until six-thirty. Both Abby and Jennifer get up at six-thirty."

"And she usually gets up at six-thirty and gets your daughter up?"

"Yes."

"Where do you work?"

"AMETEK Dixson in Orchard Mesa."

"Okay, and your wife is a stay-at-home mom?"

"Yes, she usually helps at school."

"She works at the school?" the dispatcher repeated.

"She doesn't work," Mike clarified, "she volunteers."

"Okay. So you don't know if she went. Is there anybody that can be called to see if your daughter or wife went to work or showed up at the school?"

"Dianna Shirley. Jennifer and Dianna are best friends, and they usually work together at the school."

"Okay, we'll call her."

"Okay."

"You're doing real good, Mike. Come on, let's keep breathing. Just breathe deep and breathe slow, okay?"

"Ohhh," Mike cried out.

"Mike, when you were looking around the house, did you notice anything else missing?"

"I only went in the master bedroom and upstairs."

"You have an upstairs home then?"

"Yes. It's two-story."

"And you said you were in the garage and the car is still there?"

"Yes."

"So you didn't look in any of the other rooms?"

"No."

"That's fine. We'll let the deputies do that, okay?"

"Okay," Mike agreed.

"Do you have weapons in the house?"

"Yes. There's a pistol in our closet."

"So it's in the master bedroom?"

"Yes."

"Does your wife know where it's at?" the dispatcher wanted to know.

"Yes, she does. We don't keep it loaded, though."

"Okay, we're just letting all the officers know this that's en route, okay?"

"Okay," Mike's voice choked again as he replied.

"Come on, let's breathe again," the dispatcher urged. "Just breathe deep and breathe slow. We want to kind of maintain control here. You're doing good. That's good, Mike. And, Mike, just to confirm, your last name is *Blagg*?"

Mike corroborated that it was.

"Have you had any problems in your neighborhood?"

"No, we're in a very calm neighborhood. It's mostly older couples that live here," Mike explained.

"Okay, just continue breathing for me."

"What's your name?" Mike wondered, asking a question himself for the first time in the conversation.

"My name is Vickie."

"Thank you, Vickie," Mike sniffled.

"You're welcome. That's what I'm here for, is to help you," Vickie replied, adding quickly, "Let's continue breathing, okay? And I'll let you know when they get there, so you won't be startled. What's your wife's first name?"

"Jennifer."

"And what's your daughter's name?"

"Abby."

"And Abby's in what grade?"

"The first grade."

"Okay, the other dispatcher is going to call so we can find out about school, but just keep breathing for me, all right?"

"She's in Miss Fausnaught's class."

"Okay, he's calling for me, that way I can keep you on the phone."

"Thank you."

"You're welcome.

"Come on, you're doing a real good job, Mike, and I know it's really, really hard," Vickie urged. "Okay, let's just keep breathing, Mike, until they get there."

Mike could be heard trying to take steady breaths.

"You didn't call and talk to your wife any time during the day?" Vickie wondered.

"I tried about four times and never got through."

"Oh, so the phone just rang?"

"Nah, we've got an answering machine."

"Oh, so did you leave messages?"

"Yes, I tried her on her cell phone and I tried her at home."

"And she does have a cell phone? Did you notice if that was missing?"

"No. Do you want me to go in and look?"

"No, let's just stay outside until they get there, okay? We don't want to . . ."

"It would be in the master bedroom, but I don't want to go back in there."

"Okay, Mike, can you take your phone and . . . Let's walk to the front yard and sit on your front porch there."

"Okay."

"Let me know when you are out front, okay?"

"Okay, I'm going through the side yard now."

"Do you have any dogs or anything?"

"No," Mike said. "Okay, I'm in the front yard."

"Okay, and you are sitting on your front step?"

"No, I'm still walking through the grass."

"Okay, Mike, continue breathing for me."

"Okay, I'm here," Mike announced.

"Okay, sit down, the deputy must be getting terribly close.

"Does your wife have any medical problems?"

"Yes, she's got . . . She's got a, um . . . Oh, give me a second to think . . . She's got a mitral valve prolapse. She's got . . ."

"What does that mean?"

"It's similar to a heart murmur," Mike explained. "She's got a vulvar vestibulitis, which is a chronic problem with the vestibular glands down in her genitals, she had a gall bladder removed, she had her female organs removed, she's had so many problems . . ." Mike's voice trailed away in tears.

"Okay, so she does have problems . . ." Vickie began before being cut off by Mike's sobbing.

"Okay, come on, Mike, let's take some deep breaths, okay?"

In a garbled wail, Mike tried to explain about his anniversary.

"Huh?"

Mike tried to bring his crying under control as he barely managed to say, "Friday is our tenth anniversary."

"Today's your anniversary?"

"Friday is."

"Oh, Friday will be?" Vickie clarified.

"Yes," Mike replied.

"How many years?"

"Ten."

"Ten?" Vickie repeated.

"Ten," Mike echoed in a plaintive wail.

"Have you lived in Grand Junction the entire time?"

"No. We've moved around. I've been in the Navy," Mike began to explain as sirens could be heard getting louder in the background. "I've been in AlliedSignal and now I'm in AMETEK . . ."

"Okay. Let me know who that is that's showing up. I think that might be the ambulance."

Mike had been on the phone for sixteen minutes when Mesa County Sheriff's Deputies Tim Orr and Jeff Doty pulled up to the scene, radioing back that they were parking next to the white 1998 Dodge Stratus that was out in front.

From the outside, the pale yellow house with the light gray trim couldn't have looked calmer. A large pumpkin left over from Halloween was in the side yard, a child's swing set was visible in the back. But getting up from the front porch and walking toward the arriving cruisers was a very worried-looking Michael Blagg.

"How are you doing, sir?" a deputy asked.

"Not so well," Blagg replied, holding out his house keys.

Orr and Doty went in, doing a quick counter-clockwise sweep through the first floor to check for victims before Doty brought Sergeant John Coleman, who had just arrived, back inside for another quick look at the bedroom and especially the blood. Then everyone cleared the residence, called Investigations, and strung up crime-scene tape while they waited outside for the forensic technicians to arrive and begin what was obviously going to be a painstaking examination of the entire property.

Police officers can end up in the presence of blood just about as often as EMTs can, and both Coleman, who'd investigated nearly forty suicides over the years, and Doty, who'd been a member of a search-and-rescue team, had seen a lot of it, so they had a good sense of what even large amounts of blood would look like as time passed. What they saw in the Blagg residence did not look extremely fresh. Just by eyeballing the thickest, partially dried puddle on the floor, the officers were able to estimate that it had been there at least three to five hours, but less than twenty-four hours.

# 4

**SHERIFF'S** Investigator George Barley was off duty and heading downtown to his favorite barber shop when the dispatchers began sending cruisers and EMTs over the river to the Redlands. As Barley listened on his police radio, the reports of blood in the home and a missing mother and daughter were updated, but by the time he parked in front of "Your Hair," the deputies still hadn't put out a call for detectives.

Known to his friends on the department as "Big Daddy," at 51, Barley was an affable bear of a detective who'd grown up in Eastern Tennessee before spending twenty-eight years in law enforcement out in Colorado. He loved the vast terrain where he could lose himself in his off hours doing as much hunting and fishing as possible. Shy and self-effacing almost to a fault, Barley practically hid from things like publicity and press conferences, but over the years he had taken on some of Mesa County's most difficult cases and sawed patiently away at clues like a gem grinder, willing to put in whatever amount of effort and time it took to produce a result.

Despite a job which could wake him at any hour and force him to sift through the motives and possessions of the very worst of people, Barley loved the ordinary routines of normal life, and his every-other-week buzz cuts were a ritual he'd looked forward to and carried out faithfully for twenty-one years. But even as he reached the door of the shop, he hesitated, unable to shake the thought that kept rolling through his head: "This doesn't sound good." With a sigh, Barley turned and walked back to his car. As he switched on his emergency strobes, he just knew he was going to be working right through the night.

Steve King was another of the sheriff's investigators who'd decided to skip the formalities and step on the gas pedal after hearing the radio traffic. King, a black belt in karate, who often trained new officers on the finer points of police work, possessed easily the most telegenic hair in the department, and as a result, the other detectives often pushed him to the front whenever cameras began hovering around crime scenes. But in the twenty years he'd been with the sheriff's office, ever since coming down from Michigan to attend college in Grand Junction and, like Barley, falling in love with the region, it wasn't his good looks and Western-style mustache that had moved him up the ranks—rather it was his ability to sense what was really going on under the surface. Echoing Barley, his gut feeling on the ride out to the Blagg residence was, "This isn't good."

King kept thinking it was pretty unusual to get a call about blood all over a bedroom at 4 o'clock in the afternoon. It was the kind of call he would've expected to get paged out of bed for at 2 or 3 in the morning.

King was struck by the location as well. He thought of the Redlands as squarely in the top 25 percent of Grand Junction's neighborhoods, and the dispatchers were saying this was happening to a businessman with a wife and small child, not the kind of people who were usually mixed up in violent situations.

Barley at last pulled into the cul-de-sac, which was rapidly filling up with police vehicles, and went to speak with the patrolmen who had secured the house. Michael Blagg was sitting in an ambulance while EMTs tried to keep him breathing calmly. Barley, who would have been just as happy sitting unnoticed with his wife of twenty-seven years and their friends in the corner of a Cracker Barrel restaurant, nonetheless began to show why the county had hired him to do exactly this kind of thing. Within moments of being briefed on what little was known, he began dictating a schedule for the staff of the sheriff's department. He turned to King, who had just rolled up to the scene, and told him he wanted Mike taken to the sheriff's office and interviewed as soon as possible. He also needed search warrants and serologists and evidence technicians, and a lot more cops to knock on area doors, and several dozen phone calls made quickly.

As Barley swung into gear as lead investigator, methodically starting the large operation into motion, it occurred to him that the incident unfolding on Pine Terrace Court had the makings of a serious case, and that it needed to be treated as a potential homicide. This was going to be taking up his time for the next few days . . . or years.

As more investigators began arriving at the scene, Barley had both of Mesa County's coroners, Dr. Robert Kurtzman and Dr. Dean Havlik, called in to take a look at the blood in the bedroom. Because there was no body, it was unclear who had been bleeding. Jennifer jumped to mind because it was her bed, but that didn't necessarily mean anything. The blood could also belong to Abby or some unknown third person. The forensic pathologists' opinions were that the volume of blood on the bed was so substantial that it indicated whatever type of injury that had taken place there was sufficient to cause serious bodily injury or death to a small 6-year-old girl or even to an adult if it was left untreated.

Barley was racking his brain trying to figure out what he was looking at. Was this an attack by a stranger or by somebody who knew the Blaggs? Who had actually done the bleeding and where were they now? It was the wife's side of the bed, but if she had been assaulted, why, then, would the young daughter be missing too? Barley was leaning to-

ward the theory that she had snapped, killed her child while
her husband was at work, and then taken off, probably with
the intent of killing herself, perhaps throwing her daughter
in the river and then jumping in herself. Her mini-van was
still in the garage, but this part of the Redlands was riddled
with bike trails and hiking paths that worked back and forth
from the Colorado River and on out into the surrounding
hills.

Meth use around Grand Junction, like much of the rest
of the West, was an extreme problem, and meth users were
known to rob, steal, and burglarize property all the time in
order to come up with money to buy their drugs. But if
that's what the open door and the missing jewelry were all
about, then Barley couldn't figure out why they had removed Jennifer and Abby from the house and yet hadn't
bothered to grab the other money that Barley had seen lying in plain sight around the bedroom. There was also the
question of how they'd come and gone. The back of the
property that abutted Greenbelt Drive was walled off by a
wooden palisade fence, and there were plenty of neighbors
close by who might have seen strangers dragging a woman
and her child out to a waiting car.

Barley knew that with anything this weird, there was
also another possibility, which was that the husband had
committed the crime. Mike was still sitting out in front of
his house collecting himself in the ambulance with Ray
Shirley, who was both his minister and best friend.

King climbed in the back and introduced himself and
asked Mike to come downtown to the sheriff's office to
help figure out what had just happened.

As King drove out of the cul-de-sac, followed a moment later by Ray Shirley, who'd agreed to drive Mike
downtown in his Jeep Cherokee, Sergeant Wayne Weyler
was busy calling both St. Mary's Hospital and Community
Hospital. When Weyler confirmed that neither facility had
treated anyone matching Jennifer or Abby's description,

Sheriff's Investigator Scott Ehlers began typing up a
search warrant for 2253 Pine Terrace Court to be expe-
dited over to a judge for a signature.

He listed the probable crimes being investigated as
second-degree assault and second-degree kidnapping.

# 5

AT 5:15 P.M., Mesa County Sheriff's Investigator Steve
King showed Mike into the tiny interview room.

"Go ahead and take a seat. Water?" King offered.

Mike shook his head, pulling his chair up to the round
wooden table and glancing around at the empty white
cement-block room with its drab acoustic-tile ceiling
and brown carpet. The only distinguishing feature was
the poster-sized observation window on the wall that re-
flected Mike's drawn features back at him.

"Appreciate you taking the time to come down and
talk to me. I know there's a lot going on," King sympa-
thized. "I need to get some real basic information from
you. For example, how do you spell your last name?"

Mike took a deep breath and began, "Blagg. B, like
*boy*, L-A-G-G." The interview would stretch well into the
night.

Addresses and phone numbers followed in quick suc-
cession as King made notes.

"And where do you work at?" King asked.

"AMETEK Dixson in Orchard Mesa."

"What is AMETEK Dixson? A paper company?"

"We make gauges for trucks, tractors . . ."

King shifted into what he hoped would come off as a
casual aside. "Oh, um, Michael . . ." he began, doing his
best to be breezy and reassuring, "if at any point you get
tired or don't want to talk, I mean, that door's not locked,
just shut so we've got some privacy. You can leave at any

time you want. You can go talk to the pastor anytime you want. I don't want you to think in any way that I'm trying to keep you here. That's not it at all. I'm just trying to get some information about this—get a handle . . ."

Mike nodded and motioned for King to continue.

"Well, I appreciate that. You know sometimes when you shut the door and you're talking to an investigator, you know . . . I don't want you to think you are under arrest or anything like that. You're not, and you can leave anytime you want, and if you need more water or coffee or anything else, just let me know. Um, I need to get a little bit of background in reference to your family. How many people are in your family?"

"Me, Jennifer, and Abby," Mike replied.

"And where does Jennifer work?"

"She's a stay-at-home mom. But she does sometimes volunteer at Bookcliff Christian School, where Abby goes."

"Oh. Okay. So what grade is Abby in?"

"First."

"First grade? How long have you and Jennifer been married?"

"Friday will be our tenth anniversary."

"Friday will be your tenth. Any other relatives that live here in town?"

"No." Mike related that his mother lived in Georgia, and Jennifer's mother and step-father were down near Dallas.

"So tell me about your day, Michael, how did that go?"

"I get up at five-thirty . . . and get dressed, um . . ."

"Is that what time you got up this morning?"

"Um-hmm," Mike nodded in agreement.

"Five-thirty? And who was there? Who was in the house when you got up?" King enquired.

"Jennifer and Abby. They both sleep in until six-thirty."

"And does Abby sleep with you guys, or does she have her own room?"

"She's got her own room upstairs," Mike replied. "The master bedroom's downstairs, and uh, I get up at five-thirty. And we have a downstairs bath that's kind of the guest bath. And the night before, I put all my clothes in there, so when I get up, I close the door to the master bedroom and go to change so I don't disturb Jennifer when I'm getting dressed."

"Okay," King said.

"Then at six o'clock I go upstairs and close Abby's door, 'cause she usually sleeps with it open. Then I get dressed and have a little breakfast sometimes, and sometimes not, and . . ."

"I'm sorry," King interrupted. "This morning—when you closed Abby's door—was she in bed?"

"Um-hmm," Michael affirmed.

"Okay, and Jennifer was sleeping when you went into the bathroom to put on your clothes and get ready for work?"

"Everything was normal."

"Okay."

"As far as I could tell," Mike added.

"All right. And you said that you got something to eat, or usually, or didn't today, or . . . ?"

"This morning I just took my . . . I take Sudafed and some other vitamins and stuff."

"Okay. So you left at six o'clock?" King prompted.

"I put the flag out at six and I go out and close the door. Lock it up. I've got the white Stratus that you probably saw parked out front. I just went in to work. Had a normal day at work. I call Jennifer at seven o'clock each morning just to see . . . make sure, number one, that they are awake . . . if they woke up. And then that everything's okay and they're getting ready for school."

"So did you do that today? You called Jennifer and . . ."

"No answer. I got the answering machine, which happens sometimes, not often, but sometimes if Jennifer's in the bathroom or something, she'll let the answering machine get it."

"And did you leave a message?" King asked.

"I always leave a message."

"Do you remember what the message was that you left?"

"Uh, 'Good morning, uh, hope you guys had a great night. I hope your day goes well at school'—because sometimes Abby will be listening on the extension."

"Okay, good, so seven o'clock, you call and nobody picks up. You get the answering machine . . ." King motioned for Mike to continue.

"I called right back about five minutes later because at AMETEK we're in the process of the open enrollment for the health care for next year, and I forgot to ask Jennifer last night if she wanted the same coverage we had for this year. I told her that unless I hear from her, I'm just gonna sign us up for the same stuff."

"Okay. So you called back at seven-o-five?"

Michael nodded. "I got the answering machine again."

"Okay, okay, and did you leave a message that time too?"

"Um-hmm. I told her unless she called back, I'm just gonna sign us up for the same stuff we had. She didn't."

"Okay, um, okay," King acknowledged, nodding for Mike to go on.

"Then just normal work stuff. I'm the director of operations. I gotta make sure manufacturing goes like it's supposed to right now. Our general manager is out of town, so basically I'm in charge of the plant for right now. Sometime later in the morning, I don't know what time, I think it was ten-ish . . . in that ballpark . . . I called back, 'cause usually she's finished with whatever volunteering she would have done by that point. I just said, 'Hey, when you get a chance, give me a call,' you know? Then I called again around lunch time. At this time, I said, 'I'm getting a little concerned. Haven't heard from you. . . .' I called her on her cell phone about that time. She doesn't like for me to leave messages on her cell phone."

"When did you call her on her cell?" King asked.

"Uh, I think it was right around lunch time. I called her back on the home phone and said, 'I'm getting a little concerned. I haven't heard from you.' 'Cause we talk two or three times a day on the phone."

"Right." King nodded.

"And, uh, and I said, you know, 'Haven't heard from you, so I'm gonna go ahead and call you on your cell phone,' which I did. She doesn't like for me to leave messages on her cell phone, but I left one this time anyway, because I was concerned. Uh, I said, 'Please call me as soon as you get a chance.' "

"You called her on her cell phone around noon, and then what happened?" King prompted.

"Then things started getting busy at work again, so I didn't get a chance to call her again until sometime around three something. At this point, having not heard from her, I was pretty concerned. Because, again, I . . . we never go all day without talking on the phone. I told her I was gonna be normal time coming home, 'cause she's always interested in that. Helps her with her planning dinner."

"Okay, so you said that at the three o'clock call, you said that, you know . . ." King started.

Mike reiterated the gist of the message: " 'I'm really concerned now. I haven't heard from you all day. Things are going pretty well here. Just want to let you know I'll be home at the normal time.' "

"And that you were gonna help with dinner?" King suggested.

"Well, usually just letting her know that I'm gonna be home at the normal time for her to time dinner," Mike explained.

As the minutes wore on, Mike sat in the chair and matter-of-factly went through a detailed account of his return home to find the blood in the bedroom and the call to 911. King was especially interested in everything that Mike had touched along the way, because the crime-scene technicians sweeping through the house would eventually need to account for every stray fingerprint.

"So tell me about your wife Jennifer," King urged.

"She's the most energetic, enthusiastic, wonderful woman you could ever want to meet," Mike began. "She's a good Christian, warm, loving woman. She's about five-foot-four, blonde hair . . . semi-blonde hair. She's letting it grow out. It was short, but it's now probably just a bit over shoulder-length. She's got brown eyes . . . just . . . just cute as can be. Never have I seen her not make friends with people. Everybody that she talks to is instantly a friend of hers. She could talk to anybody . . . She could talk to a wall and have the wall laughing in ten minutes after she started talking to it."

"You said 'Christian woman,' " King noted. "Actively involved in her church and . . ."

"We have two things going on right now . . . at Monument Baptist Church . . . That's our home church . . . The Lord led us to do prayer ministries, and so we were led to a church called New Hope Fellowship and we initiated a prayer ministry there. So we've got a prayer team built at New Hope, and we're working with Ray and Dianna Shirley at Monument. . . ."

"So I take it she knows quite a few people between your home church and what's going on," King said, adding, "You mentioned prayer teams. Is she actively involved in that also?"

"Yeah. The two of us initiated the prayer team, and there's about seven people on the core team, and there's twelve or fourteen on the whole . . ."

King steered the conversation back to the house. "Um, what time did the two of you go to bed last night?"

"Ten. Around ten," Mike recalled.

"Do you remember what time Abby went to bed?"

"She goes to bed at seven o'clock every night," Mike explained. "Usually falls asleep within half an hour."

"Before you guys went to bed, was it a fairly normal night last night?" King wondered.

"We watched the football game and . . ."

"Did you watch the football game at home or someplace else?" King interrupted.

"No," Mike assured him. "At home."

"At home," King echoed. "Okay, was there anybody else in the house?"

"No. Just the three of us," Mike said flatly.

"Okay, you said that Abby went to bed around seven. And you and your wife went to bed around ten. When you got up this morning and went out to your vehicle, where was it parked at?" King asked.

"At the same place that I always park it, right off of the driveway. Just off the right-hand side of the driveway."

"How long have you lived in Grand Junction?" King asked.

"We moved out here April of 2000, and we lived on the other side of town."

"Okay, you moved here for what reason?"

"Job change," Mike answered succinctly.

"Job change? And where did you move here from?"

"Greenville, South Carolina. Simpsonville, actually. A little suburb of Greenville," Mike clarified. "I was with AlliedSignal as an engineer. They moved us around quite a bit."

"How about Jennifer? Has she said anything to you about any problems that she'd had?" King fished.

"She had a sore throat the last couple of days, but that kind of stuff comes and goes," Mike said noncommittally.

"So, how would you characterize your marriage right now?"

"Very strong. We've got a wonderful marriage," Mike said.

"Um, what would you say would be the biggest plus in your marriage right now?"

"That we both love the Lord with all our hearts," Mike replied without hesitation.

"And what would you say is the biggest hurdle or the biggest challenge that the two of you are facing right now?"

"We both have pride issues that we, you know, we . . . We love each other so much that sometimes we let that get in the way of, you know, prayer time or social events," Mike tried to explain. "We're . . . more often than not, homebodies, because we prefer to stay . . . stay together. I'm an introvert. She's an extrovert. I mean, there's . . . there's several things there, I guess, that are differences, or things that could cause outside issues. But, nothing, . . . I mean, we've got a strong marriage. It's wonderful."

"Okay. Who would you say is Jennifer's best friend?"

"Probably Dianna Shirley. Ray's—my pastor's—wife."

"When do you think she talked to Dianna last? Any idea?"

"Yesterday at school," Mike was certain.

"Okay, did the pastor say anything to you about whether your wife had called his house at all today or anytime?"

"I didn't ask him."

"Okay, all right, what are Jennifer's parents' names?"

"Marilyn Conway. Her father's deceased, but Marilyn's remarried to Harold. They've been remarried for a long time. They live in Haltom City, Texas, a suburb of the Dallas–Fort Worth area."

"Okay, and your folks?" King continued.

"My dad passed away about five years ago. My mom

still lives in Warner Robins, Georgia. Her name is Elizabeth Blagg."

"If Jennifer had a problem that she couldn't come to you with, who would she turn to?"

"Her mom. Without a doubt," Mike said.

"How has Jennifer's health been?" King probed.

"In general she's pretty healthy," Mike answered. "She's been healthier here in Colorado than probably any other place that we've lived. She's had occasional allergy problems, like when a strong front comes through or something, she'll have some symptoms. She'll take some Allegra or something like that. She has had her female organs removed, so she does estrogen replacement therapy. In the past, she's had thyroid problems, so she's on Synthroid. She does have mitral valve prolapse, which is kind of a fluttering of your heart muscle sometimes, which we have to keep an eye on periodically."

King asked about Jennifer's hysterectomy and wondered if, up until that point, the couple had been planning to have more children.

"No, no," Mike said, without hesitation. "She had a few complications with Abby when we had Abby, and we prayed extensively about that, and we believe the Lord led us to not have any more children. I had a vasectomy about six months after Abby was born, and so we weren't planning any more children."

"Okay, so before you left from work to go home, when was the last time that you called home? Let's go through that," King prompted.

"I think it was in the three o'clock time frame. Three to three-fifteen, somewhere in there. I had called her and said, you know, 'I'm getting pretty concerned now. I haven't heard from you all day. I hope everything's okay. Please give me a call. I'm expecting to be home at the normal time'—which is between four-fifteen and four-thirty, typically."

King was curious why Mike would place so many calls each day.

"I call almost every morning at seven o'clock for two reasons," Mike explained. "One of 'em was, I want to say 'Hi,' see how things are going, but also I want to make sure they woke up at six-thirty and that they're moving toward being ready for school, 'cause Abby's got to be at school at eight-fifteen. Eight-fifteen A.M. to three-fifteen P.M."

"When your wife does the work at the school, does she work in Abby's class?"

"Yeah, she typically would be in there grading papers or picking up work books, and Ms. Fausnaught, the teacher, will sometimes have Dianna and Jennifer work pretty close together. She's—they're best friends—pull out, like, to-morrow's assignments, you know, so that . . . for twenty kids, that's a little bit of work to be able to do that. So they'll do that, and it's typically a couple hours that she'll be working now, getting stuff done on Tuesdays and Thursdays. On Mondays, Wednesdays, and Fridays she goes to Jazzercise with Dianna in the morning."

"Tuesday and Thursday she goes to school, right?"

"Right," Mike confirmed. "Tuesdays is chapel, so more often than not, she'll be there. There's a prayer group that meets in a room and prays during the chapel services in the morning, so that's why I thought ten o'clock would be a fairly safe time to call on Tuesdays, because she's usually home by that time. Chapel is at nine. They pray for about forty-five minutes. It's about a fifteen-minute drive coming home."

"If Abby wouldn't have shown up for school, would the school have called you?" King wanted to know.

"I would have thought so. They should," Mike said.

"Would that be normal?" King asked.

"She's had perfect attendance, so . . ." Mike had to think.

"So it would be pretty normal if Abby didn't show up

for school and they couldn't get ahold of your wife, that they would call you at work," King concluded. "Have you ever had that happen before?"

"No." Mike thought for a second and then added, "But that's a question I'm gonna ask them when I get the opportunity! Why didn't I get a phone call?"

"Unless, of course, Abby was at school," King noted.

"Well, Ray said that he talked to Dianna, who was at school today, and she said Abby wasn't there, so . . ." Mike trailed off.

"When did he tell you that?" King asked. "When you guys were . . ."

"Yeah, at my house when I was sitting in the Cherokee," Mike interjected.

"Okay."

"That was one of the sheriff's deputies' questions— Was Abby at school?" Mike continued, adding, "And Ray called Dianna to find out, and she said, 'No,' that Abby wasn't there."

"Right," King interjected. "Would Jennifer ever just leave?"

"I can't think of any time or any reason she would do that. No, I don't think she would, no," Mike concluded.

"Has there ever been, in the ten years you've been married, anything else that would be anything like that— surprise-wise—in the last ten years, that she has done?" King pressed.

"No. Nothing like that. No," Mike was certain. "And I'm not here to tell you that we have a perfect marriage, I mean, we go through the normal ups and downs of any marriage."

"Sure. Sure," King nodded that he understood.

"But," Mike added, "we've never had anything that would be really bad or serious."

"If—and understand, I'm just talking out loud and just trying to get a feel for things that might be able to help me help you—if she were to leave, could she, financially?" King queried. "I mean, does she have her own checking account or does she have her own access to money? If she wanted to just say, 'I'm leaving' . . ."

"We have a joint checking account, and we have a credit card that's got a pretty high limit on it," Mike acknowledged.

"So she would have the ability to do that if she wanted to?"

"Yeah, but . . ." Mike trailed off.

"How about Abby? How's Abby's health?" King inquired.

"She's healthy as a horse," Mike said, perking up ever so slightly at the chance to talk about his daughter. "She is just the most dynamic, energetic, fun-loving little girl you could ever hope to be around. She's got more energy than the sun. She's almost never sick. Occasionally she'll have allergy-type symptoms also, if we let her play outside. She is allergic to grass. So if you let her roll around in the grass to play and stuff like that, we have some albuterol inhaler that we give her sometimes, but other than that, she is just a tank."

"When you got up this morning and went into the bathroom to put on your clothes and stuff like that, did you talk to Jennifer at all?" King asked.

"No. She was sleeping," Mike replied.

"How do you know she was sleeping?"

"I could hear her breathing. She's got this . . ." Mike paused.

"Does she snore?"

"Not a snore, but it's kind of a heavy breathing sound."

"Good. Okay," King said.

"Technically, I guess, it's a snore, but . . ."

"So you went up and shut Abby's door. Why did you shut Abby's door?" King asked.

"Because as the sun starts coming up, the light starts coming in," Mike explained. "We like her to sleep in until six-thirty, and so we close her door. Also, I've got an electric razor, and I make a little noise when I'm downstairs getting ready and stuff. I got an electric razor and sometimes that can wake her up. So we let her sleep with the door open. We got a little mouse or something that we prop the door open with. I just push that out of the way and the door closes pretty much on its own. It's not latched. I just let it close until you can't really see any light through it."

"So does Abby wake your wife up or does your wife wake Abby up, or does your seven o'clock phone call wake 'em both up?" King asked.

"Actually they both have alarms and they are both set to six-thirty, so they both get up about the same time," Mike said. "Abby wakes up singing every morning. She sings as she's getting dressed and making her bed and everything, then she comes downstairs. By that time, Jennifer's gotten up, she's made the bed, typically, and is most of the way dressed at that point. Then she usually turns on the TV and lets Abby watch a little TV while she finishes getting ready, and that's usually the seven o'clock time frame when I call. Abby's just turned on the TV and Jennifer's finishing getting ready."

"So what do you think happened?" King pushed.

"I don't know why anybody would wanna hurt anyone in my family," Mike replied. "I can't imagine anything that would cause that. I would hate to think that somebody would hurt for material things, but Jennifer does have a lot of jewelry, and she wears it, so the potential could exist that somebody may have seen something . . . I mean, I haven't got a clue who would . . . would have any malice in their heart at all for anyone in our family. Abby's a beautiful little girl. Wonderful, energetic little girl. I didn't see any blood in her room when I was up there, so that gets some scary thoughts going in my mind about what could be happening or could have happened to her. There are sick people in this world and I, honestly, I just, I . . . I would rather not let my mind go to where some of those things . . . some of those scenarios . . ."

"Do you guys have any weapons in the house?" King asked.

"I've got a Colt single six that we keep in the closet unloaded," Mike said. "It's more of a deterrent than anything. It's a twenty-two-caliber pistol. We decided to keep it unloaded once Abby got big enough to be able to start climbing on things. I've also got, deep in our storage under the stairs, a twenty-two-caliber rifle and a twelve-gauge shotgun. They're in their cases, but it'd take some digging to get into either one of those."

"And the Colt, where is that again?" King asked.

"It's in our closet. It's on the third or fourth rack from the bottom, under some clothes. I've got a black gun case and it's just slipped into it."

"And you said that it's unloaded. There's no rounds in it?" King asked pointedly.

"Yes," Mike confirmed.

"Are there rounds for it?" King asked.

"No. We don't have any rounds," Mike said.

"There are no rounds in the house for it?"

"No."

"Okay, so when you say *deterrent*, you're saying the idea is that . . ."

"Wave it if you had to," Mike shrugged. "Maybe you could scare somebody off."

"So, other than those three weapons, anything else in the house, gun-wise?"

"Gun-wise, no."

"Do you hunt?" King asked.

"No, but I did when I was in high school," Mike said.

"Okay, Michael, can I get you some more water?"

"Yes," Mike answered.

King left for several minutes and then returned with a cup of water and a colleague in tow to resume the interview.

So far, what Mike had told King seemed to be making sense to the officers, who were taking turns looking through the one-way observation window and listening to the audio of the interview, but at times Mike was speaking so calmly it was almost a monotone, and they wanted to see what would happen when they turned up the heat.

# 6

"HEY, Mike, I'm gonna make some phone calls and do some more follow-up," King said, stepping back into the interview room for just a moment and introducing his shorter, dark-haired associate. "This is Wayne Weyler."

Mike didn't know it yet, but Weyler was known in the department for his questioning skills and his ability to sort out big cases. He was here to take another hard look at everything Mike was telling law enforcement.

"Hey, glad to meet you under the circumstance," Weyler said, shaking hands briefly with Mike and settling in to the only other chair in the room.

"Wayne is a sergeant. He just got here," King said. "If you could get him up to speed on what's going on and what you know, then I can go and do some of the follow-up stuff. If you can help get him up to speed, that would help us out a lot."

Mike nodded.

"I apologize, we're probably gonna go over a lot of things you just talked about," Weyler began. "Like I said, I'm just coming in and trying to get caught up on things and, sometimes, if another person asks, you might remember something else. Sometimes it helps. You doing okay?"

"Yeah, like I've been hit by a truck, but . . ."

"What are you feeling?" Weyler prompted.

"Depressed. And sad. And scared for, uh . . . Honestly, if . . . if we can't find Jennifer and bring her back home, I don't know what I would do without her. We have been such a part of each other for . . . for so long now."

"Uh-huh," Weyler continued to listen.

"I feel a little lost. Where do I go from here? What do I do?" Mike wondered. "You can do all things through Him who gives you strength, and I just keep repeating that to myself. The Lord is gonna strengthen me and give me the sustenance to be able to make it through. I know that, and that's where I am right now."

"What do you think happened? I mean, what's your gut feeling?" Weyler wanted to know.

"I don't know. I've got . . . I've been running scenarios over in my head," Mike began. "I have no idea what could have happened to them. There's nobody . . . nobody that I can think of that would have any animosity toward anyone in our family. But I saw a lot of blood. A lot of blood."

"Mike, some of these questions are really tough, but we gotta ask 'em, you know," Weyler said firmly.

"I know."

"But how do you explain a whole bunch of blood where you saw it, and on the ground, but not going out of the room, and your wife's not there?"

"I haven't got a clue how it would not . . . how it wouldn't trail someplace. I don't know. I don't know how that would happen," Mike said.

"How do you feel about Abby? I mean . . . just . . . close?"

"She's the light of my life," Mike exulted. "I just love

her to pieces. She is just a ball of energy. She's wonderful. When I come through the door, even though she's six years old, she still . . . 'Daddy!' Comes runnin' to me, and . . ."

"Got any pets?"

"No. But she wants a dog pretty bad, though."

"You know, standard questions that we ask, we have to ask them. I apologize. I know it's hard, but we have to just go through the whole gamut of things," Weyler began as he got set to zero in again on Mike. "Any problems between you and your wife? Physically?"

"No. You won't find anyone that loves each other more than we do. It's a wonderful marriage."

"Any sexual problems?" Weyler asked point-blank.

"No."

"Okay. Any . . . We'll get the hard questions out of the way. It's not easy, but it's easier to get out of the way, then we can get the rest. Um, last time you had a fight?" Weyler pressed.

"Uh, maybe a couple of weeks ago. I don't really remember."

"What was the fight over?" Weyler asked, keeping the questions coming one right after the other.

"Uh, we had an argument about . . . I get calls from recruiters about once or twice a week, looking for job possibilities. We both believe the Lord has led us out here for a reason. And on the spur of the moment, impulse decision, one of them asked me, you know, 'Are you interested?' and I told him, 'Well,' you know, 'it never hurts to talk.' And when Jennifer and I started talking about that, we started . . . She was like . . . 'You know, we're here for a reason.' I mean, 'What's . . . Why would you even open the door to something like that?' " Mike tried to explain.

"So you get a lot of offers from throughout the United States?"

"From manufacturing, yeah."

"And, you considered it 'cause of more money and things . . . and that led to the argument?" Weyler asked.

"There . . . Actually, we hadn't even gotten to any of that. It was a cold call, for one thing, and when we came out here, it was from a recruiter that did a cold call and just asked for a business unit manager, they put him through to me. No intent of talking to me ahead of time that I could tell. And this was a similar situation. We know that the Lord led us out here from that phone call in Simpsonville. And usually the calls that I get from the recruiters, you know, they call and they ask for, you know, Mike Blagg. You know, 'Hey, I got your name from so-and-so.' Not this one. This one was just a cold call . . . 'Hey, we got this opportunity on the Front Range. Are you interested?' Never hurts to talk."

"Sure, you went, 'We're settled. We're staying'? Okay. Been here about a year? . . . Been in that house the whole time that you were here, or . . ." Weyler asked.

"Well, actually, we got here April of 2000 and we lived in five hundred and ninety-five Grand Cascade over there by the fire station right off of Patterson. We lived there for a while and then they wanted to put that house, which we were renting, up for sale. We started looking around and found this house as a rental and moved there in January. So we've been there since January."

"And what's the rent there?" Weyler probed.

"Twelve hundred dollars," Mike replied.

"How are you guys doing financially?"

"Doing pretty good," Mike said, sounding sincere.

Sergeant Weyler switched topics and asked Mike about his arrival back home, and his walk up to the front porch after he'd parked his car out front.

"Did you see a package in there?" Weyler asked.

"No," Mike said, confused.

"From anybody? UPS package or anything?" Weyler prompted.

"Yeah," Mike suddenly recalled what Weyler was talking about. "There were two packages. One was in the mailbox and one was at the door. Jennifer had just ordered some medicine to help flush oxidants out of your system and . . . because she's got some pain that she thinks is related to oxidants. So I brought that stuff in. I just . . . Once I saw the stuff on the floor in the master bedroom, I just dropped everything and went back there to look."

Again Mike described his ordeal walking inside, seeing the pool of darkening blood spreading over the bed, and racing to dial 911. Weyler was curious about his trip upstairs to check on Abby.

"Which door? There are two bedrooms," Weyler noted.

"As you're coming up the stairs, hers is the right-hand bedroom," Mike clarified. "I turned the light on and her bed was pulled down about halfway, I guess, give or take a little bit, her baby doll was still on the bed. And the fan was still running, so, in general, Abby's procedures in the morning are, when her alarm goes off, she gets up, she makes her bed, she puts her clothes on, which we lay out the night before, turns the fan off and comes downstairs. And the fan was on, and her clothes were still laid out where I put 'em the night before."

"Which was where?"

"She's got like a Fisher-Price picnic table in there."

"What were those clothes?"

"It was a yellow vest, white shirt, and blue-and-yellow flowery tights," Mike recalled.

"Long-sleeved shirt?"

"Uh, the white shirt was long-sleeved and the vest was not."

Steve King stepped back into the interview room and picked right up on the line of questions Weyler was asking.

"Does Jennifer usually put out her clothes, or do you?" King asked.

"Usually I do," Mike said. "I put her down at night, typically."

"Oh." King was a little surprised it was Mike and not Jennifer who did that. "And you said that she went to sleep consistently at seven o'clock in the evening?"

"We put her down at seven o'clock every night, and then usually she's up there, she either sings or does whatever she does for about a half an hour . . ."

"So, what was Abby doing before she went to bed last night?" King asked.

"Well, we read. We've got a devotional up there. We read the daily devotional and sometimes we'll read a book," Mike recounted. "Last night we didn't read a book. We got started too late, so all we did was the devotional . . . She brushes her teeth, she goes to the bathroom . . ."

"How come you got started too late?" King wanted to know.

"We were just doing stuff throughout the day. If we start at about a quarter till seven, we have time for a book and a devotional and all the bathroom stuff. But last night, it was ten till. Or something like that."

"So what were you and Jennifer and Abby doing last night before bed? You guys . . . How did that evening go? You have dinner at home or . . . ?" King trailed off.

"Oh, yeah, we had dinner at home," Mike assured him. "We had tacos last night. About five, five-fifteen, somewhere in there. By the time we got dinner finished, it's after six, had to take a bath at that point. By the time all that stuff was done, it was about ten till seven and we didn't have time for an extra book last night."

Weyler chimed back in, "So the other room that's there, did you go into that room?"

"No. That's her playroom," Mike explained. "That's where she keeps her games and toys."

"There's a bed in there?" Weyler asked.

Mike said there was, and for several minutes the two detectives led him on a detailed inventory of every single sheet, blanket, comforter, pillow, and spare blanket he could think of, and exactly where it should be found within the house.

"Did you ever go back in the house after that?" King asked.

"After Abby, uh, no."

"Do you have insurance policies?"

"Through work, we've got life insurance on both Abby and Jennifer," Mike responded.

"How much are those policies for?" King queried.

"Ten thousand, I think, for Abby, and I think it's fifteen for Jennifer."

King moved the questions ahead. "So did Jennifer make dinner last night?"

"Yeah."

"And you said you guys had tacos. When you and I were talking, you said you'd watched the game together . . . You guys sat down and watched the game," King prompted.

"After we put Abby down. It was the Monday night football game. Ravens and uh . . . It was a pretty decent game."

"Do you remember who won?" King asked.

"We didn't watch the end. We, uh . . . I took my shower about nine-forty-five so we could get ready for bed."

"So, watching the game in your bedroom? And . . . I don't know if . . . You have a TV in your bedroom?" King said.

"Yeah. We were watching in my bedroom. I was also doing a little bit of homework, so to speak. I've got a computer that I bring home from work sometimes that I can do some stuff on. So I was working on that while Jennifer and I were talking and watching the game and . . . trying to get some stuff done," Mike answered.

"Have you been married before?"

"Uh, yeah, I've been married once before. Right after college."

"How long did that marriage go for?" Weyler asked.

"A year . . . a year."

"What brought about the end of that marriage?"

"I was in the Navy and doing a lot of travel, and she was a professional woman that didn't want to be doing all that traveling, so we did a summary dissolution," Mike explained.

"Have any children?" Weyler asked.

"No."

"You hesitated when you said you had been married once. I mean, were there other relationships? Women . . . relationships . . . or anything?"

"Oh, yeah. Yeah."

King jumped back in. "How about Jennifer . . . has she been married before?"

"No."

"Where did you meet her?" King wondered.

"Jennifer? In San Diego. She was going to school at National University in San Diego, and I was in the Navy."

"What's National University? Sorry, I've never heard of that," King said.

"It's a nationwide chain of universities. It can also be correspondence."

"Okay, so you could learn from a computer . . . What was she studying?" King asked.

"Business Administration."

"So, did she have relationships prior to you?" Weyler prodded. "Live-in relationships or anything?"

"Not live-in relationships. She had boyfriends, but

not . . . No live-in ones. She was living with her mom in San Diego. Probably would have never met her . . ."

"How much younger is she than you?"

"Four years."

"You were married how long after . . . How long after you ended your first marriage did you meet Jennifer?"

"A year, year and a half, something like that."

"Weren't forced to get married because of pregnancy or anything of that sort?" King wondered.

"No. No. We had Abby three years after we got married or something like that."

"No other pregnancies or miscarriages?" King asked.

"Oh, no. No, no, no," Mike said insistently.

"How long have you been a Christian for?"

"Um, actually, I became a Christian in 1987."

"And Jennifer?"

"When she was fourteen," Mike said.

"Okay. Wild past for you before 1987?"

"Yeah, I had pretty much the standard Navy time," Mike said. "You know, I had a good time when we were on cruises and a lot of stupid drinking and stuff like that. Doing the dumb things that, fortunately, I've been able to get away from."

"Usually we have a pretty wild early past and God delivers us from a lot of different places so . . ." Weyler prompted.

"Yeah," Mike agreed.

"You have lots of problems?"

"Yeah. I had lots of girlfriends. I had lots of drinking. No drugs."

"Anger?"

"No. I haven't ever had any kind of anger problems."

"Okay. You ever been arrested for anything in the past?" Weyler pushed.

"No."

"Trouble for anything?"

"No."

"As a kid, as a juvie?"

"No."

"Any mental health problems at all?"

"No."

"Difficult questions. Do you understand why I have to ask 'em?" Weyler asked again.

"I understand," Mike acceded.

"Okay. I don't want you to know for a second we forgot to explore everything. How about Jennifer . . . any mental health problems?"

"No. Occasionally, she'll battle depression," Mike admitted, "but not with medication. Sometimes she'll be unhappy . . . When we first moved out here, we had a bunch of good friends in South Carolina. So probably the first four or five months we were out here, she was battling depression. She was having a hard time the first few months we were here. But she made new friends, found some good churches. We realized that the Lord brought us out here for a reason."

"You talked about a fight two weeks ago. Any other fights recently?" Weyler broached.

"No," Mike said.

"Financial problems? Financial fights? Everybody has financial fights," Weyler offered.

"Yeah, we're actually . . . Our financial problem is that we're renting. And we both would like to have a house out here, but we've found the kind of house that we want to have is unfortunately out of our price range. The house we had in South Carolina was a beautiful, wonderful house. But it was in a close-out neighborhood and we had to leave. There were like ten spec homes that the builder was really discounting, so for us to compete with that, we had to really take a bath on our house. We basically lost our deposit is what it boils down to, so we were here building . . . trying to build a deposit up to be able to put a down payment on a house."

"So you lost your deposit in South Carolina. How much are we talking?" Weyler asked.

"We lost about eight thousand dollars."

"Ooo!" Weyler exclaimed.

"That was a big hit," Mike conceded.

"What's your salary here?"

"Hundred and ten thousand."

"Geez. How much do you take home monthly?"

"Uh, after all the deductions and everything? It's about twenty-five hundred a paycheck, so . . . twice a month."

Changing gears, Weyler asked sharply, "Are you having an affair with anybody?"

"No," Mike answered.

"Have you, recently?" Weyler persisted.

"No. Never."

"How about credit card debt? Any credit card debt?"

"No. We try and pay it off each month when it comes in," Mike explained.

"What are you as far as ranking within your business? How high up are you?"

"There are essentially three of us. There's a general manager, of course, that's over everything, and then there's the chief financial officer, and me, that's the hierarchy."

"Do you have a company vehicle?"

"No."

"Have you been in a company vehicle the last few days?"

"No."

"So what problems were you and Jennifer having?"

"Well, we have a very good marriage," Mike said.

"Explain it. Tell me about it," Weyler challenged.

"Uh, well, we're very loving. We're very open with each other. We talk about everything. I mean, we talk about what happens at work, even mundane little nothing things. We're very touchy . . . I mean, open with our affection for each other. We genuinely care about what's going on in each other's lives and we do whatever we can to help the other person through any kind of issues that are going on. If I have a bad day at work, she is there to help talk me through it or, 'Hey, let's go get some ice cream,' or, you know. Just little things that add up to show what an incredible love we have for each other. We hold hands all the time whenever we go anyplace. Abby picks up on it because she tries to get between us all the time and hold hands with all of us. We're just a very loving, affectionate family."

"Sexually, you and your wife, how often a week, a month?" Weyler asked.

"Um, once a week probably."

"Okay, any mental problems in that area or anything?"

"No."

"Okay."

"I mean, we took it easy there for a little while," Mike said, thinking back to the sex question and referring to the hysterectomy.

"Sure," Weyler acknowledged. "Describe Jennifer for me, physically."

"She's about five-foot-four. She's got kind of sandy blonde hair that's down about to her shoulder now. She's growing it out. Brown eyes . . . Just cute . . . Beautiful as can be. About a hundred and twenty-eight pounds, something like that."

"Describe her build . . . Thin? Medium? . . ."

"I think she's thin, yeah."

"Okay, and what about Abby?"

"Abby is a stick. She's about forty-eight inches tall and just about forty pounds. She's skinny and lanky with blonde hair and blue eyes. A beautiful little girl."

"Michael, would you do anything to harm your daughter or wife?" Weyler asked earnestly.

"No. I would never do anything like that," Mike insisted.

"Did you take 'em somewhere?"

"No, I did not. I would never do that." Mike was adamant.

"Tell me what happened . . . What you think happened," Weyler urged.

"I don't know what happened. But I can tell you the time frame. I left at six o'clock and they get up at six-thirty, so something happened between six and six-thirty and, uh . . ." Mike said.

"Who would have been watching the house? Or done something like that?" Weyler pressed.

"I don't know."

"Any thoughts, ideas, anybody at work? Anybody been trying to pick up on your wife that you heard, that she said?"

"No. And she would talk about that," Mike said.

King picked up the theme. "If Jennifer was gonna leave, where would she go?"

"To her mom's," Mike replied.

"She'd drive to . . ." King paused.

"She'd probably fly," Mike said. "What I would anticipate is that she would take a flight out of Walker Field to Dallas. But I don't see that as a real option. But you could call Jennifer's mom, I mean, I haven't gotten a chance to talk to her since all this . . ."

"Oh, we will be, we probably will call Jennifer's mom," King avowed. "One, it saves you having to do it, and it makes her aware that there's a problem. I think the best way to do it would be to get ahold of the people in that city and have them, go and be with them, because obviously we don't want to make her health any worse.

We don't want to stress her out. If I were Jennifer's mom, I would definitely want to know that there's a problem."

"Oh, yeah," Mike agreed.

"At this point, we're looking at all the possibilities. And I would be remiss if I didn't try and hit every possibility that I could think of, and you know I don't say that with the idea of stressing you out. I say it with the idea that knowledge is important here, and any possible alternative needs to be looked at."

"But I've tried to be really good about answering every question that you guys . . ." Mike said plaintively.

"Oh, and I . . . I totally appreciate the time and effort . . . and I realize that this is not easy," King replied.

"Can I ask you some questions?" Mike requested.

"Sure. Absolutely," King agreed.

"Do you think there's any chance that she's alive?"

"I think that . . ." King began slowly and then hesitated.

"Please be honest," Mike urged.

"I think there's always that possibility," King sidestepped. "I . . . I . . . My question would be, Why would you think she's dead?"

"'Cause the blood . . . I saw lots of blood," Mike explained. "I've never seen that much blood before in my life, and that scared me."

"Okay," King noted. "What about your daughter?"

"Well, the scenario that's going on in my head right now with my daughter is not a pretty one right now," Mike admitted. "Because, I . . . She is such a. . . . I don't . . . I don't have any pictures, but if you could come with me to work, you could see. I've got a Plexiglas top to my desk, and it's just full of pictures of my family. And one or two looks at my daughter and you would fall in love with her. I mean, that's how pretty she is. She's just wonderful. She's just the most . . . And as equal as her cuteness is, her beauty is . . . is her attitude and enthusiasm. It's every bit as contagious. And I gotta tell you, the scenarios that are going through my head right now are not real pretty about the fact that there's no blood in her room, and she's gone. I mean, that . . . that scares me. From a father's standpoint . . . , I can see you're married . . . I don't . . . Did you, did you tell me you have children?" Mike wondered.

"Yeah, I have three," King said.

"As you can imagine, a missing child is a nightmare that you wouldn't want to have to go through," Mike conjectured.

"No, I . . . Absolutely right," King agreed. "And that's why, believe me, I'm just one person in a team of probably twenty-five or thirty people that are right now looking at every possibility. And, I mean, just because I'm spending the time to speak with you, it is with the idea that I might come up with something that I can pass on to them that might help with this situation. There are many other people out there doing other things, working on your behalf, trying to figure out what's going on here."

"I know . . . I know you guys have a full-court press going on with this, and I appreciate that. From a father to a father, I can tell you, I appreciate that," Mike said.

"And I guess, I mean, you asked me outright, you know, whether your wife is still alive," King recalled. "My feeling is that a couple things . . . One is that any type of blood a lot of times looks like a lot of blood."

"So I'm just being paranoid of that, do you think?"

"Well, I don't know," King offered. "All I know is that I tend to look at these types of things with an attitude of not going to the dark side unless there's a reason to. I think that there are many things that, over the next twelve hours, that we'll figure out. And I think part of that you're a key to, with the time that you've spent and the information that you've given, and your cooperation."

"I know you guys are working hard," Mike countered.

"I know . . . I know . . . I know . . . And I know it's late and probably horrible for you guys to have to go through all of this. But I can't tell you how much I appreciate it. She is, on this Earth, she is my life. I love my daughter to pieces, but there's a biblical backing to your spouse comes first."

"Right," King went along with Mike.

"And she does. And I'm having a hard time thinking about what I'm gonna do if the dark-side things are what happened. I mean, I guess what I'm saying is: What can I do? Where can I go? What . . . Is there anything I can do to help, or is there . . . is . . ."

"I can't . . . I can't imagine . . . I can't tell you anything other than the help you've given so far," King said supportively. "You tell me where you think they might have gone, and I'll be happy to send someone to go look. That's . . . See what I mean? . . . There's no point in you going out and driving around. Tell me where any . . . Give me any place in this valley, and we'll go look. Any place in Colorado, and we'll go look. Any place in Colorado–Utah, and we'll go look. I mean, those are the options. But when you say, 'Is there anything I can do?,' we're doing it. We're coming up with different scenarios, different options, different ideas and information . . ."

"Can I just give you a little background into me, too?" Mike asked.

"Sure." King nodded.

"From when I started working in the corporate world, about seven years ago now, my jobs have always been in quality engineering, continuous improvement, problem-solving scenarios."

"Right," King acknowledged.

"And the idea of not being able to do anything has kind of just ripped my guts out, you know. You know what I'm saying?"

"Solving the problem," King summed up.

Weyler began the next round of questions by saying, "The good news about something like this is where you talk to everybody and get all the questions that we ask you about is . . . I know you're tired . . . but the more information we get, the better it helps us. That make sense?"

"Yeah, that's what we were just talking about," Mike agreed.

"I mean, if we're gonna ask a few strong questions, we're gonna ask questions about you, 'cause we gotta look at everything. Okay?" Weyler asked. "So hopefully you can bear with us and not get too pissed and just help us in every way you can, okay? When you called 911 you didn't know if your daughter had gone to school or did go to school?"

"Didn't . . . I don't think I had any idea at that point," Mike replied. "I don't really remember saying anything about that, but I do remember saying, when we started talking about Abby, I had to go upstairs and check her room to see if she was there."

"It concerns me, Mike, a little bit . . . Why . . . You come home and you're very concerned about your wife. Why wouldn't your daughter enter into your mind?" Weyler wondered.

"Because my first concern was for my spouse."

"Okay. Give me the reasoning there. I mean, everybody thinks different, so tell me why that is with you," Weyler urged.

"I love . . . I love my daughter and I love my wife both. But my wife is the light of my life here on this Earth," Mike said. "That's . . . That's . . . That's the way it is for me. And when I saw that initially . . . that's where the fear was pulling me, 'cause I saw stuff that I wasn't expecting to see there."

King and Weyler had Mike stand up and turn around so they could see if any blood had gotten on his clothing from his time in the house. Then they asked him to list every single item of clothing he'd had on in the past twenty-four hours and where it would be found now inside the residence.

"After Jennifer had Abby, did she go through any type of post-partum depression, any type of mental stress as a result?" King resumed the questions.

"Yeah. Let me walk you through the whole thing, then," Mike offered.

"Okay," King agreed.

"With the pregnancy, Jennifer and I decided to have a baby right before one of my cruises in the Navy," Mike began. "So we worked real hard and were successful before a cruise. It was about a two-month period of time before I had to leave on cruise. So, for six months, she was at home—this is when we were living in San Diego—so she had Marilyn and her mom and Harold there to help her through pretty much the whole time. But she had six months there where she had some difficulties with the pregnancy. She wasn't gaining weight as the physician hoped that she would. When she went in for one of those amniocentesis things—the needle things—they couldn't draw liquid . . . couldn't draw fluid because there wasn't enough fluid there. Abby kept shifting around every time they put the needle in there. The first time they were able to get fluid from the amniocentesis—I'm learning all this through letters that she sends back and forth—but the first time, it came back as a potential Down's baby. So, of course, there were follow-up tests that had to be done with that. Of course, Abby didn't have any of that, but still, she [Jennifer] wasn't gaining weight like her obstetrician wanted her to. So she prescribed her a vitamin supplement: Ensure. It's just a liquid vitamin she can buy in the grocery store, but it's got a high fat content. So it was the only vitamins that Jennifer could take that she wouldn't throw back up or have complications with, so that's what she took. And she took it for about four months during the pregnancy and she gained seventy-something pounds. Abby was an eight-pound child. You figure double that for the placenta and everything . . . sixteen, twenty pounds' top worth of baby in there. Fifty pounds' worth of excess weight."

"Right," King said, nodding for Mike to continue.

"She had never been big before in her whole life, and it was devastating for her. We talked a little about depression, I think. I forget who we were talking to about that, but she has battled depression off and on since then. But she has gotten the weight off and she's looking good now."

"At any point in that battle was she medicated?" King asked.

"No."

"At any point did she see someone about her depression?"

"No, but she did see people about her weight. Trying to lose weight," Mike said.

"Could you tell when she was depressed?" King asked.

"Oh yeah," Mike said.

"How could you tell? I mean . . . How did you know when she was depressed?" King persisted.

"'Cause she's a very, very . . . I think I was telling you . . . She could talk to a wall and make the wall laugh . . . She's that kind of an outgoing person," Mike said before continuing, "But when she's depressed, she's quiet and doesn't like to discuss things. And she may ask, you know, 'How was your day?' But she doesn't really want to know how your day was."

"Ever to the point of talking about suicide?" King suggested.

"No. No. She had a strong enough belief that she knew that when it was time for her to go, the Lord was gonna take her, and it wasn't gonna be her doing it. She never discussed any of those things with me. I know you guys are gonna call Marilyn and talk to her about all this kind of stuff, too, but I would bet you almost anything you wanna bet that she never talked to Marilyn about suicide. I would be very surprised if she did."

"Have you ever thought about that?"

"No. Too much to live for," Mike insisted. "I told you, she is the light of my life here on this Earth. And for the past ten years we've been married, and then four years before that. We were dating the last fourteen years, you know, and I had plenty of reason to stick around."

"Okay, and she got pregnant with Abby . . ."

"We had Abby in March 1995, so nine months prior to that," Mike recalled.

"So on your last tour she got pregnant . . . Surprise pregnancy . . . or . . ."

"Oh, no. We planned it," Mike said.

"Planned it? Wasn't that kind of bad timing, you know, you going on tour and she gets pregnant?" King asked.

"Well, there were a couple of things going on right then," Mike explained. "One of the problems, physical problems, that Jennifer had is called vulvar vestibulitis. I'm not sure if you're familiar with that, but it's sort of an infection of the vestibular glands in the genitalia area. One way of fixing that problem completely is with a hormone boost beyond all hormone boosts—which happens when you get pregnant. So we'd been talking about having children for a while before that. So after talking to this doctor that said that's one of the cures for this, we said, 'Okay, this is the time.' So we started working on it."

"Still, you going on tours, six months if I remember correctly," King noted, "you go out to sea. Six months. I mean, most people don't plan to get pregnant and then on leaving, 'See ya six months later.' I mean, any hardships and difficulties with you guys, disagreements on that or anything?"

"No, actually, we thought it would work out pretty good. Because I was there for the first couple months," Mike replied. "Then selfishly, the middle part . . . I was gonna be away for it. However, I knew Harold and Marilyn were . . . At that point we were living a quarter of a mile away from each other. Something like that. In San Diego. I knew she was gonna be well taken care of, and I knew that this was something that was gonna solve her problem. The problem with the vestibulitis was so bad that she couldn't sit still for any length of time. She described it as sitting on a hot coal all the time."

"Back then, sex wasn't good, I assume, when she had that," King commiserated.

"Yeah, there was about a six-month period of time that she was in a lot of pain."

"Probably couldn't have sex at that point."

"No. But, we're creative," Mike said. "We do other things also, and . . ."

"Not that I'm gonna get that personal . . ." King added, perhaps a bit late.

"Yeah, I understand." Mike shrugged.

King continued, "What I'd like to do is have you help us fill out this consent to be able to go into your house and so forth. One of the other things that I'd like to do is, because of the fact that you were in the house, from a processing standpoint, I would like to be able to look at your clothing with a black light, which shows fibers, those type of things. Do you have any problem with that?"

"No problem whatsoever," Mike replied as he began to fill out the form.

When King and then Weyler left the room briefly to get Mike some more water, the tape recording that was being made of the interview picked up Mike whispering one word over and over. "Please . . . Please . . . Please . . . Please."

Weyler walked back in and handed a cup of water to Mike.

"You have a cut on your finger. What's that from?" the sergeant asked.

"Yeah, from moving the workbenches," Mike explained. "Part of what we're doing is moving into the shipping dock, so I end up with scratches and scrapes on my hands all the time."

"You're a smart man. You're intelligent. You've got a very high-paying job and a prestigious position," Weyler replied. "But you understand we have to ask questions. When we look at something like this, we always look at everything."

"I understand."

"Yeah? Okay. When we see cuts, we're gonna ask those things. We have to ask you if you did something. You know, it just kind of hit me that your anniversary's coming up. I guess I have to appeal to you as a Christian and as a father and as a husband. If something happened last night that was an accident, you need to tell me. You need to tell me now so we can get out and can find what's going on. I mean, you might know something—you guys had a fight, you had an argument and you're scared about hiding something. You just need to be honest with me and tell me, because we need to figure out if things just got out of hand or whatever. But you've got to be honest and tell me."

"I understand. I appreciate you asking the questions. But there was none of that . . . that went on," Mike said.

"Okay," Weyler said.

"I know you have to ask that stuff," Mike added.

"We do, and I guess I go back to what you saw in the house," Weyler said. "You saw blood on the bed and blood

on the floor. And there's no other blood. Where's the blood
for your daughter? Where is the drag mark carrying her
out? Where's your wife?"

"I don't know. I wanna know. I wanna know where my
family is, and want you to bring them home to me. That's
what I want," Mike replied.

"Is there anything you can tell me to help me?"
Weyler proffered.

"All I can tell you is what we've already talked about.
I wish I knew more. I wish I had recommendations. I
wish I could look into a crystal ball and tell you, although
I don't believe in that. But I wish that there was some
magic wand I could wave. Anything to get them here.
Whatever it takes. I think I've been trying to be very co-
operative . . ."

"You have. You have. Absolutely," Weyler agreed.
"And all this information, very important—outside, family, home, and everything. But we've also got to look
at you."

"I understand."

"We gotta look at you and we gotta ask a lot of questions."

"I understand," Mike acknowledged.

"I mean, I wish I didn't have to, 'cause part of me says,
you know, 'Doggone it, you didn't have anything to do
with this one,' making me feel guilty, rotten, and all these
different things," Weyler said, before adding, "The other
part of me says, 'The majority of the statistics say it's
somebody that the person knows.' That's the reality. You
remember JonBenét, that case, right? So we always have
to look at spouses, close friends, you look at relationships . . . there might have been an extramarital relationship, anything of that sort. We gotta ask those questions.
I've gotta feel . . . The majority of these statistics say that
when there's a situation like this, that usually it's an accident. A fight happens, things got out of control. A person

is scared to tell. And that's why we have to ask those questions. So I've got to appeal to you as a man, as a . . . You know, I don't have a doubt that you cared for your wife. You convinced me of that. No doubt."

"I love her beyond all . . ." Mike began.

"No doubt about it. The question of you loving her," Weyler said. "The next thing I've got to get resolved is, did you do something accidentally?"

"No. I didn't. I didn't," Mike said. "I appreciate the question. I understand the need for it. I don't like the need for it, but I do understand. I would have asked the same questions."

"Right. You would. You would. You would, and history is on my side in saying that it's usually somebody they know. Doesn't make sense—I mean, you're not a millionaire—for someone to kidnap your daughter and harm your wife. Take her out . . ." Weyler said.

"I was renting a house, for goodness' sakes, I mean, I didn't even own it, so, I mean, there's not a lot of money there. No," Mike agreed.

Weyler tossed in a curveball. "Why did your van come home at three-thirty?"

"I don't know," Mike replied.

"It did, it came home at three-thirty, neighbors saw."

"I have no idea."

"Do you know who was driving it . . . who could have been driving it . . . who has keys to it?"

"Jennifer and I were the only ones who had keys for it."

"One garage door opener for each car?"

"And we changed the code when we moved in so that the previous owners wouldn't be able to get in," Mike noted.

"Can I ask again, who drove your car home?" Weyler pressed. "Any idea? Who drove the car home? Did you drive it?"

"No, I didn't. I would have no reason to be up at three-thirty in the morning," Mike said.

"Did you leave work at all today?"

"No. I was at work the whole day," Mike insisted.

"Somebody can account for your actions all day long?"

"I believe so, yeah. There should be lots of people that could."

"Did you leave for lunch?" Weyler continued.

"No, actually we had lunch in today," Mike answered.

"You had lunch in? Is that normal?"

"It's part of that training that we were gonna . . ."

"Is that normal?" Weyler cut him off.

"It's abnormal, actually," Mike said.

"Do you normally go out to eat lunch, or do you go home?"

"Usually, I just work through lunch," Mike replied.

"Okay. Would, do you have family that has money? Brothers, sisters, parents, grandparents?" Weyler wanted to know.

"Not significantly, no. I mean, just standard middle-class family."

"Fired anybody lately?"

"Nah . . . Not in six months or so. Maybe eight months."

"Anyone upset at you at work 'cause of the way you manage, or anything of that sort?"

"I don't think so," Mike said. "I think, when you talk to those people—my co-workers—I think you'll find that I've got a very lenient management style."

"Abby have any problems, has she come home in the last couple of weeks telling you about concerns—maybe anybody approaching her, or anybody following her . . . anything that seems suspicious to you?" Weyler asked.

"No."

"Anything, anything . . . Can you think of anything that would help?" Weyler reached.

"Not that I haven't already told. I can't think of any reason why anybody would do anything to our family. Just doesn't make sense."

"Cars driving by? High rate of speed the last few nights? Anything that's sort of annoying? Any mailmen, newspaper people leaving anything out of the ordinary?" Weyler queried.

"No. Usually it's dark when I go into work and I don't really see much of anything when I go," Mike said.

"What were you guys gonna do for your anniversary?"

"I was gonna . . . Well, hopefully, if this babysitter was gonna work out tomorrow, I was gonna go to Chefs'. I got her some earrings she's been asking for. I was gonna give her the earrings at Chefs'."

"Where are those earrings at?" Weyler wanted to know.

"I've got 'em hidden in Abby's playroom upstairs, in the closet. There's a pink clothes hamper. That's where I've got most of the Christmas presents and stuff hidden."

"Tell me this . . . How did she get out, do you think? I mean, do you think she walked out, or was carried out, or what?" Weyler demanded.

"I don't have any idea. I don't know how she . . . I keep going back to the blood. It was a lot. In my opinion, it was a lot of blood," Mike noted.

"I haven't seen it," Weyler acknowledged.

"And I don't know how she could have done anything. I don't . . . I mean, with that amount of blood . . . And maybe it wasn't as much as I think, but you'll see that when you go, and you take a look at it. But it was more than I'd ever seen before."

"Okay, so how would you get her out?" Weyler insisted. "Did she walk, you think, based on the blood? And what would your wife be like if somebody was taking her out and she was bleeding bad, what would she do?"

"She'd fight. She would fight. She's a fighter. She would fight with everything she's got in her," Mike said.

The men took a break from the interview for a few minutes to let criminalist Mike Smith come in with an ultraviolet light and, dimming down the room lights, he looked over every inch of Blagg's clothing and shoes to see if there was any indication of even tiny specks of blood anywhere on him. The search was negative and when the lights came up, it was Steve King's turn again.

"Okay," King began, "it gets to be a certain point where— I call it the "coming to Jesus" questions. Obviously you feel that something was amiss at your house when you called us. Did you have anything to do with any possible injury or the disappearance of your wife and child?" King asked.

"No. I did not."

"Okay. The next question I would ask is, again with the idea that we need to be able one hundred percent to eliminate you as a suspect in this case, I would ask if you would be willing to take a polygraph in reference to the questions I just asked you."

"Whatever it takes so that you can find the person that did this," Mike replied.

"I appreciate that. I mean, that's a step, a big step, in the right direction towards being able to focus more so on someone out there," King said.

"Let's do it," Mike agreed.

"Okay, Michael, in your training in the military, did they . . . What kind of training did you have in reference to interrogations or possibly being captured in a foreign country? Did you have training in that?" King inquired.

"Yeah, I went through a one-week course called S.E.R.E. School—Search, Evasion, Resistance, and Escape training. It's basically, you get thrown out in the woods for a week and you go hungry and then, for a ten-day period of time they put you in a little prisoner-of-war camp. Put you in a little concrete box where you have to stay, and they pound on the box periodically and they play weird music to try to get you to, say . . . go nuts or whatever. That's about it."

"Did you learn anything from that?" King asked calmly, even though Mike's answer had now thrown serious doubt on the first several hours of the interview.

"Uh, well, I learned that it's better to escape than to be captured . . ." Mike gave a small laugh. "Better to not get shot down."

"I have to tell you that I . . . I have to tell you that I . . . I have this strange feeling, and I don't . . . I can't put my finger on it," King began. "And I don't know if it is because of your religious beliefs and your military training that you handled, or are handling, this extremely well. As in, I'm not sure if, if my child and my wife were gone and I came home and saw the things that you saw, if I would not be at St. Mary's right now being medicated in reference to this and . . . and one part of me, it concerns me, and the other part of me is saying . . . 'He's doing the things he needs to do to get through this.' Any insight there that you might be able to give me?"

"It is only through the strength of the Holy Spirit that I am able to be standing . . . sitting here in front of you right now," Mike replied calmly. "Every fiber, every core member in my body wants to scream out and shout and grab somebody by the neck and say, 'You did it!' and tear 'em limb from limb. We're talking about the two most important people in my life are missing right now and— You're both fathers, you know the situation. I'm telling you, I'm concerned out of my mind about Abby, because of the lack of, uh, harmful evidence. There's no blood that I saw in there. She could be being abused in ways that I don't even wanna . . . don't even wanna have go through my head right now. And my number-one concern is getting to the point where you guys say, 'All right, let's go find the person who did this,' I mean, I know you guys are doing that now, but . . ."

"That's good," Weyler interjected. "That's exactly what we're saying. We want to take our focus off you . . . Not that we're not looking other places. But our job right now is to focus on you and make sure we clear you or put you in the loop."

"Well, and that is important for us too, from a support standpoint," King added. "I mean, I want to know in my heart that you had nothing to do with this, and that way, when it comes to . . . tell me what's going on and everything . . . We're doing, showing you the one hundred and ten percent and the amount of people that are involved right now. I think that it is a big step. And you have cooperated in every way possible. I appreciate your candor in reference to those questions that I have. It is a tribute to your religious beliefs that that's helping you through this."

"When I told you the van was seen coming home, what's your thoughts?" Weyler asked.

"I don't know how that could happen," Mike said.

"Okay. What time did I tell you that happened?"

"I think you said three-thirty."

"Three o'clock, actually," Weyler corrected. "And was that morning or afternoon?"

"You didn't say," Mike noted.

"What do you think?" Weyler bluffed.

"Well, I was there in the morning, so it couldn't have been in the morning."

"And I wanted to make sure you got that perception, 'cause I didn't mention P.M. or A.M. You believe it was in the afternoon? Okay. And nobody else has your keys? Okay," Weyler said, moving on. "You know, I asked you about carrying a body out. Where could somebody put a body around your house? I don't know the neighborhood real well, do you have any ideas?"

"Yeah, there's an open field back behind the house that I've seen horses and ponies and things in back there."

"Back behind on the other side of . . ." Weyler fished for the street name.

"Greenbelt. That's the only close non-developed area."

"What about that area where the house was falling down? What about something over there? Is that fairly easy to get to from your house? Seems to me it's just right up the street," Weyler said.

"Yeah, if you're driving someone, then you could get over there pretty easy. But if you are carrying someone, I don't . . ." Mike replied.

King changed tacks. "I don't know if Wayne asked you this— Is there any possibility, even a raw possibility, that your wife had met someone else? A man?"

"Everything inside me says no, but if you ask, 'Is there a remote possibility?' I can't positively say no," Mike said.

"Do you have suspicions?" Weyler followed up.

"No. I have no suspicions."

"Never have had?" King pressed.

"Uh-uhh." Mike shook his head.

Mike was answering the questions well—maybe a little too well—but he was doing it in a voice bordering on a monotone and, as Weyler tried to figure out what was bugging him about this man who should perhaps be more distraught in such a moment of crisis, a thought occurred to him. "In your military background, did you have prisoner of war . . ."

King stopped him. "Yeah, we talked about that, and he did. And we talked about that flat affect and he did learn some stuff from that. He answered that to my satisfaction."

King continued the conversation. "Okay. You said that

Jennifer did aerobics. What else did she do for fun? What did she like? You said she'd lost all that weight . . . that fifty pounds. Did she diet to do that?"

"Yeah, we're all on . . . We both do the Sugar Busters diet," Mike told them, "so, I mean, that was one of the most positive signs that Jennifer has had in a long time. She actually had been losing weight. She's fitting into some eights that she hadn't fit into in a long time."

"That ought to make her feel good," King noted.

"Oh yeah," Mike agreed. "She keeps clothes for a long time in the hopes that she'll be able to get back into 'em."

"So she was doing aerobics. Anything else that she liked to do, I mean for fun?"

"She spent a lot of time at the school, and then spent time with the Intercessory Prayer Ministry. And that's it. Sometimes she'd walk in the mall. She likes to do that too, sometimes. And then on weekends we would always ride our bikes. We had a good time riding bikes. Abby had just learned how to do her bike without the training wheels."

"Had you guys been down the river for a trip? Do you know where that's at? Across the street . . ." King wondered.

"Yeah. When we first moved into that house we went down there quite a bit and then— I forget when it was, but they put a sign up that said that there was a mountain lion down there," Mike recalled.

"Yeah, there was. In fact, there is," King noted.

"So after that, we stopped going down there."

"Yeah, apparently that mountain lion's been sighted down there four or five times. Never gone after anyone, you know, but just the mere fact that they're being seen down there . . . Yeah," King recalled.

The conversation drifted to a halt for a moment and Blagg became pensive.

"You guys are gonna find 'em, right?" Mike finally

asked. "I went through a lot of questions. Bring 'em home."

King nodded in agreement.

It was time for the polygraph, and Lieutenant John Hakes came into the room and introduced himself to Mike, inviting him to come over to his office to take the test. Mike returned to the interview room an hour later with Wayne Weyler.

Polygraph tests are notoriously unreliable, and the sheriffs were aware that Mike had been schooled by the military in how to resist interrogation techniques. Since a wide variety of factors can influence the outcome, the question of whether a subject answered truthfully has to be inferred by the examiner in a process that is as much art as science. Mike's test result was inconclusive at best, and, although he wasn't filled in on the details, he was told they were satisfied with the answers he'd just given, and the questioning resumed.

"Do you have your wallet with you?" Weyler asked. "I wanna make sure that she or somebody else didn't get into your accounts . . . Besides the two credit cards I got, is there any other credit cards in there?"

"Yeah. In the dresser drawer on my side is the—the left side . . . the top left side, underneath the socks, on the right side there—I've got a bunch of credit cards that we just don't use."

"What's the amount of money you have in the accounts?" Weyler asked.

"Uh, got about four thousand in Wells Fargo checking. About another four thousand in Wells Fargo savings. And another three thousand in Navy Federal," Mike recalled.

"Anything else? And what I mean by *access* is, can someone force her to get money out? The other thing that we have to keep open is, maybe she left on her own. Have to look at that, okay? Any inkling or possibility she may have?"

"I can't believe that, no."

"All right. There is a bunch of people from the church out front. I hear they . . . I just found out about a half-hour ago that they've been here two or three hours, maybe longer. They want to talk to you. Also, your mother-in-law wants a phone call. You can talk to them tonight. Your pastor, and all your friends from church, are saying, 'No way he's staying in a motel, he's staying with us.' Well, we'll leave it up to you, so you need to go up front."

"All right," Mike agreed wearily.

"Only thing is, I gotta hang out and make sure who you're gonna be with, so we can get ahold of you. Any questions you have for us?" Weyler asked.

"Do you really think that she could have left on her own?" Mike wondered.

"It's an option," Weyler said.

"Just one of many," King noted, adding, "Let's get you out of here."

It was now 2:30 A.M. on Wednesday morning, ten hours since the 911 call, and there was still no word on Jennifer or Abby.

"Do you have my sleeping medicine?" Mike asked. He had requested his sleeping pills earlier, and police said they'd try to retrieve some from the house.

"Um, no, not yet," King replied.

"I'm pretty beat, so I might be able to sleep on my own," Mike sighed, "but my mind is going."

# 7

**MIKE'S** friends from church had turned out in force to collect him following his marathon interview with the detectives.

While Mike spent a fitful early morning attempting to catch some sleep at the home of his other minister, Art

Blankenship, Grand Junction awoke to the news that there had just been some sort of brutal kidnapping in the Redlands.

One of the first things detectives did was listen to the tape on the Blaggs' answering machine. They knew Mike said he'd been calling, but they also wanted to know if Jennifer might have gotten any other calls that could shed some light on what had occurred.

The tape wasn't particularly helpful. There were seven separate messages from Mike throughout the course of his workday looking for Jennifer to call him. Later in the evening, there were two calls from women who were friends of the Blaggs'. They'd just heard the first alarming news reports and were trying to confirm whether it was the same Jennifer Blagg they knew who was missing.

Mike's messages were short and indisputably sweet.

"Good morning, gorgeous. It's me, just calling to see how you and Abby are doing," was the first.

Mike had called back mid-morning. "Hey, where are you? I was just calling to see how you're doing. And I guess I'll just keep trying to get ahold of you."

At noon, Mike tried again. "Hello, my beautiful bride. Hope you're having fun. I hope you're out and about, doing all kinds of cool, nifty things."

"Hey, where are you guys?" began the next. "I hope everything's going okay. I love you. I miss you."

It wasn't until the last call that Mike, although still sounding upbeat, began to inject a note of worry into the message. "Man, where are you guys?" he wondered. "It's three-twenty-two and I haven't talked to you all day long. I love you, sweetie. I hope everything is going well for you."

Mike's messages struck the sheriffs as kind of mushy, but so what? The cloying endearments were said only for Jennifer to hear. They were never meant for a bunch of guys at the Mesa County Sheriff's Office to study—or were they? The investigators strained as they listened, trying to pick up any hint of a cover-up in what Mike was doing. They wondered if Mike could have harmed Jennifer and Abby before he left for work and then spent the rest of the day using his answering machine to try to throw police off his scent.

By mid-morning on Wednesday, the complicated process of sifting through the Blaggs' house was well underway. Three members of the Colorado Bureau of Investigation who specialized in processing crime scenes were on hand to help the Mesa County sheriffs go inch-by-inch through the home and both cars, looking for fingerprints and any other traces of blood.

The main purpose of a crime-scene investigation is to find clues—yet the most mysterious thing about the house on Pine Terrace Court wasn't what was actually there, but rather, all that wasn't.

There were no victims, no signs of forced entry; there was no trail of blood leading away from the blood-soaked bed, no weapon, no ransom note; nothing appeared to have been stolen, no unusual messages were on the answering machine, and nothing other than the jewelry box and the purse had been disturbed—except perhaps for the wide-open back door, which had an inexpensive little portable motion alarm hanging on the handle whose battery had been removed.

The jewelry box was empty, so whatever had been in it was taken; however, assuming that the same person had dumped out Jennifer's black purse and set it back on the dresser top, there was an odd anomaly at work. It wasn't possible to be certain, but it looked as if nothing had been taken from the purse. Currency, change, credit cards—some of them unsigned—identification, car keys . . . everything of value that logically belonged in a woman's purse was all still right there, either on the floor or on top of the dresser.

Some sweat clothes were lying on the floor near the

items that had been dumped, and since a pair of underwear was still nested inside the sweatpants, it was clear that whoever had worn them must have hooked their thumbs into the waistbands of both garments and removed them simultaneously. It looked likely that they belonged to one of the Blaggs, probably Jennifer.

Beyond the bed and dresser there wasn't anything anywhere in the house that could even remotely be interpreted as a sign of struggle. No broken objects, nothing knocked over, no more spattered blood . . .

George Barley and Steve King stood in the bedroom looking left and right at valuable things that would have been so easy for an ordinary criminal to pick up and take. There was the handgun in the closet. At first glance it didn't appear to have been recently fired, but police seized it anyway and sent it off for testing. There were several portable safes that certainly looked like they could contain valuables. There was cash lying on the floor from the emptied purse, and there was also a bag of coins, complete with handles, in plain sight against a wall. If it hadn't been for the appalling amount of blood, there was almost nothing to indicate that it was a crime scene.

"This just doesn't look right," became the refrain throughout the day as Barley, King, and other investigators made their way around the house.

The detectives considered the possibility that a burglary had barely gotten underway when Jennifer surprised the thief or thieves in the act, provoking a violent reaction, followed by a panicked flight. But why, then, would such housebreakers-turned-attackers make the effort to take away a bleeding victim, but not anything more valuable than the contents of a jewelry box?

As the detectives checked out the Blagg residence, they began to consider other, more elaborate, possibilities.

Mike seemed to have an alibi for the workday, and he'd been extremely convincing during his extended interview the night before, right down to the polygraph exam and the fact that police using a black light hadn't found any traces of blood on his clothing.

Investigators continued to wonder if Jennifer could have snapped and killed Abby, grabbed the child's body, and taken flight. In that case the overturned purse and missing jewelry could have been a ruse to deflect suspicion from herself and cover her disappearance. Alternatively, they had to wonder whether Jennifer was involved in an affair and had either killed her lover or vice-versa—and then, whoever was still standing had removed the other person's body before taking off with Abby. Without knowing who'd bled on the bed, the detectives were up against a full range of wild possibilities.

As deputies interviewed the Blaggs' neighbors, one of them, Judy Currie, reported that she had seen what she was sure was Jennifer Blagg's maroon-and-beige minivan coming into the cul-de-sac from Greenbelt and heading toward the Blagg residence between 3:00 and 3:30 P.M. on Tuesday. Currie had been sitting in her sewing room at the time and she didn't notice who was in the van, but she told police she was familiar with it because she often saw the mother who normally drove it and her small daughter heading back and forth during the day.

The question of when anyone last had contact with Jennifer was of critical importance to the investigation. They knew when she was first missed—both at school and during Mike's series of phone calls—but questions remained as to when she had last been seen. Mike said that when he'd left, his wife and daughter were asleep. Then there was Currie's sighting of Jennifer's van being driven just about an hour before Mike returned home.

Police in Texas had sent officers out to contact Jennifer's mother, Marilyn Conway, who was frantic with worry after hearing that something ominous had befallen her daughter and granddaughter. The last time she had seen Jennifer and

Abby was two-and-a-half weeks earlier when they—and Mike—had come down for a visit on October 25 and 26 while Abby's school was off for parent–teacher conferences.

Conway told the investigators that the last time she had spoken to Jennifer was a phone call on Monday evening. Jennifer hadn't seemed upset or distressed, and Conway didn't recall there being anything unusual about the conversation.

Conway was undergoing cancer treatment, and she'd been expecting a call back from her daughter first thing Tuesday morning because of an important doctor's appointment Conway had scheduled for 9 A.M. Jennifer usually called her mom and prayed with her before such visits, and Conway found it very unusual when Jennifer hadn't done so that morning.

Helen West, a neighbor who lived directly across the street from the Blaggs, said she'd chatted on the phone with Jennifer about 8 P.M., and also thought Jennifer sounded perfectly normal. "She was not acting like a woman who was about to disappear the next day," West recalled.

Even though the Redlands Mesa area is just over the river from the municipal boundary between Grand Junction and the rest of Mesa County, the sheriffs quickly included the Grand Junction Police Department in the Blagg investigation. Grand Junction sent a canine unit over and the dog was given samples of Jennifer and Abby's clothing to sniff, hitting on a possible scent that took the dog, his handler, and accompanying officers out the door on a quarter-mile jog down the hill toward the Colorado River.

The dog's "track" to the river was another puzzle for investigators. On the one hand, it was one of the few solid leads to date; on the other, it was hard to imagine Jennifer, or whoever it was who had been bleeding, leaving the house on foot with an injury of that magnitude in broad daylight—possibly accompanied by a child—and making their way down to the river without being noticed, not to mention without leaving so much as one other drop of blood behind on the way. It was equally hard to picture any time between 6 A.M. and 4:15 P.M. on that Tuesday when an intruder would have been able to bundle up one injured or dead person, let alone two, and drag them down to the river through a populated area without being noticed.

What investigators were also struggling to figure out was whether the Blagg family was really the intended target of whatever had happened. Did some pedophile try to snatch 6-year-old Abby and kill her mother in the process? Did someone assume Abby was at school and initially try to rob, rape, or abduct Jennifer, only to have things spiral out of control? Was all this really some elaborate plot by someone who was angry with Michael?

There was the possibility that none of this had anything at all to do with the Blaggs. Maybe a burglar had entered the house thinking that everyone had left for the day, and was startled. Maybe someone bent on doing violence to another resident of Pine Terrace Court had mistakenly entered the wrong home on the cul-de-sac, where the houses, built at the same time, using a common architectural style, all looked similar.

There were at least a couple of the Blaggs' neighbors with high-ranking jobs in law enforcement, enough so that they might conceivably be targets of someone disgruntled by their interaction with the justice system. Tammy Eret, the deputy Mesa County district attorney, lived right next door to the Blaggs, and Grand Junction Deputy Police Chief Marty Currie lived across the street.

The Blaggs had only lived in this particular house for about nine months, which made police wonder if perhaps the home invasion might actually have been directed at a previous resident by someone who didn't realize the house had changed hands.

One of the first places investigators looked for answers was at the Bookcliff Christian School. The staff members were deeply shaken by the sudden turn of events, but tried to be helpful. Everyone seemed to remember that Abby had had an excused absence on Tuesday.

Investigators were briefly intrigued, because it sounded initially like someone must have called the school claiming that Abby was sick. But when they checked further, there was a far less mysterious explanation: a school official had been aware Monday that Jennifer had a cold, and when neither mother nor daughter had shown up on Tuesday, just wrote Abby down as an excused absence, assuming that both had come down with the same bug.

By Thursday afternoon, Mesa County District Attorney Frank Daniels had already made three trips out to the house to look at the scene and speak with the forensics investigators. But, aside from getting chemical confirmation that the gory stain in the bedroom was indeed human blood, there was nothing new that the technicians could venture as to what had happened.

Abby's bedroom on the second floor of the house was one of the least helpful spots to the investigators.

Her bed looked slept in. Claire, her favorite doll, was still on her pillow. Her room fan was still whirring and her school clothes were neatly laid out and waiting for her. The Mickey Mouse savings bank that she kept her birthday money in was still in her dresser drawer with $25 in it.

Nothing appeared to have been removed from the room, expect perhaps for Abby herself.

Downstairs in the entry foyer, Abby's pink Barbie backpack was still sitting on the floor with a note from Jennifer saying that Abby had completed her homework.

The technicians carefully marked a number in the corner of every single tile on the foyer floor and dusted each one for prints, coated them with luminol to check for blood traces, and then photographed them. They climbed up onto the roof and searched the rain gutters, and poked into the orange-colored swamp cooler to see if anything had been hidden in plain sight. They crawled through the crawl space beneath the house, and ran a tracking dog around and around the grounds to sniff for anything that had been tossed.

The only other place within the entire scheme of the house that yielded up something interesting was Jennifer's 2000 Ford Windstar van. The criminalists had searched through it using chemicals that allow blood to react and fluoresce when exposed to ultraviolet lights. Working in the darkened garage with the special handheld lamps, they had found several droplets, specks mostly, of what appeared to be human blood, both inside the driver's compartment and outside on the metal body of the van.

Inside, there were trace amounts of blood on the steering wheel, single pinhead-sized drops of blood on the brake pedal and the driver's-side door handle, and a thin smear a few inches long on the interior frame of the sliding door. Outside, there were two distinct drops near the bottom of the van's sliding side door on the driver's side.

Blood is incredibly durable, so just the fact that there were a few drops in a family vehicle wasn't that startling. A 6-year-old with an ordinary nosebleed can leave enough droplets around to make a place seem like a crime scene when it's forensically tested. But the find in the van might prove interesting if investigators could determine how fresh the blood was and, more important, whose it was. They would just have to wait to see what DNA tests could tell them.

# 8

**WITHIN** the master bedroom zone of the house, police found two separate notes that struck them as possible clues, one written by Jennifer—the other by Mike.

Taped to the mirror in the bathroom was a note that had been written out on a small form that had the title "Urgent Prayer Request" printed right on it. Jennifer had written her own title underneath, "The Key to Peace," and the entire note read:

> *Jesus has the keys to life and death. But, He's left me some keys also, health, marriage, material; and my will as to what I do with these keys. The Key to Jesus' peace is to give Him the key to my will. Trust Him with the keys He's left me. Give them back and trust Him w/ them. I'll have peace, because he says I will.*

The second note had been found folded up on the floor among the items apparently dumped out of Jennifer's purse. It was an undated letter that had been printed out on a computer, apparently from Mike, which read:

> *Jennifer, I love you! I am sorry that we have ruined this day and the opportunity to spend our lunch time together. I don't know what went wrong. My intent was to spend a wonderful time with you and coincidentally get some Christmas shopping done. That obviously went horribly astray. The Lord tells me to not let the sun go down on my anger and so I won't. You are the light of my life. I ask for your forgiveness for any wrongs I have done to you and I also forgive the wrongs I have perceived against me. I do not want us to waste a weekend being an-*

*gry with one another. I would love to take some
time today to talk through the problems we are having. I will send this as an e-mail and also I will
bring it home to you. After Paul says to not let the
sun go down on our anger, he says, do not give the
devil a foothold. Eph 4:27. I am sorry if I have
given the devil a foothold. I will always love you.*

While the work inside the house was proceeding
painstakingly through each room, with every single item
in every dresser drawer and shelf being looked at individ-
ually, the activity outside on Pine Terrace Court was moving at a much quicker pace.

The Redlands was still less of a neighborhood and
more of a collection of subdivisions rapidly taking shape
across what had been steep dusty scrubland sandwiched
between the Colorado River and the Colorado Monument.

A haphazard maze of hiking trails and even less-
defined mountain biking routes criss-crossed Redlands
Mesa, and for every neatly squared-off and fenced-in little cluster of back yards there was a much larger patch-
work of wide open fields where the streets had yet to
arrive, and cattle and coyotes still wandered.

Police were racing to try to figure out where someone
could have hurriedly taken one or two bodies in broad
daylight without being seen. Their main problem was that
in and around the Redlands, there were all kinds of locations that fit the bill.

The most obvious place was still the river. It was only
a quarter-mile from the Blaggs' house and it was downhill all the way. The first search dog had led them to the
river, and a couple of days later, a pair of bloodhounds
that were loaned by the Jefferson County Sheriff's Office
also followed a scent track that led from the house in the
general direction of the river before abruptly ending a
short distance away.

While fifty volunteers from both the churches the Blaggs attended fanned out to put up missing persons flyers and search the hiking trails, sheriffs in boats set out on the narrow stretch of the Colorado River, using long poles to probe the water for bodies. Nothing, not even a piece of clothing, turned up. At the end of the day, the searchers were right back where they'd started. A crucial forty-eight-hour period had passed with no trail, no trace, not a single real clue.

The clear hope among the residents of Grand Junction who were following the unfolding drama was that what had taken place was some sort of kidnapping rather than the potential homicide the police were treating it as— partly because with a kidnapping, it's possible to hold out hope for a rescue of the victims, and partly just because random homicides are rare in Grand Junction.

For reasons no one has ever really been able to get a handle on, Mesa County, with its 116,000 residents nestled in amongst some of the most awe-inspiring scenery on Earth, has one of the highest per capita suicide rates in the nation—nearly 40 percent more than the national average. About half of those who kill themselves are oil and gas workers, but there is also a real problem with people literally driving themselves like lemmings off the edges of the Colorado Monument. However, for all of the self-inflicted trauma, Mesa County historically has had a low homicide rate.

The city of Grand Junction once had eight murders in a single year, but that was something of an all-time high. Normally the half-dozen police agencies that are found within the entire thirty-mile length of the Grand Valley would see one or two homicides annually, maybe four or five in a particularly bad year.

Grand Junction is not a city where people worry a lot about getting killed, and the question that residents kept asking themselves was whether this was a random crime or whether there was anything weird about the Blaggs that would have made them a target.

The Blaggs had been in town less than two years, but praise for them among their acquaintances seemed universal.

"They are swell people, Christian people, and I don't know a finer couple," Fran Calvert, the church secretary at Monument Baptist told a local paper, adding, "They were involved in the music and children's programs, and Jennifer was involved in summer Bible school. Mike has a lot of support and we are all trying to be by his side."

"Mike's a great guy," AMETEK Dixson engineer Harold Watson, who lived less than a mile from the Blaggs, told the *Rocky Mountain News*. "I can't see him involved in this. His office has pictures of his family and his daughter's finger-paintings on the wall. We're baffled.

"We weren't always religious about locking the doors, and now we are," Watson added. "You really have to wonder."

Chris Durham, the Blaggs' current landlord, described them as "dream renters" who kept the Pine Terrace Court home in immaculate condition, but he noted that he really didn't know them very well. In part, Durham recalled, that was because he and his wife had eventually given up on their attempts to befriend the Blaggs after Mike and Jennifer failed to pick up on repeated invitations to come over to the Durhams' house.

That seeming insularity the Durhams had noticed certainly wasn't proof on its own of any broad anti-social streak, but as the days wore on without any sign of mother or daughter, there were others who also came forward remembering an odd, almost reclusive side to the Blaggs.

Tammy Eret, the deputy district attorney who lived right next door to them, said she'd actually paid close attention to Mike's arrival home at 4:20 P.M. that particular Tuesday because it was so rare for her to even see him.

Eret told the investigators, who came to interview her as part of their sweep of Pine Terrace Court, that in her limited contact with the Blaggs earlier in the year, they had always been "nice and friendly," but she was particularly surprised by the turn of events on November 13, because she'd actually thought they'd moved away earlier in the fall.

Eret had assumed they were gone because weeds were growing in the yard, the blinds all over the house had been drawn tightly closed, and she hadn't seen Abby out by the swing set for months.

After Mike waved to her that afternoon, Eret had gone inside and changed before dashing back out to a gym for a workout. She must have left while Mike was still inside his house on the phone with the 911 dispatcher, because she didn't notice anything dramatic happening on the tiny street when she left, but by the time she returned, Pine Terrace Court was swarming with sheriff's deputies and investigators. After picking up the gist of what was going on, Eret went back to her home and wrote a note to herself so she would remember the time Blagg had returned, in the event that it became important later.

Eret also wrote in her note that Mike's actions during the minute or so that she'd seen him driving slowly around their end of the cul-de-sac before coming to a stop struck her as "weird."

"It caught my eye," Eret would later explain. "Obviously that's what stopped me in the middle of the roadway. And then when I saw him pull in and park in front of his house, I just thought to myself, 'Well, that's kind of unusual.'

"He looked happy," Eret recalled. "He didn't just turn around and walk away."

On Friday, November 16, while detectives widened the circle of places where they were requesting interviews from people who knew the Blaggs to include the states that the Blaggs had lived in during the decade before they'd moved to Grand Junction—California, Texas, Arizona, and South Carolina—Mike came out of seclusion to talk directly with reporters at a press conference.

"Anyone who knows anything about my wife and daughter, I pray that you'll come forward. That's all we want. I just want them to come home," Mike said, urging the press to get the word out. "Just allow them to come home. That's all I can ask. Please allow them to come home."

Jennifer's mother, Marilyn Conway, stood by Mike's side and added, "If you know how to pray to the Heavenly Father, pray to Him. Ask Him to bring these precious people home."

It wouldn't be a press conference without a rude question, so Mike was asked point-blank whether or not he'd had anything to do with the disappearances. "No, I don't have any idea what happened to them. I want to know what happened to them," Mike replied firmly.

Asked if he'd retained a lawyer, Mike replied, "There's no need. An attorney would just get in the way right now."

Mike revealed that he'd placed the series of calls throughout the day on Tuesday trying to reach Jennifer at home, and said that he was as baffled as everyone else as to who could have wanted to harm his family. "My wife and daughter are the most loving people in the world. There's no one in the world that would hold any animosity towards them," he said. "Nobody . . . Nobody I can think of."

On Saturday over a dozen sheriff's deputies expanded the radius of their door-to-door canvassing efforts out several blocks in every direction from the Blagg residence, but still nothing particularly useful was turning up.

Sheriff's spokeswoman Janet Prell also changed the tenor of the official statements noting that, with four full days having passed with no sign of anyone, the detectives were now thinking that whoever had bled that much in the bedroom was likely to have died.

"We presume there's at least one death in this case. Whether it's one or two, who knows?" Prell said.

Mike Blagg refused to be drawn in to the pall that was descending. He always spoke about Jennifer and Abby in the present tense, and he began making little white cardboard pins wrapped in lavender ribbon that said "Hope— Jennifer and Abby," handing them out to his friends who were searching and to the many people who were stopping him around town and offering him their sympathy and moral support.

IT was clear that before November 13, 2001, very few people in Grand Junction outside of their churches had occasion to know the Blaggs. But within days of the disappearances, the police, the press, and the residents of the Grand Valley were rapidly coming up to speed on their shared history together as a couple and a family.

Mike told the investigators that as a born-again Christian, his life was an open book, and he would cooperate in any way possible in order to get his wife and daughter back. At every turn he appeared to be true to his word, consenting to interview after interview, and signing waivers so police could access bank, phone, and medical records.

Colorado's last major mystery involving a 6-year-old had shaken the state and grabbed national headlines five years beforehand, when child beauty pageant contestant JonBenét Ramsey was found murdered in the basement of her home in Boulder. Early on in the Blagg case, it was clear to reporters that whatever had happened on Pine Terrace Court had the potential to be equally baffling.

Looking closely at the Blaggs, there was just nothing sketchy about them. There was no history of contacts between either Mike or Jennifer with law enforcement in Colorado or the states they'd previously lived in. Neither had any criminal record. There was no indication they'd ever been involved in any public controversy or scandal.

Mike had been born a Roman Catholic in Sherman, Texas, and had moved frequently as a child, growing up, along with two brothers and his sister, on Air Force bases from Hawaii to Georgia because their father, Air Force Colonel John Blagg, was a career military attorney with the Judge Advocate General's office.

Mike spent his teen years in Georgia, attending Warner Robins High School. He was a quiet, polite kid, and certainly smart—an "A" student throughout. Neighbors remembered him constantly washing and polishing his car in the driveway and helping out around the street. He played some football and ran some track, but he was much more of an academic. He was a member of the Governor's Honor Program in his junior year and a recipient of the Georgia Certificate of Merit in his senior year—coveted awards for the absolute best students in the school system, all of which helped assure his rapid acceptance into college after he graduated from WRHS in 1981.

He enrolled in Georgia Tech and studied nuclear engineering, delivering pizzas to help pay his way through school. He also joined the Navy ROTC, so when he graduated in September 1985 with a bachelor's degree in nuclear engineering, Mike went straight into the Navy and soon began helicopter flight training.

At the age of 21 Mike also went straight into his first marriage—and then right back out again with an "amicable" divorce just a little over a year later. Investigator

Steve King contacted Blagg's first wife to see if there'd been any hidden sides to him that the police ought to know about, but she told King she had "nothing bad to say" about the year they'd spent as husband and wife.

After a few periods at sea and "lots of girlfriends," accompanied by "lots of drinking," Mike began to think about toning it down a bit. As part of that introspection, in 1987, he left behind his Catholic upbringing and became a born again Christian. It would take a bit longer before he completely left the wild partying behind.

In 1988 Mike's helicopter squadron was stationed in San Diego, where he went to a beach party with one of his best friends and bumped into Jennifer Loman, a student at nearby National University. Mike's buddy happened to be dating Jennifer's best friend at the time, so finding out her number afterward was no trouble, and Mike called to ask her out. Despite having been "warned off" Navy pilots as a general rule by her girlfriends, Jennifer remembered the imposing 6'1" aviator, quite favorably. Their first date would have an easy anniversary to remember: July 4, 1988. They had dinner at a Japanese restaurant, then took in a movie—*Who Framed Roger Rabbit*—and ended it with a spectacular view of the fireworks from atop Mount Carmel.

The confident young naval officer, who'd usually spent his nights out on the town with his hard-drinking, hard-partying buddies, was soon smitten with the gregarious 21-year-old brown-eyed blonde from small-town America.

Jennifer had grown up on the southern edge of Oklahoma, in the oil-rich country halfway between Oklahoma City and Dallas–Fort Worth, which helped explain why she was such an avid Dallas Cowboys fan.

Her parents had divorced when she was young, leaving Jennifer, her older brother David, and their mother, Marilyn, to form a fiercely loyal family unit.

"My mom's one of those cool moms in the world,"

David Loman would recall. "She would let you know pretty quick if you were making some tragic mistake, but Mom let us grow up and let us learn right and wrong."

David was just enough older—three years—that he fell easily into the roles of best friend and protector of Jennifer, nicknaming her "Bear," short for *teddy bear*, when they were both still toddlers.

As they grew, the pair would conscientiously take turns doing the things that interested each other, playing with David's toy cars for a while and then switching to Jennifer's dolls.

Jennifer developed an interest in ballet and playing the piano, taking lessons in both. Later she liked dancing, water sports, and just hanging out with her friends in a typical Midwestern town.

Smack in the middle of the Bible Belt, both children were raised to have a strong sense of Christian principles and a deep belief in God, making it all the more loathsome when Jennifer was molested sexually at the age of 12 by a male relative who took advantage of a young girl without a father to protect her. As an adult, Jennifer would feel compelled to witness in church as a sexual abuse survivor, and would tell her best friends that she had struggled with anorexia and depression as a consequence.

Whatever emotional and psychological trauma Jennifer had suffered silently as fallout from the molestation, her friends saw nothing but a successful teen.

The siblings spent a year together at Ardmore High School when David was a senior and Jennifer a freshman.

David made it a point to leave his Wednesday evenings open, because that was always "Jennifer's night," when he would join his sister at home to eat nachos and watch *Dynasty* with her.

As a teenager, Jennifer was well-liked and popular, an upbeat, energetic all-American girl with a crush on

Michael J. Fox. She loved music, and sang in choirs at school and in church. She made the drill team at school, was in the pep club, and had a part in Ardmore High's production of *Grease*.

As a teenager she'd been especially active in the Northwest Baptist Church's youth group, and she went on the annual spring ski trips to Colorado with her friends.

"She was a typical young lady," David remembered. "She did everything that normal girls do at that age. She socialized, she went to church, and she had reasonable boys for boyfriends."

As they got older, David and Jennifer remained tremendously close, making time whenever they could to go fishing together, more for the experience of hanging with each other than for any particular love of the sport.

Somewhere in their distant childhood, the siblings had agreed never to end any conversation or good-bye between them with anything other than the words "I love you," even if it was only to be for a few minutes. So when David learned that Jennifer was missing, he knew with absolute certainty what the last words they'd spoken had been.

Jennifer had graduated from Ardmore High School in 1985, the same year Mike graduated from Georgia Tech, and she'd spent a couple of years attending Oklahoma State before moving to San Diego with her mother. She was taking classes at National to finish her business administration degree when she met Mike.

As their relationship bloomed, it was Jennifer who was determined not to rush things. At one point she even threatened to break things off with Mike if he didn't quit his drinking and the type of partying that came with it. Mike continued to work to bring himself into alignment with Jennifer's expectations, and she continued to live with her mother in San Diego while dating Mike. They were dates that were punctuated with long absences when his carrier battle group sailed out on extended "cruises" to the Pacific, the Indian Ocean, and eventually the Persian Gulf, where he wound up serving two tours of duty in the combat zone off Kuwait and Iraq.

After three years of dating, and the war clear on the other side of the world, Mike and Jennifer, now 28 and 24 respectively, were married on November 16, 1991, surrounded by bridesmaids in iridescent purple dresses and the twenty epic Medieval-style stained-glass windows of the Broadway Baptist Church, a gothic landmark in Fort Worth, Texas.

Throughout their moves after they were married, including a brief stay in Corpus Christi, Texas, Jennifer kept in close contact with her brother and especially her mother, calling Marilyn on the phone and talking every day.

Abby arrived four years into the marriage on March 21, 1995, and even though it was Marilyn who was in the delivery room with Jennifer, Mike being at sea on the U.S.S. *Kitty Hawk* at the time, Abby effectively marked the end of Mike's career with the Navy. Soon after her birth, he began the transition from newly minted lieutenant commander to full-time family man.

Jennifer's pregnancy had been difficult on several levels, first because of a scare during an initial amniocentesis that indicated the baby might have Down syndrome, and then because Jennifer had gone from failing to gain enough weight, to gaining too much. After Abby was born, Jennifer continued to struggle for a time with her weight and with a severe bout of post-partum depression.

Later that year, Mike's first job as a civilian, with frequent military contractor AlliedSignal, moved the Blaggs to Phoenix. It was during those next couple of years in

Arizona that Mike's friends would notice he'd really cemented his conversion to evangelical Christianity.

By 1997 when AlliedSignal moved Mike to Simpsonville, a suburb of Greenville in the northwest corner of South Carolina, he had adopted a literalist interpretation of the Bible and viewed the world in the stark black-and-white terms of good versus evil. "There are angels out there, and there are fallen angels working for Satan," he would say.

Just going to church on Sundays wasn't enough for the Blaggs. As a couple, they became founders of a chapter of the Intercessory Prayer Ministry, part of a network of volunteers spread out across the world who set out to shower God all twenty-four hours of the day with prayers on behalf of believers who fill out forms requesting them. "This is a ministry that Satan hates," Mike would tell people. "Satan wants to cause problems to stop this ministry."

If there were demons scuttling around the manicured lawns of the Woodruff Lake subdivision trying to undermine the Blaggs' efforts, the neighbors certainly never saw them.

About the only thing that struck neighbors as out of the ordinary was the Blaggs' decision to downscale their cars—for the sake of the Lord. Mike was making good money, and he and Jennifer had come to South Carolina with his-and-hers BMWs. But they soon replaced them with Dodge Neons. Friends said the Blaggs told them that the matching Beemers had made them "uncomfortable," because "the lifestyle associated with driving BMWs interfered with their ability to witness as Christians."

From their two-story red-brick "starter home," set squarely amidst the nebulous swaths of suburban Simpsonville, the Blaggs struck those around them as a perfectly normal "God-loving" young family. There was nothing reclusive about them in South Carolina. They would walk Abby over to talk with neighbors on pleasant summer evenings and Jennifer would join the other young moms up and down the street to see a movie or have lunch somewhere.

The Blaggs seemed happy and, while it was clear to close friends that overall they had preferred living out West to their new situation on the East Coast, they didn't appear to be under any sort of strain. If anything, they seemed stronger than ever as a couple, with Jennifer especially having overcome some tinges of shyness she'd displayed earlier in her life, and stepping more confidently into her role as a mother and member of the community.

Karen Loman, Jennifer's sister-in-law, would recall that at some point, Jennifer had wanted to become a counselor for young women, because she believed that a lot of their problems stemmed from low self-esteem and, based on her own experience, Jennifer was convinced that if they could learn to overcome that, they would succeed in life.

The Blaggs were active in the First Baptist Church congregation, with Mike helping to teach the Sunday school group they attended for young couples, and Jennifer singing in the choir.

Less than three years after they joined, Mike was nominated to be a deacon. Pastor Randy Harling would later recall that it was an unheard-of honor for someone so new to the church, especially given its large size, but he said it was merited because they'd both had a big impact on First Baptist in the short time they had been there. Jennifer helped start a women's Bible study group and Mike taught one of the Sunday school classes for teenagers for about a year until his ultraconservative positions on abortion and homosexuality actually caused complaints, and he was eased out of the position—something that Jennifer had found highly embarrassing, according to her friends.

In her Thursday morning Bible study group, Jennifer came across as warm and empathetic. The women who came, mostly young mothers like herself, remembered both her commitment and spiritual depth on the one hand, and her ability to just laugh and live in the silliness of the moment on the other. "She had this terrific laughter. She would throw her head back and just roar until tears rolled down her cheeks," Nita Lyda, who helped teach the class, recalled in an interview with the Cox News Service.

Jennifer Coker, another friend from church who was interviewed, remembered that Jennifer "spent considerable time in prayer before ever saying a word. I remember at times asking her what she thought about something, and she would say, 'I don't know. I'm gonna have to pray about that first.' I've been a Christian for many years, and am still in awe of how strong her faith was."

Despite Mike's quiet, steady commitment to Christianity, and Jennifer's spiritual depth, the family member who made the deepest impression on Pastor Harling was actually Abby. In an interview with reporter Charlie Brennan of the *Rocky Mountain News*, Harling recalled sitting down with Abby shortly before her baptism in the fall of 1999 when she was still 5 years old.

"She had a real unambiguous desire to know more about God," Harling said. "She, in some ways, had a depth of understanding that a five-year-old should not have had. She was beyond her years.

"I must have asked her, 'Why do you feel like you're ready to do this now? Why do you want to consider becoming a Christian, now?'" Harling related to Brennan. "And her words were almost like, 'Well, you fool, you should know, you're a preacher.' So matter-of-fact.

"She said, 'Because God told me it's time.'"

When the family prepared to head to Colorado in the spring of 2000, friends noticed the understandable sadness that they would be leaving both people and a community they knew well. But overall, the Blaggs seemed to be looking forward to the move and Mike's new job.

Pastor Harling recalled that Jennifer had visited him several times for counseling prior to moving to Colorado, but he later told another reporter, "It was never anything marital. It was never anything of that nature, at all.

"There was never a time when she hinted, or plainly spoke, of any problems of discord. When she came to talk to me, it was other topics, other issues, unrelated to them or to their marriage," Harling said.

The Blaggs had arrived in Grand Junction and rented their first home on the northeastern side of the town, in a densely packed neighborhood that was home to many older residents. They made a good impression among the handful of neighbors who knew them, but privately they were off to a rocky start because for nine long months, the house they'd left behind in South Carolina languished on the market. Finally they took a hit on the price and got it sold, but in the interim, they had deeply depleted the savings they'd been building for a decade.

In her phone calls back to friends in Simpsonville, Jennifer said she wasn't entirely thrilled with life in Grand Junction. She felt it was fundamentally a blue-collar town where there wasn't much to do, but she noted that while Mike had been "miserable" in his job back in South Carolina, he was now happy, and Jennifer said that as long as that was the case, she could tolerate a few more years on the Western Slope.

Reverend Art Blankenship and his wife Rhonda met the Blaggs at their church in 2000 and were immediately taken with them. The Blankenships regarded the Blaggs, especially Jennifer, as open and friendly, the kind of "ideal family" whose portrait a photographic studio would probably single out to hang on their display wall. Art said that when they'd heard something terrible had happened inside the Blagg household, their first thought was "Is there some escaped prisoner on the loose?"

Mike and Jennifer became active in not one, but two

churches in Grand Junction, Monument Baptist Church and also the New Hope Fellowship Church, where they quickly began recruiting more "prayer warriors" in order to set up another new Intercessory Prayer Ministry chapter.

Jennifer had volunteered as a teacher's aide when Abby began attending classes at the Bookcliff Christian School, and across the board, friends said that the Blaggs appeared in every way to be a happy couple who were solid in their faith and enjoying raising their daughter in the shadow of the Rockies.

Jennifer decided to be a stay-at-home mom for Abby's sake, and friends said Abby showed every sign of being well-cared-for and loved.

Hardly shy, she would reach out to shake hands when introduced to adults, and stick around to talk. Endlessly energetic and inquisitive, Jennifer's friends laughed that Abby could sit them down and "talk until your ears ached."

A miniature Jennifer—as Mike liked to call her—Abby would go to bed singing, and wake up singing again in the mornings. Abby was an enormous fan of cookies-and-cream ice cream. She loved to go swimming and take hikes on the Colorado National Monument with her parents. She couldn't keep a secret and liked to be in the thick of activities in her first grade classes. As an only child, Abby was excited to be around other kids, but at the same time, she could happily spend hours on end amusing herself with her Barbie dolls, her collections of rocks and jewelry, and playing house and dress-up. In the evenings she would play just outside of the kitchen while Mike and Jennifer cooked together and then they would read story books and peruse a few religious devotionals before Abby went to bed at 7 P.M. each evening.

# 10

**IN** the days immediately after the disappearances, the entire investigative staff of the Mesa County Sheriff's Office had been up at all hours working on the few "hot" leads.

Tips were being phoned in, "lead sheets" were being assigned to officers for follow-up, a steady flow of interviews were coming in and being transcribed, and hundreds of items taken from the house were being sifted through for additional clues.

The town was rife with theories. Methamphetamine use was a real problem throughout the West, and certainly in Grand Junction, where there were thousands of remote places to hide labs in the surrounding countryside. Meth users are legendary for going off the deep end and doing psychotic things.

There had been run-ins in the past with "coyotes" smuggling illegal aliens through the region to job sites, and there were even roving bands of gypsies who'd caused trouble. There was speculation that some crazed child molester might have set out to kidnap Abby, and killed Jennifer in the process.

As the searches of the river and the Redlands continued, Mike was joined in Grand Junction not only by Marilyn Conway, but also by his own mother, Elizabeth "Betsy" Blagg, a retired corporate attorney; and by his sister Clare Rochester, a school administrator from Baton Rouge.

Clare Rochester had been in Mike's wedding to Jennifer and had met Conway before, but had never actually met Abby. Like the others, she was desperately concerned about what was happening, and wanted to be there to support Mike. The devastated little family group stayed in a bed & breakfast operated by a member of one of Mike's churches, where they tried to monitor the search operations, put up MISSING posters, and do whatever else they could think of to help.

Detective Steve King was working on the case around the clock and also meeting with Mike on behalf of the investigators as various questions came up. Mike was always eager to sit down with King whenever the detective had the chance, because their visits were his main window into what was going on behind the scenes. In friends' homes, relatives' hotel rooms, diners, and even in King's car on occasion, the men would chat about aspects of the case.

Friends described the Blaggs' "fairy-tale marriage" to investigators in tones tinged with awe. But some had also noticed that while Jennifer was the outgoing member of the pair, Mike could come across as distant and remote—maybe even obsessive and controlling.

King asked Mike to name the three things that he loved most about Jennifer. That was easy, Mike replied, they were her love for the Lord, her love for her family, and her "service heart" toward others. "She would do just about anything for anybody," Mike said.

King pushed further. He told Mike that he was painting a really nice picture, but it sounded almost too good to be true. Every relationship has its faults and challenges. What, King asked, had been the dark side to the Blaggs' marriage?

Mike paused and said that while there hadn't been a dark side, there was "an embarrassing side," because of Jennifer's cascading history of medical difficulties, which had made sexual intercourse increasingly painful for her.

"The Bible says you won't withhold your body from your mate," Mike told King. "She takes that very seriously. I do too." Mike explained that he and Jennifer had set about researching and trying "other things" they could do to please each other, especially oral sex.

Mike hesitantly explained to the detective that in the wake of Jennifer's hysterectomy, they'd been looking up porn websites on their computer as an "educational tool."

King nodded along in agreement, but in the back of his mind he was thinking, "Okay, that just doesn't play right." Mike and Jennifer were unquestionably quite religious, but that didn't mean they were completely naive. Considering that oral sex isn't particularly difficult to figure out, to the point that adolescent sexual behaviorists were still bemoaning an "epidemic" of it among the high-school-aged population, King didn't think Mike's life experiences as a college student, naval aviator, and twice-married man would have required him to do in-depth research on the subject.

# 11

ON Tuesday, November 20, exactly a week after Abby and her mother disappeared, Mike stood in front of an ABC television camera crew and took his appeal for help to the large national audience on *Good Morning America*.

Anchor Charles Gibson recapped the mystery that had taken place in Grand Junction before turning to Blagg.

"You have described this as 'a nightmare,'" Gibson noted over the video linkup from his studio. "How are you doing?"

"Well, right now, we're just taking it day by day," Mike sighed.

"I guess it's a hopeful sign that it's still a missing persons investigation?" Gibson prompted.

"Well it's always a hopeful sign when no one has been willing to say anything beyond that. It's a hopeful sign for me, because Jennifer, Abby, and I serve a God of hope. And we know that the Lord will bring them home to us. We just have to wait in His time."

Gibson asked if anyone had received a ransom note.

"No. And we've been waiting on all the phones that Jennifer or anyone would be able to call. We've been listening and waiting for that," Mike said.

Picking up on the elephant in the room, Gibson politely explained that he had to ask—could Mike assure everyone that he wasn't involved?

Mike could. He praised the investigators for their thoroughness and said he had been cooperating "in every way, fully and completely . . . leaving no stone unturned."

"Mr. Blagg, I hope—everyone hopes—you get good news out of all this," Gibson concluded as the interview was wrapping up.

"Charles, that's my prayer too," Mike replied. "I just pray that if anybody has seen Jennifer or Abby, please, please, Lord, let them call the Mesa County sheriff's department."

While Mike was talking to the nation, Sheriff's Investigator Beverly Jarrell was sitting down to interview two of Blagg's neighbors who had just returned home after spending a week on vacation.

Gary and Vona Murphy remembered the morning of November 13 quite clearly, because that was exactly when they'd left for Vegas. The couple told Jarrell that they did recall one strange encounter as they were pulling out of Pine Terrace Court between 7:00 and 7:15 A.M.

The Murphys described seeing a white female in a coat with a stocking cap covering her hair walking from Greenbelt Drive into their cul-de-sac. They thought the woman had a stocky build and stood between 5'2" and 5'4", but what caught their attention was the "intense, deranged, cranky, angry" look on her face as she headed into Pine Terrace Court.

The Murphys didn't know the Blaggs, but they told Investigator Jarrell that when they'd returned from Las Vegas, and saw Jennifer's picture in the paper, they were "ninety-eight to ninety-nine percent sure" that she was the unhinged woman they'd seen walk past them early on the morning of November 13.

# 12

A week after Jennifer and Abby vanished, the sheriff's office sent copies of their closely guarded initial reports and the information they'd gleaned to date from the crime-scene investigation over the Rockies to someone they knew would be able to keep a secret.

Retired FBI Agent Ron Walker had spent twenty years working for the Bureau, including assignments as a senior criminal investigative profiler, before becoming a private criminologist in Denver.

The sheriffs wanted Walker to take a look at the big picture on behalf of Grand Junction. What kind of crime, they wondered, was this likely to have been, and who would do something like this?

On November 21, a delegation of detectives from the Blagg investigation went to meet with Walker and look at his preliminary conclusions.

Walker was adamant: he felt the Blagg disappearances were almost certainly a double homicide that had been carried out by someone intimately related to the victims—and his chief and only suspect in that regard was Michael Blagg.

The massive pool of blood in the bedroom was an obvious indication, as far as Walker was concerned, that a homicide had taken place right on the bed and, since she'd slept right there, the logical decedent in that scenario was Jennifer.

The single most important and damning thing that stood out about the crime scene from a behavioral science point of view was the fact that Jennifer's body was missing.

Walker stressed that a mother and child at home in the morning in a peaceful upper-middle-class neighborhood were "low-risk" victims to begin with—and whenever murders do occur in that situation, it is extremely rare for the victims' bodies to be removed from the scene.

As a profiling "rule of thumb," Walker said that body removal indicated an intimate relationship between murderer and victim. Low-risk victims killed in their own homes are almost always targeted—and, as a matter of pure statistics, Walker told the detectives, 99 percent of the time in a case like Jennifer Blagg's, it would be an intimate partner who'd killed her.

Walker pointed out that if a burglar had been surprised in the act and lashed out in fright, killing the residents of the house, he would have fled as quickly as possible. A rapist would have done the same. Each might have paused to retrieve a weapon or to obscure some particular piece of evidence, but they wouldn't have any reason to take the body away, because doing so would increase their perception of risk.

Obviously, something bad had happened to Abby too, and Walker's strong suspicion was that she had been murdered instead of abducted. His reasoning stemmed from the same major clue, namely that Jennifer had been deliberately removed from the house after she had been bleeding profusely. Walker felt that if the intent had been to take Abby, and Jennifer had just been killed to somehow clear a path for kidnappers bent on seizing the child, then once Abby had been secured and Jennifer killed, they would have already accomplished what they'd come to do. Adding Jennifer's body to the list of things they had to deal with as they left the house with Abby would make little sense for an organized effort—or a disorganized one, for that matter. Walker argued that if someone had kidnapped Abby for money, it would have worked to their advantage to have Jennifer's body found by Mike with a note demanding immediate payment or else.

A victim's dead body is a tremendous burden for any killer, and being caught with it is the worst possible scenario for someone trying to avoid detection.

Most people who kill, especially in haste, distance themselves as fast as possible from their victims. Someone who was not expected at the Blagg residence to begin with, yet who ended up committing a murder there, would leave the bodies behind and just take their chances out in the wide world that the crime wouldn't be linked back to them.

Even far-fetched scenarios that Walker looked at, like some kind of professional "hit" killing or some long-simmering family or work-related vendetta targeting Jennifer and Abby as a way to get back at Mike, wouldn't have created any need for the killer to remove the bodies from the house.

Walker told the investigators he thought they were looking at a "staged domestic homicide," and that Jennifer was both the primary victim and the reason behind the murders. Abby was simply an "ancillary" victim. He also thought that Jennifer's killing had been planned in advance and meticulously carried out.

For Walker, too many things about November 13 didn't add up. The items dumped on the floor all belonged to Jennifer, and all the items that were missing appeared to belong to her as well. He concluded that the "ineffectual staging" was the work of someone trying to make it look like a break-in when they really didn't have any experience with what an authentic burglary looks like.

A real ransacking is a disastrous thing to befall a home. A burglar who doesn't care in the least what they harm—especially one potentially willing to kill a homeowner—can be expected to tear through a house like a tornado. Drawers, shelves, cabinets, dressers, closets, bags, boxes, cupboards, storage bins . . . all are pulled out and apart, rapidly raked through, and thrown anywhere and everywhere. Anything valuable is stolen and everything else is tossed, walked over, crushed, kicked, and generally treated like worthless trash before the burglar gets right back out the door in the shortest possible amount of time.

On a relative one-to-ten scale of typical burglaries, the Blagg residence didn't even score. What happened in the bedroom was way too neat and confined to really count as a burglary. The burglar had supposedly taken just Jennifer's jewelry and passed right by things like cash, guns, a laptop computer and other electronics, and three small safes. Those were all things that, for practical reasons, would actually be more valuable to the average burglar than jewelry.

"Burglars would canvass the entire home looking for valuables," Walker told the investigators.

He thought the real significance of the burglary scene in the Blagg bedroom was that it was there at all.

If the perpetrator had bothered to stage a little ransacking tableau for the police, then why did he think it was needed?

Walker's answer was that it was meant to divert attention. It was a billboard left for investigators meant to say, "An anonymous robber did all of this!"

Walker knew that if the person who had harmed Jennifer really thought that they would be unknown to any investigation that would eventually follow, then there would be no reason for them to try to divert suspicion to "someone else." All they had to do was get out of the house as quickly as possible.

But if Mike was responsible for what had happened,

then he would have a large checklist of things he needed to do in the house if he was going to successfully shift the blame elsewhere. Mainly he would've had to account for the fact that he hadn't seen what happened. There would be no way he could just leave Jennifer's body lying right there and then "discover" it when he returned home from work. First of all, even if Abby slept through her mother being killed, she would have to get up sooner or later—most likely sooner when both alarm clocks went off at 6:30 A.M.

Abby would have quickly found her mother's body and summoned help. Any investigation that kicked off within a few hours of Mike murdering Jennifer would quickly have been able to determine from her body temperature and other medical clues that her time of death had occurred before Mike left for work, thus destroying any chance of his having a plausible alibi. The only solution would be to remove Jennifer's body from the house.

Once Jennifer was gone from the equation, the cold math of the moment meant that Abby had to go away too.

Just as Mike's alibi couldn't hold up if Abby found her mother's body that early, it also couldn't survive if Abby woke up to an empty house and a mysterious bloodstain that appeared to be more than an hour old, right where her mother had been sleeping.

The only solution to the puzzle would be to remove every single person from the house who could vouch for the time-line of events that day, in order to try to widen the window when the trauma could have occurred to include the hundred or so minutes between Mike's departure for work and Abby and Jennifer's 8:15 A.M. arrival time at the Bookcliff school.

Ron Walker told investigators that the facts suggested that Mike had killed his wife and then his daughter before spending a considerable amount of time during the pre-dawn hours re-arranging things within the house.

Right from the beginning, the detectives had picked up on the fact that there was no smeared trail of blood from the bed across the carpet and down the hallway to the van, so something quite strong and impermeable had been used as a body bag to remove the corpse and the pillows from the bed in order to make the transfer.

Walker felt that whoever had set up the crime scene was juggling several competing needs. There was a need to adjust the time-line and a need to deflect suspicion away from those who belonged in the house. But at the same time, the level of restraint that had been shown in the amount of damage inflicted on the house and upon the personal property within it suggested to Walker that someone with a "proprietary interest" in the residence was making the decisions. Overall he saw what looked like a subconscious limit on the destruction they were prepared to inflict on their surroundings.

What burglar, hitman, child abductor, crazed meth head, roving band of gypsies, illegal immigrant smuggler, or homicidal friend, relative, or co-worker willing to kill or maim Jennifer and her daughter would care whether or not they got additional amounts of blood on the carpet?

Under Walker's scenario, "the perfect family" had nearly become "the perfect crime," except for two intractable pieces of evidence—the blood on the bed and the blood in the van.

Although they were polar opposites of each other— the bed was drenched in blood that couldn't be missed, while the van had traces so small they couldn't be seen without the aid of forensic techniques—the two areas where blood had been found became the bookends that set the limits for everything else in between.

Because of the location of the bloodstain and the lack of any blood spray or "cast-off" spatter patterns typical of stabbings or beatings with a blunt instrument, Walker felt that Mike had most likely shot Jennifer right in the head as she slept by placing a pillow over the gun to muffle the sound of the shot. He thought that would explain why two pillows were missing instead of just one.

A shot fired into the head while Jennifer was asleep with the covers pulled up to her neck, according to Walker, could also explain why there was blood on the edge of the covers, which were subsequently pulled down to the bottom of the bed.

Many well-planned murders throughout history have come undone because the perpetrators failed to appreciate just how much of a complicating factor large amounts of blood would present. It's a strange point of reference, because while everybody has blood, there are—fortunately—very few people who have much experience with large amounts of it being spilled around. Walker couldn't be sure if leaving the bloodstained bed intact was a last-minute change of plan necessitated by an insurmountable mess, but he was convinced that the blood traces found in the van were purely a mistake.

It was hard to imagine the profile of someone not directly connected to the household who would kill Jennifer and Abby and decide to remove their bodies from the house. It seemed preposterous to imagine that such a person would need to use Jennifer Blagg's van to remove the bodies and *then* return it to the garage, try to clean it of any traces of evidence, and put her keys back in her purse before dumping it over in her bedroom.

Walker thought the only reason the blood was still in the van was that the killer had failed to see and remove it. If it wasn't for the chemical luminol, the police might not have seen all of it either, but once the van came into play and Walker saw reports that there were water droplets on the foyer floor, which indicated it might have been mopped, he realized that considerable time had been spent trying to tidy up a murder scene.

Someone had clearly been up to no good in the Blagg residence, and whoever that someone was had spent precious amounts of time doing things there. Walker felt that indicated a "high comfort level" with the house itself, and an innate knowledge that they were very unlikely to be surprised in the act by, say, a returning husband. As far as a profile of the murderer was concerned, Walker felt all signs pointed to Mike.

# 13

**EVEN** before Walker's damning assessment, the sheriffs had been looking at Mike for any sign of involvement. But he'd passed their initial polygraph exam and they just didn't have any direct evidence tying him to the crime. Furthermore, for all of Walker's extensive statistical reasoning as to why Mike fit the criteria as the most likely perpetrator, his analysis wasn't designed to figure out a motive, and the sheriffs just weren't seeing one.

Time and again the investigators had heard about what a "good Christian" Mike was, and how the Blaggs were altogether just "the perfect family." When they'd pressed both Mike and Jennifer's relatives for any history of marital discord, or any hints from Jennifer that Mike had ever been abusive to her or Abby, the police weren't only met with denials, but downright disbelief and other angry reactions.

Jennifer's mother in particular wanted to know why the investigators couldn't shake off their perpetual interest in Mike and spend more time out looking for Jennifer and Abby.

The sheriff's problem was that twenty-hour gap from

the time any person other than Mike had talked to Jennifer up until the bloody bed was discovered the next day. There was nothing other than Mike's word to rely on for fully half of that time period, and as the sheriffs thought the case over, there were several things about Mike that continued to gnaw at them.

There was, for instance, a curious bit of information from Jamie Peden, Abby's Sunday school teacher, who recalled that on Sunday, November 11, 2001, Abby had mentioned that before she'd come to church that morning, her mother and father had fought over the last glass of orange juice. Jennifer Blagg wasn't in church that Sunday—the explanation was that she had a mild cold—and Mike had left before the service began.

It wasn't much to go on, but the notion that the argument the 6-year-old had witnessed was really all about orange juice seemed a bit unlikely, and, when combined with Mike's note of apology, it gave the sheriffs some hint that tensions might have been boiling over in the Blagg household just a day or two before Jennifer had vanished.

Interviewing one half of a couple about the quality of their relationship without the other person available to verify the information is a dubious errand, so the detectives decided to see what they could learn about the Blaggs' marriage by turning the spotlight on Jennifer.

Whenever he talked to police, Mike was effusive in his praise for Jennifer. He'd mentioned his deep religious faith right off the bat, even going so far during his first long interview on the night of November 13 as to have a sort of *Sophie's Choice* scenario worked out in his head as to whether his wife or his daughter was more important to him, based on some Bible verses.

The Blaggs had lived almost their entire lives in some of the major stops on the Bible Belt, and Mesa County itself was no stranger to evangelical fervor.

Grand Junction has a lot of churches per capita, but there are plenty of agnostics and even some full-blown atheists haunting the bars and enjoying the sushi in the trendier blocks downtown. There are also a few bow-legged loners with six-shooters straight out of a Wild West cattle drive, a handful of Rastafarianated college students who hate the world, and enough jittery methamphetamine "tweakers" bouncing through the side streets and yammering away in the backs of buses to cast a re-make of *Night of the Living Dead*. But, for all of its varied collection of subspecies, the population of Grand Junction is one where you can easily find plenty of faithful in Jesus' flock.

It was against that backdrop that the investigators began to examine the role that religion had played in Jennifer Blagg's life.

One of the first things that investigators came across when searching the Blagg household was a collection of Jennifer's diaries, notepads, and Bible study workbooks.

Having access to a diary written contemporaneously by the victim of a murder is just about the Holy Grail of homicide investigations, and detectives wasted no time flipping to the back pages of the big spiral-bound notebook to see when Jennifer's entries had ended.

Although the earliest sections, dating back to the Blaggs' years living in South Carolina, appeared to contain almost daily notations, Jennifer had made only three entries in the two weeks preceding her disappearance:

*10-30-01*
*Mike and I believe God has told us we will leave G.J., Co. in one-and-a-half years. I still pray about Abby's schooling, where to put her in 2nd grade? Where will we go? God will guide and lead us forward—that I'm certain of.*
*\*God is transforming me. Smoothing the rough*

*edges. He will help me with my weaknesses i.e. depression, anxiety. I just bought a book "Loving God with all Your Mind". I pray I'll be open to the Lord. I pray He'll continue to increase my love for Him. I can trust God to deal with me as he see fit and in His time.*

*11-5-01 Tue. In Colo.*
*I went to "Mom's In Touch" this morning. I felt that everyone else's praying was dead but mine. I prayed some "good stuff" with a lot of emotion and expression. When I left I felt, angry, confused about "their" dryness in prayer. I cried out to God about it. I went home ate and rested a little. Then I was ready to hear Romans 12:3-8 "transformed by renewing of mind," don't think more highly about myself than I ought. "God gave people different gifts." God indeed heard me and answered me. I was screaming, praising, crying, praying, thanking, asking forgiveness (repenting) asking for Him to change me. I love it when you speak to me Father, the sinful woman I am, yet you speak to me. I've asked that you'd "renew my mind." I believe you are and will. Thank you Father. May you get all the Glory.*

*11-11-01 Sunday in Colo.*
*I was sick with a mild cold so I stayed home from church. So, God spoke to me at home.*
*I watched Dr. Stanley's* <u>The Key to Peace</u>. *[Written by Atlanta minister Dr. Charles Stanley, one of Jennifer's favorite celebrity pastors.] I learned Jesus holds the* <u>key</u> *to life and death. He knows when you're gonna be born and die. But he left us some keys as well. Health key, financial material, relationships, future desires keys. I must give Him all*

*these keys. I had some prayer time. I prayed and acted like I was picking up health key, future key, reached out next to me and handed Jesus the keys. I may have to do it every day but, for today, He's got the keys and I've got peace. Thank you Father.*

On top of the TV stand in the living room the investigators found one of Jennifer's religious books titled *Winning Over Worry*. Examining it, police found a notation penciled into the margin at the side of page 55 which stunned them:

*Fought w/Mike on Fri. I unexpectedly got sick this weekend. 11-12-01 Colo. But, staying home from church, God blessed me w/Stanley's* Key to Peace Sermon. *And I had an incredible prayer time with Him about giving Him the keys to my life.*

It wasn't clear why Jennifer had included the date right in the middle of the short statement, but it was a godsend to the detectives, because it showed them it had been written on Monday, the last day anyone could verify that Jennifer had been alive.

The detectives quickly made the link between the fact that Jennifer must have watched a videotape of a sermon by Dr. Stanley about "the Keys to Peace" before she wrote the PrayerGram with the same title and taped it to the mirror in the bathroom. Taken along with the "Fought with Mike" reference, the "Don't let the sun go down on our anger" note from Mike that had been found in her purse, as well as Abby's statement about an argument over orange juice, the police were quickly building a picture of a tumultuous weekend of marital acrimony.

Police also found a much lengthier notation that Jennifer had written hours before she vanished, on a page of the self-help book entitled *Winning Over Worry*. Under-

lining several places for emphasis and adding stars next
to still others, Jennifer once again mentioned having
watched the "Keys to Peace" sermon the day before,
which indicated that that note too had to have been written on November 12:

> *God is ready to assume full responsibility for the
> life wholly yielded to Him.*
>
> *I also give God the things in my life . . .*
>
> *Giving God everything means giving Him my-
> self, my things, and the people I care about as well
> as the physical, the practical, and the emotional
> concerns of my life. All of these are His to do with
> as He likes. This complete commitment to God of
> all that I am and all that I have is another way I re-
> spond to God's love and try to love Him with all my
> mind—and making this commitment daily is (key).*
>
> *The Key to Peace. Dr. Stanley Sermon yesterday.*
> <u>*Although I have a plan, I want God's will for my*</u>
> <u>*life. I therefore hold my plan loosely and stand*</u>
> <u>*ready to defer to what He would have me doing dur-*</u>
> <u>*ing the course of the day.*</u> *After all, He is the One
> who enables us to meet Christ's challenge to deal
> with today's "trouble" and today's trouble only. . . .*
>
> *In other words, not only <u>do we not need to worry
> about tomorrow, but we also don't need to worry
> about the next hour.</u>*
>
> <u>*As you proceed with your plan and remain open
> to God's plan, you will find yourself walking with
> God through the day and not worrying about to-
> morrow.*</u> *That's obedience to the command of
> Matthew 6:34.*
>
> *1) You've prepared for the day,*
> *2) Made your plans,*
> *3) And lifted them before God in prayer.*
> <u>*Now live this day fully by experiencing the joy of*</u>

*the Lord, walking with Him as you go from task to task, meeting the needs of your husband, children, and others, and handling whatever God brings— and doing all this in His power and without anxiety. Then wake up tomorrow and do it again.*

*As C.S. Lewis wrote, (Important!)\* "Relying on God has to begin all over again every day as if nothing yet had been done.\*\*\**

It was the grimmest of ironies; the detectives couldn't help but notice that for all of her emphasis on not worrying about tomorrow, Jennifer appeared to have been killed later that very night.

# 14

**SO** often during the course of major investigations police end up wishing they had some real understanding of the victim's state of mind, some sense of why his—or her— routine was like it was, what he was capable of, any tiny window into what he really thought of the people around him . . .

Sitting on the TV stand in the middle of the living room in a simple spiral-bound notebook was an absolute treasure trove of insight into the very soul of Jennifer Blagg.

For nearly three years and 200 pages, Jennifer had kept a diary, sometimes fitfully, sometimes uninterrupted for weeks on end. Jennifer had intended for it to serve as a reminiscence of her journey to finally find and know God, and from the very first day she began it, it was written like a series of letters to Him.

Many of the entries for each day, written out in her exuberant handwriting and filled with her own idiosyncratic abbreviations, were little more than hastily shouted exhortations to God's greatness and praise for His name, replete with increasing numbers of exclamation points meant to show enthusiasm and sincerity. But threaded throughout the white noise of rapture and enthrallment were plenty of entries that finally gave detectives a real idea of who Jennifer Blagg was and what she had been thinking in the months and days before she and Abby vanished.

In an age of skepticism, and sometimes even cynicism, toward religion, Jennifer Blagg's most personal writings showed a sincere woman who never once expressed a doubt about God's existence. Nonetheless, it is clear from reading the voluminous entreaties she wrote to God that she assumed she was going to get something concrete in return for her devotion, and what she expected and desired from Him the most was answers.

Perhaps not surprisingly, Jennifer felt that God, as an omniscient being, would know how to solve whatever issues vexed her day-to-day existence. Throughout the journal, with varying degrees of patience and humility, she constantly asked Him to reveal to her the "right" answers to very specific decisions facing her and her family. Should Mike take a job back in Phoenix or in Indiana? Should she switch doctors or try a new medication? Jennifer was sure God could make the difficult decisions for her and that if she prayed long and hard enough, was good enough, and was willing to listen, He would eventually tell her what were the correct choices.

Jennifer seemed to view God as a substitute for the father she'd lacked growing up, going so far as to refer to Him coyly as "Dad" in a couple of her journal entries, while constantly searching for signs that He was trying to communicate directly with her. Although the journal is at first enthusiastic, almost playful, over time it's hard to miss the sense of desperation that crept in as Jennifer's health took turns for the worse and Mike's career prospects became murkier and more difficult.

The journal began during the first days of 1999, and as

the detectives combed through the hundreds of individual entries, they noticed that there had been profound mood swings on Jennifer's part as she went from asking and hoping and waiting to plaintive cajoling, then eventually wheedling and what looked like outright efforts at divination, trying to puzzle out the very mind and intent of God Himself in the years, months, and weeks leading up to her disappearance.

*1/11/99*
*God's blessings are countless.*

*Help me to keep this daily. Born from a lie (sin), May I be forgiven for that, do it no more and keep this going.*
    *BLESSING: Depression gone. Since New Year feel happy and energized.*

*1/14/99*
*As you know God, we've been praying about a move or to stay in South Carolina . . . ? And you worked it out where the Human Resources person called Mike in and asked what he was going to do instead of Mike having to go to Human Resources first. Praise, Praise, Praise. Then the guy from Phoenix called about the Lean Manufacturing stuff.*
    *Whatever your plan is Lord, I will do. I desire to be faithful and patient. Both of those desires come from you. I will not take credit for them. Lead us on and help me to care for others.*

*1/18/99*
*Blessing: Praise. God you are involved in Mike's work decisions. We don't want to react (against) the way you are working your plan out. We want to*

*move in the exact way you'd have us to. Thank you
for my family and the love you've given us.*

*1/25/99*
*I'm still sick but God is faithful. I've been praying
I'd be able to stand up under this and I have.
Praise him!.*

*I'm enjoying the Left Behind series. We are still
seeking your will Father about Mike's job move.
Mike said today he thought you said to him, "Relax,
don't worry, I'm working in this." Your Will be done!*

While Mike appeared to think God was urging them to
both take it a bit easier, it was actually Jennifer who, by
her own account, tended to be the family member most
prone to bouts of anxiety.

*1/28/99*
*Not a great day.*
    *I blew up at Abby.*
    *CMA is threatening to send us to a collections
agency.*
    *Mike is never at this desk and hasn't been an-
swering my pages quick enough for me . . . :0*
    *I'm mad and I can't believe someone is going to
send us to a collections agency.*
    *God help me to remain Christ-like in this situa-
tion. I need Wisdom and encouragement to be
Christ like to act properly.*
    *Toward the p.m. things started getting better.
CMA is giving Healthsource until the 15th of February.*
    *We watched a Billy Graham Crusade "Running
from God."*
    *Thank you Father for a changed attitude.*

2/1/99

*I've done Dr. Stanley's "Listening to God" Bible study. God you speak to me thru him often. Thank you. You've made him a blessing!*

*Today has been good. We are still waiting on [you] Lord for an answer to the job change. No answer, no change. You're God. What you say goes. Amen!*

2/2/99

*Lord, I pray for patience with Abby. She gets "time out" almost every day. What to do? Should we do what that article says—make the punishment be more than the crime? I.e if an 8-year-old breaks a rule in the house, sent to room for rest of day? Thirty minutes late coming in after date, grounded for two weeks? How do we handle this. She won't listen. It drives me bananas.*

*Praise you Lord, that you gave her to me.*

*Deadline ends on that job in Albuquerque, New Mexico today. Wonder what will happen? Whatever the Lord says will happen. You're my authority Lord. Gracious, perfect Heavenly Father! You know the best for us.*

*Mike got a call from that job in New Mexico that said, "we got your resume and we'll call you in about a week." God you only know the outcome. I'm excited <u>for now.</u> That you move us all over the country. On the move for you. Lord, teach me in your time.*

Jennifer had been having frequent stomach aches and wondered if God's unwillingness to heal her had to do with her not being spiritual enough, but she continued to write Him almost daily, willing to include Him on decisions large and small, imploring Him to take her under his wing . . .

*2/6/99*
*Great day. Park with Abby. Colored hair back to original color. Lord you allowed me to feel fine with it. Thank you.*

*2/8/99*
*No news on the job front for Mike. No problem, we are gonna be obedient and prayfully gracious about it. I don't want any regrets afterwards or to grieve the Holy Spirit.*

*2/9/99*
*Teach me about you. Reveal yourself to me. Please supply me with everything I need to do your will. May I always PRAISE YOUR NAME. You be my rock and my security. Help me to claim your promises. Teach me to love you and to want to go to you first with everything, not later, after I've tried stuff myself. You are my peace.*

*2/14/99*
*Praise your name Lord God! Your ways are perfect! Mike painted and finished the garage, built cabinets. It looks awesome. He also gave me chocolates, 100 roses, cut off the stems and floating in a flat beautiful vase. 2 snake chain necklaces and out to eat. But later was the best! Thank you Lord for my husband! He's the best part of me.*

Jennifer's health problems continued: her gallbladder was removed; her stomach aches didn't cease, and she wondered if they ever would. Her journal showed that she increasingly viewed the things that happened to her in a day's time as all part of a direct reward–punishment system meted out by God. Bad things that happened to her were punishments for some fundamental transgression, good things were rewards handed down from the heavens . . .

*2/27/99*
*Took Abby in today. Dr. said if she's not a lot better by Monday evening we may need to do an X-ray to see if she's got pneumonia. God please let her be better TODAY! I didn't let the Lord work me at all today until 9 p.m. when I was convicted to pray for forgiveness for the way I have acted all day. How dare I leave the Lord out of my day? Who do I think I am? I did pay for forgiveness and I believe He has forgiven me. I am truly sorry.*

*3/1/99*
*Abby is still coughing, still sounds syrupy. She has a 2:30 appointment today. Maybe they'll do a chest X-ray to see what's going on. Lord—I know you are in control. You won't forsake us.*

*Lord thank you for the tax refund. Please tell us how to use it. It's your money. Should we give ten percent back to you? How do you desire us to use it?*

*Lord, as you know Abby was diagnosed with asthma. Is that a correct diagnosis? I'm not sure but I want to hear from you. I desire to raise her and take care of her the way you'd have me to. I asked if we could have her evaluated for ADD. Lord—You have got to control this. I'm clueless where this could go. Only, I want (need) to trust you completely for her well being.*

*3/16/99*
*BLESSING! Wonderful Father I pray for my (your) Mike again today. For peace, calm heart and mind,*

Together, Mike, Abby, and Jennifer Blagg struck those who knew them as "the perfect family." *Mesa County Sheriff's Department*

2253 Pine Terrace Court was an ordinary house on an ordinary cul-de-sac in the Redlands when mother and daughter suddenly disappeared.

*Eric Francis*

Blood pooled on the floor next to the bed in the Blaggs' master bedroom.
*Mesa County Sheriff's Department*

Police thought the items dumped out on the floor of the master bedroom looked like a "staged burglary," not a real ransacking.
*Mesa County Sheriff's Department*

**PLEASE HELP**

**Jennifer and Abby Blagg**

disappeared from their Grand Junction, CO home on November 13, 2001.
The circumstances surrounding their disappearance have led
Investigators to believe foul play may be involved.

- All Information is Valuable -

**If you have information—Get Involved, Help this Family**
Mesa County Sheriff's Office (970) 244-3500
Crime Stoppers (970) 241-STOP

Thousands of missing posters like this one went up all across the American West.
*Mesa County Sheriff's Department*

George Barley, known as "Big Daddy" to his fellow detectives, was the lead investigator on the Blagg case.

*Eric Francis*

The "smoking gun"—Jennifer's keys to her minivan—were right underneath her overturned purse.

*Mesa County
Sheriff's Department*

plan is quite different from my plans.

I remember reading about <u>Thomas Edison's reaction</u> as his laboratories were burning and his life's work was going up in flames. He exclaimed, "Son, go get your mother quick! She's never seen a fire like this!" When looking over the smoldering ruins the next morning, he was able to say, "Just think. All our mistakes have been

*Fought w/ mike on Fri.*

*I unexpectanly got sick this weekend. 11-12-01 colo. but, staying home from church, God blessed me w/ Stanley's Key to Peace Sermon. And I had an incredible prayer time w/ Him about giving Him the Keys in my life.*

Jennifer's handwritten note that read "Fought w/ Mike on Fri." and "11-12-01" was a pivotal clue. *Mesa County Sheriff's Department*

A camera at Ametek Dixson showed Mike arriving at the factory at 5:56 A.M. on November 13, 2001.                     *Mesa County Sheriff's Department*

Police suspected the bodies had been placed in a large blue industrial dumpster at the Ametek Dixson factory loading dock.                     *Eric Francis*

Sheriff's Investigator Steve King on the landfill deck where he and his colleagues spent "53 days of burning hell" digging for clues.          *Eric Francis*

Sheriff's Lieutenant Dick Dillon led the grueling search of the landfill that cracked the case.          *Eric Francis*

The sheriffs hand-searched nearly 5,000 tons of trash in hundred-degree heat at the Mesa County Landfill. *Mesa County Sheriff's Department*

Dr. Rob Kurtzman, one of Mesa County's coroners, identified Jennifer Blagg's body. *Eric Francis*

Attorney David Eisner was the public defender who zealously defended Michael Blagg at his lengthy trial.

*Eric Francis*

Prosecutor Frank Daniels called nearly a hundred witnesses and nailed Michael Blagg with a conviction for first-degree murder.     *Eric Francis*

The excavation into the landfill found Jennifer, but the sheriffs are convinced Abby remains somewhere in its depths.

*Mesa County Sheriff's Department*

revelation, not pride. When pride comes in have the Holy Spirit convict him to pray. Lord, I thank you for having a sense of humor. I said you didn't but Lord you do. Praise your name, you know we've been struggling (four months worth) with finding Safeguard's telephone number. This morning a van in front of him, Mike wasn't happy. When he looked more closely and it was a Safeguard van with an 800-number on it. Oh _me_ of little faith. You are so good. Thank you Lord! You just made my whole day. Thank you!

3/24/99

My appointment is today at 1 p.m. with Dr. Harris. I have prayed for calmness, healing, confidence, lack of timidity, but also power and wisdom. You say I can ask you for anything in Jesus' name and it will be given so the Son can give you glory. I believe this. Give me faith.

It's 12:40 I'm a bit nervous probably because I'm going to talk to someone I don't know about my difficulties. Not always very easy.

The appointment went pretty good. Severe PMS is increasing anxiety in me. He put me on Effexor. I've prayed Lord you will help me get better and be done with anxiety and depression. I believe you will. I have to believe. My faith is in you. You perfect my faith and trust. All glory goes to you!

3/25/99

Horrible reaction to Effexor. Worst one I've tried yet. God is faithful however.

3/26/99

Mike put in for another job in Ohio. Lord, your will be done.

*4/6/99*
*Abby said today that every time she sees the "cloud" left by a plane that it made her think of Jesus coming to get her back. How <u>cool</u> is that? She's amazing Lord.*

*4/7/99*
*Abby and I and everybody from church had a blast at the Park. Mike got a call about a position in Texas. Only you know Lord. I'm not sure about any of these places. I'll go anywhere you say Lord, just change my attitude if I don't comply. I know your will is perfect.*
*Mike got an offer from Ohio. Is that our confirmation Father? Or is that a distraction from your will? Is it here, Ohio, or Texas? With Allied Signal or without? Lord, calm my heart down. Stressing is not trusting.*

As the job search dragged on, Jennifer tried to keep her spirits up, writing almost every day about what struck her, from a hike in the park with Abby to her concern that Satan was behind the high school shootings in Littleton, Colorado. But throughout it all, she never seemed to have an unkind word about Mike, hinting occasionally at episodes of discord, but always blaming herself for them . . .

*5/1/99*
*I went to see "October Sky." Good movie I told Mike he should go see it. Lord, I get mad at Mike for really no reason. I've been off the Natural Phases [a homeopathic PMS remedy] for two weeks and, sure enough, I'm one-and-a-half weeks short of starting and the anger has started. I can get so angry. Help me with this please. Give me the wisdom and knowledge to deal with this. I always*

*end up back here. Where's the answer? I know you
have it.*

*5/31/99*
*Mike and I got fried down at the pool. I hate it when
I do that, stupid, stupid. I forgot the sunscreen. I bet I
don't again. Lord, help me to remember to take and
to put sun protection on. This is the skin you gave us
and to abuse it this way is sinful.*

In June of 1999 Jennifer's father died in Oklahoma
and she stopped writing for several weeks as she traveled
out West to attend his funeral, wracked by difficult emotions. In August she was back out on the East Coast and
within a month, she got to see in person two of the people
whose books, videos, and sermons had had such a profound impact on her thinking and her life . . .

*8/8/99*
*I got to see Dr. Charles Stanley preach at his church
in Atlanta this morning. What an awesome gift you
gave me. I left it in your hands and you allowed us
to go, see him speak about "drifting away from
God", AND you allowed me, Mike, and Abby to
meet him. How awesome it all was. I thank you so
very much for your gift Lord. You even worked it out
for us to sit in the second row center. This church
was gorgeous but I'm not sure how I feel about all
the "showy" stuff. He's big time Lord but not arro-
gant. Praise your holy name for using him the way
you are.*

*8/12/99*
*The power went out at 3 p.m. today when it was
about 105 degrees. I panicked. We prayed and
prayed with Abby and Lord I knew you'd take care*

*of us. However, in all my fear and faithlessness on
my part I said to Mike, "If the power doesn't come
back on and we are in a hotel I'm not going to the
Beth Moore conference." Oh, how Satan was rejoic-
ing. Thank you Lord, you fought for me even when
my faith was nowhere to be found. The ugliness
came to me like a blast furnace and I would have
missed out on you completely Lord. You spoke to me
so gentle—go, my child, go.*

*9/13/99*
*Beth Moore seminar in Columbia.*
　*GET OUT OF THE BOAT!*
　*Praise God unashamedly. Focus on Him and let
the chips fall where they may. Will I let the Holy
Spirit jump in me.*
　*SHOUT TO THE LORD!*
　*"Be ye filled" Beth wrote in my book.*
　*"Lord, blow my mind"*
　*"Lord, you are WILD!"*

*9/16/99*
*Started feeling sick. Sinus symptoms. Lord you are
the VICTOR. HELP ME! Satan is truly trying to
discourage me Lord—heal me. Give me faith with no
doubt. Put Satan in his place. Don't allow him to in-
vade my body with an infection. Protect me FA-
THER! Heal me. I do feel worn out but help me
fight. Send your angels to fight this thing please.
I want to be found faithful in this!*

In February of 2000 the Blaggs got the job offer from
Colorado that would change their lives. They felt God
had finally spoken to them, and in a few short weeks they
had made their move out to the edge of the Rockies . . .

5/4/00

*We haven't found a church yet, however, you are faithful Lord. I'm praying about a community wide Beth Moore study or a church wide study. Lord I know you will answer me. Today I felt horrible and pulled a muscle in my back. Could Satan's demons have something to do with that?*

5/13/00

*Abby told me Satan hated her. Was she right? I told her Yes. But god loved her and would help her. He was bigger than Satan. I cried, she makes me Lord. I pray Abby's desire for you increases everyday. And she lives for you. How awesome you are. You love us so much.*

5/20/00

*We went to the Rockies (30 minutes away) Your creation Father is beautiful. I was so moved I was in awe. You knew what I'd like. Thank you Dad.*

5/23/00

*I've just finished "Healing for Damaged Emotions" Lord thank you for sorting all this out for me. I know you are in the process of healing me. You will turn it all good and have a lot already. I thank you for being my Perfect Parent and protecting me all these years. You're not going to stop. What do I need to pray? Who do I need to forgive? How do I be "the real me" and not the false me? How do I raise Abby without teaching her to be false and people will like your patterns? How do I know which voice is yours and not mine or Satan's?*

*6/17/00*
*Mike and I had a serious talk about our lack of communication abilities. It was very serious, Lord—I feel hopeless, but I shouldn't, after we talked I prayed and you gave me Ps. 142. How comforting you are for me. So faithful when I'm faithless.*

*6/18/00*
*Father's Day. We went to Bookcliff and it was a message for us. First, fathers are to be the spiritual leaders of family. Second, in your own gentle way you are leading Mike and I to a better marriage as better Christians. More mature. That takes time and surrender. Lord, thank you for growing me and Mike.*

*7/24/00 [six hand-drawn stars for emphasis]*
*GJ CO*
*God asked me to have a heart undivided toward him.*
    *Deu 30:6 The Lord your God will circumcise your hearts and the hearts of your descendants, so that you may love him with all your heart and with all your soul and live.*
    *He allowed me to see the ugliness of my heart. T.V., Mike, Abby, laziness, most everything else ahead (instead) of him. Most of all a self-centeredness, a selfishness about my heart.*
    *I want what I want for my future: the house to sell in South Carolina, a great house here in Colorado with a pool no less, a sport SUV car. God desires to give me things, but somehow my heart isn't right to accept His gifts.*

*2/19/01*
*On February 14th Mike took me and Abby on a Valentine's treasure hunt. At the end was a beautiful 2000 van. Lord—he is a gift straight from*

*your hands. I don't deserve him or your love. It's*
*mercy and grace from you.*

Throughout the next couple of months, Jennifer began
to worry on for pages that she might be getting a tumor. In
late April she underwent an MRI scan and then spent days
writing about her anxieties while she awaited the results.

*5/2/01*
*I found out my MRI was normal. And I wasn't ready*
*for that for some reason. I stumbled big time when I*
*received the news. I really thought it was going to*
*show a tumor. It is still confusing to me. I desire to*
*please God so deeply. You know that Father.*
　　*I was scared during the procedure. I asked God*
*to give me a picture of him. Boy, did he. Jesus came*
*and <u>attached</u> Himself to me. Face to face. Hand to*
*hand, legs to legs. He stayed that way the whole*
*time. He never left me. Mom wrote a poem about it.*
*She had no idea what happened to me during the*
*MRI but God did and he had her write about it. It*
*was very like what I went thru. It was so God.*

# 15

ON Monday, November 19, 2001, seven additional detectives from the Grand Junction Police Department
joined the fifteen Mesa County sheriff's investigators already working on the case. The extra manpower was
pulled in to help with a number of interviews that remained to be done among the 180 employees working at
AMETEK Dixson, as well as the staff and volunteers who
worked at the Bookcliff Christian School.

　　Two boats were still out checking the Colorado River.
The Colorado Bureau of Investigation had taken 150

pieces of evidence from the Blagg home to their crime lab in Montrose for a closer look, but nothing was making much sense.

In the absence of any clearer leads, Mike had from the start been rather resigned and understanding about his automatic status as a potential suspect—as long as it was expressed in the broadest possible sense of the term. However, as November became December, it didn't seem like the investigation was moving in any other promising directions. Mike was obviously becoming increasingly grated by his constant introduction in press reports as the guy who "hasn't been named as a suspect, but hasn't been ruled out either . . ."

The press had picked up on Tammy Eret's description of Mike's strange demeanor when he'd driven home the day of the disappearances. The public also made note of her perception that the Blaggs had seemed weirdly reclusive during the short time they'd lived on Pine Terrace Court. Mike dismissed Eret's comments, particularly the one where she said she'd thought the Blaggs had actually moved away until she saw him that afternoon. Mike said it seemed like a misunderstanding, and that any tendency toward insularity on his and Jennifer's part was just a sign of "closeness."

Mike vehemently denied that his marriage had been under any stress, arguing instead that he felt the past two years had been the strongest out of the ten they had been married, an assessment that Jennifer's mother Marilyn told investigators she agreed with, based on her daily phone conversations with her daughter.

When the crime-scene technicians had finally examined and cataloged every bit of minutia they could find on Pine Terrace Court, the sheriffs took down the yellow tape that had been sealing off the property for seventeen days straight and officially released the house back to Mike, along with those remaining contents that they felt couldn't possibly have any evidentiary value.

Reporters who called Mike as he prepared to go back in and inspect the property again asked him the big but inherently tactless questions that were on everyone's mind about whether or not he was somehow involved, and if he knew where his wife and daughter were. "I absolutely had nothing to do with their disappearance," Blagg said, trying to manage a weak smile. "If I knew where they were, I would have brought them home."

Mike paused and then added, "I am a follower of Christ, and I want to also say that Jennifer and Abby are Christians. If they don't come home to me, they are home in Heaven, but my selfish hope is that they will come home to me."

Steve King had come along, officially to hand the house over to Mike, but unofficially to observe Mike's reaction to being back inside the residence he'd shared with Jennifer and Abby for nearly a year. The sheriffs weren't really sure whether they were turning property back over to a victim or watching a murderer return to the scene of his crimes.

As they reached the door, Mike visibly began to shake, and after he'd walked inside, he at first seemed almost afraid to look around. When he reached the small kitchen he sat down at the table and began to cry. After he'd had a chance to regain his composure, King asked him if he would check the hall closet to see if any of Jennifer or Abby's winter coats were missing. The investigators had seen some hanging there, but they wondered if there were others that either of them might have worn out the door on November 13.

As Mike flipped through the items that were still hanging on the bar, one of Abby's coats fell off its hanger onto the floor. Mike picked it up, held it against his face, and began to sob silently as King intently watched his every move.

# 16

**IT'S** difficult to say what the "correct" attitude or response really is when something unprecedented happens in someone's life. Different people really do react very differently to things like stress, emergencies, grief, and bereavement, and despite his willingness to put a brave face on it, Mike was feeling a great deal of frustration with the sheriffs' unwillingness to officially clear him. He could tell that even among his friends and his co-workers, there were seeds of doubt. People were taking a close look at him, weighing his answers, judging whether his emotions and reactions "seemed right" or "seemed off."

He began to worry that the lingering suspicion would eventually cost him his job.

"Are there investigators that still believe I did this?" Mike asked Steve King during one of their informal meetings. King explained that unless and until Mike could establish a complete alibi—including the nighttime hours before he left the house for work—there were going to be detectives who had doubts about him.

"Our goal here is to eliminate you as a suspect in this case," King kept saying. "So how can we do that? What information can you give us so we can eliminate you?"

Mike argued that without Jennifer to verify that he had been in bed with her the entire time, he was caught in a chicken-and-egg dilemma. King said that he understood, but that that also meant it wouldn't be possible to fully clear him until the killer was found.

"Well, I'm very disappointed," Mike replied. "I want to get to the point where I'm not a suspect."

Once again Pastor Harling from South Carolina stepped forward to defend Mike, telling the *Rocky Mountain News* in an interview that Mike's "stoic and reserved" nature shouldn't be taken as a sign he was hiding something, because "Mike has always been an outwardly unemotional person." Harling added that back home in Simpsonville, "Literally thousands of people are praying for him by name."

Mike began another round of high-profile media interviews in an attempt to get the word out across the country about Jennifer and Abby. The disappearances would normally have been a much bigger story, but they had a tough go of it when it came to getting air time because there was still so much news echoing around the world in the wake of the September 11 terrorist attacks.

Rather than just remaining sanguine about it, Mike began to explain to reporters why he thought he still hadn't been cleared.

"I know I had nothing to do with it, but there's a protocol they have to go through before they can unequivocally say, 'Michael is not a suspect,'" Mike said to a reporter with the *Rocky Mountain News*.

During some of his interviews Mike also began peeling the curtain back a little further, giving the press a hint about some elements the sheriffs didn't want detailed, like the wide-open back door and the missing jewelry. Those were things that only the perpetrator would know, so police wanted them kept quiet. But at the same time, Mike knew they were things that had the potential to shift suspicion in the minds of the public away from his "reclusive" habits and back onto an unknown intruder.

Mike was joined by Marilyn Conway on a segment of *Inside Edition* where he again talked about the series of calls he'd made trying unsuccessfully to reach Jennifer throughout the day that she and Abby disappeared. The anchor asked how Marilyn was holding up emotionally under the strain. "You hang on. Jennifer would expect me to hang on," Conway replied, adding ruefully, "I want to know everything. They're both beautiful children, and I want them back."

While Mike was again making appearances in the media, the sheriffs were scaling back some elements of the investigation. With over 1,200 man-hours spent on the case by over two dozen officers, the initial canvassing of people and places most closely associated with the three Blagg family members had been completed. Detectives remained on the case, but the number of deputies assisting was reduced from sixteen to nine because there were other ongoing cases around Mesa County, including several sexual assaults, that needed attention.

# 17

**THE** weather was growing increasingly cold, but the next weekend, six horseback riders went back to the point the bloodhound had originally led to on the southern bank of the Colorado, and the search began again along the river-bank. Once again, sheriffs' deputies were also back in their boats working their way along the river under the cloudy skies, but with the same frustrating lack of results.

"The dynamics of the water change from day to day," Mesa County sheriff's spokesman Chris Franz told reporters. "If we're not out here, we may miss it."

That Sunday the searches were cut short as snow began to blow through the air.

Three weeks after the disappearances, the Colorado Bureau of Investigation was finally able to provide the Mesa County sheriffs with one of the first solid clues to the case. The CBI had gone through the Blagg residence collecting toothbrushes and hairbrushes in order to get enough DNA that belonged to Jennifer and Abby to develop a reference sample that they could test the blood-stains against. It had taken time to get results, but the tests were conclusive—the DNA found in the blood on the bed, the bedroom carpet, and at various points in and on the Windstar van all belonged to Jennifer. The tests also showed that her bloodstains were not intermingled with any other people's blood.

On December 18, 2001, several of the sheriff's investigators, including Sergeant Rusty Callow, Captain Baker, and Lieutenant Dick Dillon, sat down with FBI Agent Ron Baker for a conference call with FBI Special Agent Gerard Downes, the supervising agent of the FBI's Critical Incident Response Group from the National Center for the Analysis of Violent Crime.

Like Walker before him, Downes felt the circumstances of the case were "highly suspicious" because of the removal of the bodies from the house. Downes' conclusion was that "much of the focus needs to be placed on Michael Blagg."

Detectives were deciding their next move when a cruel hoax caused a brief flurry of activity. Someone pretending to be Abby called a 12-year-old girl who was a member of one of the Blaggs' church congregations, claiming tearfully that she was in Mexico and needed help. When police contacted the phone company, they quickly learned that the call had originated from within Grand Junction.

# 18

AS one of dozens of routine requests they were making of him, Mike had given the sheriffs permission to go to his office at AMETEK Dixson and retrieve his workplace computer. The sheriffs wanted to see if anyone at work had sent him any strange emails or if there was something Mike might have forgotten about that, in hindsight, might provide some guidance as to what had happened.

What they found during their first initial examination of Mike's hard drive actually pulled them up short.

Mike's note to Jennifer that had included the memorable line, "I am sorry if I have given the devil a foothold," was in Mike's email drafts, but hadn't actually been sent. That wasn't a surprise, but investigators were shocked when they saw the time the computer indicated it had been written and printed out—3:58 P.M. on November 13!

There was no possible way a note printed just a couple of minutes before Mike left work that afternoon could have ended up amongst the contents of Jennifer's over-turned purse unless Mike had carried it into his house twenty-two minutes later and planted it there himself in the seconds before he picked up the phone and dialed 911.

When he next sat down for coffee with Mike at one of their informal chats, Steve King took the opportunity to slip in some questions about the note. When had Mike written it? Had it been a big fight? What was it about?

Mike was vague. He remembered having written it and printed it out several days earlier, probably that Fri-day, but he didn't remember the reason for their quarrel. Whatever it was, he was sure it hadn't been a big deal, just something Jennifer had taken wrong and which had blown into a tiff.

King relayed Mike's answers back to Barley and the others.

Behind closed doors at the sheriff's office, there was a definite bad feeling about Mike, but his version of how the note had come to be in Jennifer's purse wasn't unrea-sonable. Besides, it was hard to see how the alternative scenario made much sense.

If Mike had prepared an advance plan to plant a note at 4:20 P.M., then it could only mean that he had done something to Jennifer and Abby earlier in the day. But even if he'd staged the overturned jewelry box and purse to deflect suspicion away from himself and toward a mysterious intruder, how would adding the note to the purse help that scheme?

If he had harmed his wife and daughter, then this particular note, with its intimation that there had been some sort of recent "angry" spat between husband and wife, sounded like the last thing Mike would want to hastily type up and slide right under the noses of an investigation that he would have known was only minutes from descending upon him.

Mike's work computer wasn't the only thing that the sheriffs were interested in checking out at AMETEK Dixson. They were also curious to know exactly what Mike had been up to at work.

No blood had been found in Mike's white Stratus, so the investigators were pretty confident that if Mike was the person who'd removed Jennifer and Abby from the home, he hadn't taken them to work in his car trunk that morning. But still they wondered if there was anything about the factory that Mike could have used to facilitate the disappearances.

As the sheriffs poked around AMETEK Dixson, their efforts to look for anything out of the ordinary about Mike's behavior, especially on November 12 and 13, were complicated by the fact that those hadn't been typical days.

Since Mike, an executive who usually worked in his own office, had been in charge of the factory that week overseeing the transfer of production equipment to Mexico, he'd suddenly started spending large amounts of time out on the factory floor, especially around the loading dock. That made sense, because those areas were the hub of activity on the Mexican project.

No one remembered anything extraordinary happening that Monday, and there wasn't any single incident that stood out on Tuesday either, but co-workers did recall Mike eating in the company lunch room, which was unusual for him; however, Mike had already told police that that had to do with the extra computer training that was also underway.

No one was exactly sure when Mike had arrived Tuesday morning. Estimates ranged anywhere from 5:40 A.M. to 6 A.M., and the sole video camera at the factory, which was above the employee entry door, showed Mike's arrival on its time code as 5:56 A.M. During the rest of the workday, dozens of employees within the large building were able to account for Mike's whereabouts, and it didn't appear that he'd left, even for a few minutes.

If Mike was at the factory between 6 A.M. and 4 P.M., then there didn't seem to be any way he could have dumped the bodies before he got home and dialed 911 at 4:20 P.M. So if Mike was the killer, he must have gotten the bodies out of the way much earlier in the morning— or somehow gotten them into the manufacturing plant during work hours and hidden them in plain sight.

Steve King took a look around the loading dock to see if there was anything noteworthy about the fact that Mike had been spending so much of his time there that day. The thought had crossed the investigators' minds that maybe Mike had stuffed the bodies into the tractor trailers—but that would undoubtedly have been discovered when the trucks were unloaded in Mexico.

King's attention was soon drawn to the other large feature of the loading area besides the dock itself; the factory's industrial-sized trash Dumpster. The blue BFI Dumpster was connected to the building by a short metal walkway that allowed workers to take factory waste straight out the door to the big metal container without first having to descend to ground level.

King also noticed that not twenty feet inside the building there was a bathroom with a shower. Standing and looking at that arrangement, a scenario began taking shape in King's mind. What if Mike had driven the bodies over to AMETEK Dixson well before the factory opened in the morning and put them in the Dumpster? He could have added the clothing he'd been wearing to the bundles he was throwing in the Dumpster and then taken a shower right there to remove any remaining traces of blood. The crime-scene investigation had pulled every sink and shower drain out of the Blaggs' house and sprayed fluorescing chemicals over every soiled piece of clothing and underwear in the hampers, as well as every paper towel and facial tissue in the wastebaskets, without coming up with so much as one more speck of blood—but this opened up an entirely new avenue of explanation.

Back at the sheriff's office, King, Public Information Officer Janet Prell, Sergeant Rusty Callow, and Sheriff Riecke Claussen were standing in a hallway discussing whether the Dumpster could have been used to dispose of the bodies, when they had an epiphany. In hindsight, the answer seemed obvious—but no one had yet asked the question: If Jennifer and Abby's bodies had been placed in the Dumpster, where would they have gone?

"All of a sudden it dawned on us—'Oh! They'd be in the landfill!' It's not like they disappeared off the Earth," King would recall.

To decide whether there was even a chance that Mike could have pulled off the diabolical maneuver they were now envisioning, the investigators needed to figure out how often that particular Dumpster was emptied. If the big metal box had sat in the sun for a few more weeks and no one noticed an odor of decaying bodies, it could only mean there hadn't been any in there in the first place.

The detectives quickly learned that the Dumpster at the loading dock was not used for routine garbage from places like the lunch room—instead it was reserved mostly for the plastic scrap materials and packaging that the factory discarded—and as a result, it wasn't emptied on any set schedule.

Grand Junction Police Sergeant Robert I. Russell checked further and got the sheriffs to raise their eyebrows when he reported back that his investigation showed BFI waste haulers had received a phone call from AMETEK Dixson on November 13 requesting that the Dumpster be picked up. BFI had come and gotten it on November 14, emptied it at the Mesa County Landfill just a few miles down the road, and returned the same Dumpster to the factory within the day.

After some initial uncertainty, Sergeant Russell was able to pinpoint the AMETEK employee who'd requested the pickup. His name was Jim Boden, and he told Russell that he'd made the call simply because the Dumpster seemed to be full. He hadn't had any conversations with Mike Blagg about the trash.

# 19

AS a result of his place in the pecking order of suspects, Mike had actually been under constant surveillance by investigators ever since November 13.

By the end of January, with nothing new to go on and the searches largely suspended due to the winter weather, Michael Blagg began slowly slipping from the public's consciousness . . . but not from the police's. Detectives were still following him everywhere he went and watching whatever they could see him doing.

There wasn't that much to see.

For the first few weeks Mike had been living with his friends from church, but early in December the sheriff's office officially turned the house on Pine Terrace Court back over to Mike, although it was now a very different place.

Even leaving aside the pall that suffused the residence, it was obvious to Mike as he toured the property that the pitched crime-scene work had rendered his house unlivable.

Sections of carpeting, hunks of wallboard, pieces of drain pipe had all been cut, sawed, and hacked out of various significant points around the house to be tested for trace evidence at the crime lab. Every item and every surface an investigator could even remotely imagine that the perpetrators, under some circumstance, might have touched was coated in a thick layer of fingerprint powder that turned to dark sticky paste when attempts were made to clean it.

The congregations at Mike's churches had raised more than $3,000 to fund a reward for any information leading to Jennifer and Abby, and Pastor Art Blankenship told reporters that, despite the sheriffs' belief that at least one person was dead, the congregation was still holding out hope of finding one or both alive. "We pray in the present tense for Jennifer and Abby, wherever they are. We pray for that miracle breakthrough that will cause this case to come to resolution," Blankenship said.

When Mike found a new townhouse to rent on North Club Court in the northern portion of downtown, he pointed out to his friends that his new residence was big enough for three people, and he wasn't giving up hope for their return either.

As time continued to pass since the first frantic days of the disappearances, sheriff's investigators gained the benefits of hindsight, and one relatively obvious fact was beginning to stand out: Nothing else had happened.

No other women and children around Grand Junction had vanished, or been kidnapped or murdered in the days since November 13. No other strange home invasions with mysterious bloodstains had occurred in any other houses across the town. Given that background, the sheriffs made it a point to tell reporters that they didn't have any evidence suggesting a stranger was involved in the case.

Reporters instantly made the connection that "not a

stranger" included Mike. Asked point-blank again what he thought about the fact that people might suspect him, Mike replied that he prayed for those who did.

Without a house and family, without any answers, on temporary leave from his job, Mike's life had been cast adrift from the routines that once anchored it, but he continued driving out to church, even taking the reins of a youth group there. He would cry in private with close friends, but in public he was, for the most part, calm and reserved. Always willing to sit down for an interview or stand in front of another television camera to again make an appeal for information, Mike came across as a sincere, pious, sympathetic figure, always holding out hope for a breakthrough and Jennifer and Abby's eventual return. But the truth was that, beyond repeating what he'd already said, and everyone else doing what they'd already done, there was really nothing more to offer. Hour by hour, day by day, time was inexorably moving on.

As the year drew to a close, Mike made plans to return to his job. The detective detail that had been quietly shadowing him braced themselves for even longer, more boring hours watching very little transpire, while Mike spent most of his work day largely out of sight within the salmon-colored industrial metal walls of the manufacturing plant.

At his new townhouse, a noticeably wearier Mike welcomed reporters who were keeping tabs on the investigation. He showed them the Christmas presents, including a pair of gold earrings and a Barbie nightgown, that he had purchased for his wife and daughter in dogged anticipation of their return. Mike explained that he'd kept the same phone number in case Jennifer was suddenly able to get to a phone and call. Both he and Marilyn were trying to keep their spirits up in the face of the ongoing efforts to find an answer, both making refererence to their missing girls as alive. Marilyn, though, in town with her husband Harold for everyone's first Christmas without Jennifer and

Abby, admitted that as time passed, it was getting harder and harder to know how that could be possible.

Without any fanfare, Mike filed an insurance claim for almost $30,000 worth of jewelry he said had been taken during the break-in, ranging from a $50 set of men's cufflinks he'd received the year before from one of Jennifer's relatives, to Jennifer's wedding set, which was valued at $13,800.

On December 31, as the late afternoon sun began to sink behind the mesas just a few short hours before New Year's Day, 2002, the surveillance team watched as Mike Blagg and Harold Conway pulled into the parking lot of Circuit City and headed inside. They'd seen Mike stop by the big electronics chain store earlier in the week just to look around, but this time he seemed to know right what he was after.

Mike walked up to the counter and ordered a big-screen projection television, DVD player, receiver, subwoofer, and speakers to be delivered out to his townhouse. The total price tag was $5,441 dollars.

The detectives who'd taken turns tailing Mike around town for weeks had spent tremendous amounts of time watching and analyzing every mundane detail of his life, looking to see if he did anything unexpected. They were also looking to see if anyone else seemed unusually interested in him. Ultimately, they held out a degree of hope that if Mike was the murderer, he might return to wherever he had put the bodies. The surveillance was a thankless task, a mind-numbing test of endurance, a one-in-a-million crapshoot that they knew could well be directed at the wrong person. Then suddenly, in mid-January, right in the least likely of places, all those stultifying hours spent staring at nothing finally paid off big-time, when the detectives following Mike saw something very interesting indeed.

# 20

ON the evening of Friday, January 11, 2002, after most of the employees had already called it quits for the work week and gone home, the surveillance detail shadowing Mike perked up when, at 7:42 P.M., he walked out the front door of AMETEK Dixson headed for his car.

What happened next was odd for several reasons.

Instead of leaving for the weekend, Mike pulled out of his usual employee space near the factory door and drove, with his headlights off, clear across to the other side of the parking lot, pulling in and parking again amongst an anonymous line of cars on the northern edge of the property used by patrons of the nearby Orchard Mesa Lanes bowling center.

Detective Michael Clear and other members of the Grand Valley Joint Drug Task Force, which had been lending undercover manpower to the relentlessly time-consuming surveillance, then watched as Mike got out and walked briskly back to the AMETEK Dixson building, hugging the walls as he moved over to a white Ford pickup truck that was owned by the company. Without hesitation, Mike got in and smoothly looped the truck back over into the factory's recessed loading dock area, before letting himself back into the building through the side door right there on the dock.

Watching quietly from across the street and other points around the building, Sergeant Doug Norcross and the other three detectives on the detail immediately realized that what they were seeing was significant. In the hours after Jennifer and Abby vanished, Mike had been asked more than once if he'd ever used any company cars. Each time he'd immediately said no. Yet here in the darkened parking lot was Mike, comfortably squiring the company utility truck around and looking for all the world like he'd done it before.

Just a couple of minutes after he'd moved the company truck, detectives watched as Mike raised the loading dock door and scooted a table into the back of the pickup, before hopping in and driving off. While they were quietly watching Mike's actions, the detectives suddenly noticed that two other vehicles seemed to be tailing Mike around the factory as well. Two women had gotten into a van in the parking lot and were watching the building, and a man in a car was also circling the factory in a suspicious manner. The detectives began writing down license plate numbers and trying to figure out what the hell was going on.

Mike drove the pickup to his townhouse and then drove it back to AMETEK Dixson just after 8 P.M., now without any sign of the table, putting the company pickup back in its parking space, and again walking unusually quickly back across the parking lot to his own car, glancing over his shoulder several times before reaching it, and then returning directly back home.

The next morning, a Saturday, it was Sergeant Rusty Callow's turn to watch clandestinely as Blagg left home at 9:35 A.M. and drove back to the factory. Once again he made the switch over to the company pickup truck and took another table home from the loading dock.

After a quick check of the license plate numbers recorded the night before, George Barley called AMETEK General Manager Wes Hardin on Saturday and told him that detectives had noticed him driving around the plant early Friday evening, and they wondered if it had to do with the fact that Mike was also there. It did, Hardin replied. He'd gotten a call from Linda Gardiner, AMETEK's plant operations manager, who was still in the factory late in the afternoon when she noticed that Mike was moving through the building switching off several lights as he went, something that struck her as suspicious. Gardiner reported that Mike seemed to have been hanging around for no reason, and then following her and another employee, Rita Meryhew, around the building seeing what they were up to, which both women also thought was strange.

Gardiner then noticed that a large eight-foot-long assembly table had been placed on a dolly and set out right by the loading dock door. It was at that point Gardiner called Hardin on his cell phone, saying that something odd appeared to be afoot. Hardin had said he'd be coming right in, and asked Gardiner to try to stay out of sight while keeping an eye on what Mike was doing.

With Mike nowhere to be seen for the moment, Hardin had gone to the loading dock and taken a black Magic Marker, pulled out the drawer in the center of the table, and written the numbers "01-11-02 A11" on the bottom. At that point, Hardin said, Gardiner recalled seeing a brand-new paper shredder that had been shipped to the plant sitting in the same position by the loading dock, but now it was gone.

Later in the day, as Barley, Callow, and the others were still trying to make sense of the previous night's intrigues, Callow got a call from one of the neighbors on Pine Terrace Court who he'd interviewed early on in the investigation.

Judy Currie was the resident who'd been in her sewing room when she thought she saw the Blaggs' mini-van returning home mid-afternoon on November 13.

Callow asked her what was up and Currie replied that she had just seen the same mini-van drive by again. Currie was surprised, because it looked like a female was driving, and Michael Blagg was in the passenger seat this time. Callow told Currie that that was impossible, because the Blaggs' van was still being held as evidence. He didn't tell Currie at the time, but Callow also knew from the surveillance detail that Mike hadn't gone anywhere near Pine Terrace Court all that day.

Currie repeated that the van she had seen a short time beforehand looked just like the Blaggs', and the passenger looked like Mike.

Suddenly, in the space of twenty-four hours, a case that had in many respects been languishing saw two significant clues arrive back-to-back and breathe some life into it.

Mike's shenanigans at the factory had given the sheriffs a sense of just how comfortable he seemed to be carrying out shady activities after hours on his company's loading dock, and Currie's mistaken identification of a nearly identical mini-van that apparently was an occasional visitor to Pine Terrace Court put her original report of the Blagg van being in motion on the afternoon of the day of the disappearances in an entirely new light.

At 2:45 A.M. on Sunday, in the darkest part of the night, Investigator Art Smith went Dumpster-diving outside Mike's new townhouse. Smith came up with a cardboard box for a paper shredder that just happened to have a packing slip attached to it that was made out to AMETEK Dixson.

On January 14, 2002, the detectives watched as Mike went back to the Circuit City store where police had seen him buying a new home entertainment center on New Year's Eve. This time Mike shelled out $1,291 for a new computer, which brought his electronics shopping spree for the two-week period up to $6,732.

Mike had put the purchases on a payment plan. He certainly made decent money, so none of it was beyond his means, but he'd just spent over five percent of his annual income less than two months after his family had vanished. Between that and the items he'd surreptitiously removed from his workplace, detectives wondered what was going on in his mind.

A week later, on Saturday, January 19, Wes Hardin once again found himself secretly marking a piece of furniture because he suspected that Mike was preparing to swipe it.

AMETEK Dixson was preparing to hold a company yard sale to get rid of surplus equipment. Included were some tables and desks, but Hardin had gotten the impression that Mike was interested in a particular desk that wasn't slated to be sold. Hardin stuck a sign on it saying specifically that it was not for sale. When Hardin learned later that, despite his effort, Mike had come to the sale, paid for a different piece of furniture, and then come back with a truck, loaded the not-for-sale desk, and taken it anyway, Hardin called the police.

Unbeknownst to Mike, when he had moved to the townhouse in December, detectives had hidden a surveillance camera across the street that was watching his new residence around the clock. The video had captured Mike unloading the desk and the tables and carrying them in through his front door.

# 21

ON Tuesday, February 5, 2002, the Mesa County sheriffs asked Mike to come back to their office for what would become *the* pivotal interview of the Blagg case.

As he walked in the front doors of the sheriff's office just like he'd done so many times before in recent weeks, Mike didn't realize that things were now very, very different. For one thing, a team of police was forming right then back at his townhouse, with a search warrant to seize AMETEK's stolen office furniture—and, while they were at it, to see if there was anything else that might shed light on what had happened to Jennifer and Abby. Police searched the desk that had been taken and, inside the drawer, found another collage of porn images that Mike had printed off on his new computer. They also found a picture of Jennifer and Abby taped to the refrigerator door, and the Blaggs' 1991 wedding album sitting on the nightstand beside Mike's new bed.

Mike was someone who liked to view the world in absolute terms, attributing even the most mundane of events to the grand schemes of either God or the Devil, depending. But the police too have their own over-arching categories—and by stealing from his employer, Mike had moved himself in their eyes from the realm of the victim to that of the criminal.

After three months of being led in circles by Mike, the fact was that investigators could really have cared less about a table, a desk, and the paper shredder. What mattered was that law enforcement had finally been given a brand-new side of Michael to look at—one very much at odds with the ultra-conscientious God-fearing old-school biblical literalist that he'd appeared to be every time in the past when they needed to ask him a question.

Mike listened again to his Miranda rights—which he'd long since committed to memory—waived them, and admitted he'd taken the furniture from AMETEK Dixson. He said he had done it in order to set up a work station in his new home.

For nearly three months, Mike had received the benefit of the doubt, and all kinds of sympathetic treatment. The police had spoken to him nearly every day, either by phone or in person, and they'd commiserated with him over countless cups of coffee. But now the contrast in their attitude toward him couldn't have been more pronounced.

If Mike was telling the truth, then he wouldn't mind taking another lie detector test, would he? Mike said he would be willing to do so. Fine, the sheriffs replied, and they promptly introduced FBI Special Agent Bill Irwin, who happened to be right there at the ready with his polygraph.

Irwin hooked Blagg's hands up to the sensor wires and began asking him if he had harmed Jennifer and Abby; if he knew where they were; if he had stolen office furniture; if he and Jennifer had gotten into fights because he had been surfing pornographic websites . . .

For two hours, Irwin ran the test while another FBI agent took notes, before they stepped out and discussed the results with each other and the sheriffs. The other agent thought the polygraph was inconclusive, but Irwin didn't doubt the results. He felt it was clear that Mike was being deceptive.

Irwin went back into the interview room and told Mike he'd examined the graphs and didn't believe him. "It's clearly obvious you know where Jennifer and Abby are, and you can take me to them," Irwin said. Mike denied it and for the next two hours, the agent raked Mike back and forth over the problems the investigators had with the crime scene and the inconsistencies in Mike's versions of events.

Mike was not swayed by Irwin's newfound hostility toward him. He steadfastly maintained that he'd had nothing to do with the disappearances.

Mike said his visits to Internet porn sites were research he was doing in the wake of all Jennifer's many medical problems, which had made ordinary sexual intercourse painful for her.

After four hours of questions from the FBI, the sheriff's detectives came back in and joined the questioning as well.

George Barley, Steve King, and Wayne Weyler weren't interested in hearing Michael's excuses. They told him they thought he'd killed Jennifer and then killed Abby, and they spent the rest of the day and right on into the night tearing at every scrap of his story, trying to get him to admit it.

The trio started with the furniture thefts from AMETEK. Why would Mike, who was making $110,000 a year, need to steal a paper shredder? Mike's reply was that he hadn't. He had bought some of the items at a company yard sale, and the rest he was allowed to take in order to set up a home office that he was using for company-related business.

The sheriffs weren't buying it. They had already talked to employees at AMETEK, and it was clear to them that Mike had taken things that had not been included in the yard sale. Mike insisted that they had. The sheriffs kept hammering at it. They had seen Mike take the desk after darkness had fallen, other employees had seen him take it. With all the over-the-shoulder glances and skulking about the factory flicking off the lights, he hadn't been acting like someone who had a right to take it. The sheriffs' case was overwhelming, and after holding out for hours, Mike admitted that he'd actually stolen the shredder and the other items.

That small but critical victory in hand, the sheriffs shifted right back to their main target—the events of November 13.

Mike must have a theory about what had happened, so they wondered what it was.

Mike offered that it might have been a robbery that went bad. The sheriffs told him that wouldn't fly. Robbers don't leave money on the floor, robbers don't remove bodies, and they certainly don't kidnap 6-year-olds.

Mike tried again, suggesting that maybe a childless couple had seen Abby and decided to take her. The sheriffs countered that there was no evidence that this childless couple had ever been in the house, there'd been no credible sightings of Abby anywhere, and even if this hypothetical couple were crazed homicidal maniacs, they still wouldn't have had any need to remove Jennifer from the house as well.

The detectives insisted there was a lot more evidence that Mike had had something to do with events that day than any random stranger.

Had he been seeing prostitutes? Absolutely not, Mike was adamant. Had he maybe been calling up a local escort service and having women meet him in motels for topless "massage," as one of their tips from the public had suggested? Mike stood firm. No way. Never.

What then, the sheriffs wanted to know, was the big fight about on Friday, November 9, that Jennifer had cryptically mentioned in the margin of her Bible study workbook? Was it over his collection of Internet porn? Was that why he had written her that apology on his office computer about letting the devil get a foothold, on the very day she'd disappeared?

At first Mike said that he didn't recall any fight with Jennifer on the Friday before she'd vanished. Then he said there had been an argument, but he couldn't remember over what. Finally he said it had had to do with whether or not he should pursue a job opportunity that an employment recruiter told him had come up in Longmont, Colorado—clear over on the Front Range of the Rockies north of Denver. Mike said that Jennifer had gotten upset because he was even talking about moving from Grand Junction so soon after they had really begun to get settled in the community, and that that had led to a verbal row and some hurt feelings, but nothing significant. Mike's version of his last argument with Jennifer before her disappearance was actually consistent. He had given the very same description of the dispute to detectives during his first multi-hour interview on the night of November 13.

If it was a big nothing, then why had Jennifer still been carrying around the note three days later? Why was she taping messages to his bedroom mirror that night? The sheriffs wanted to know if she was threatening to take Abby and leave Mike in the next day or two. Why would he just happen to write this note and leave it in the bedroom in the hours before he discovered his wife and daughter were gone?

Mike characterized the note as nothing more than an apology over a minor disagreement, and insisted he'd written it earlier than Tuesday. He also denied that Jennifer had been on the brink of divorcing him and, when asked point-blank about the possibility of sexual abuse, he denied that he had ever done anything remotely inappropriate to Abby that would have triggered a confrontation with Jennifer.

The sheriffs pressed Mike on the sexual images he'd saved on his computer. Surely a deeply Christian woman like Jennifer, who'd told friends she didn't even want her daughter exposed to Britney Spears, wouldn't have been thrilled to suddenly discover he had a collection of hundreds of images of kneeling women performing oral sex, with men ejaculating all over their faces.

Mike squirmed in his chair and insisted that it was a bit embarrassing, but maintained that he and Jennifer both had sat down together and looked up the images about a dozen times because her hysterectomy, her bout with pelvic vestibulitis, and her other medical difficulties were forcing real changes in their sex lives.

The detectives weren't satisfied with the answer. They didn't think that Jennifer would be interested in viewing porn. Mike didn't budge. Lots of couples engaged in oral sex, he responded, and he and Jennifer had enjoyed doing exactly what was depicted in the photographs. He'd explained it to Steve King during some of their more informal interviews, and, while it wasn't something he wanted to discuss on the street corner, there wasn't anything wrong with it. He and Jennifer were married, and their sex life was their business. Besides, there were plenty of unmarried couples up to the exact same activity.

The sheriffs pushed harder. Had Jennifer ever caught Mike looking at the images alone? Was she ever upset by it?

Yes, Mike admitted, she had walked in once and caught him looking at it by himself, and been very upset about it, but he said that had been about four or five months before she'd gone missing. Further, Mike said, she hadn't been upset because of what he was looking at, but rather because he was doing it without her. Mike said Jennifer had described herself as feeling a sense of betrayal similar to the way she would feel if he was cheating on her with other women.

"Blagg claimed that Jennifer enjoyed looking at the computer pictures of men ejaculating on women," the detectives wrote in their report of the interview. "They would look at the pictures, then Jennifer would perform oral sex on him. She then would let him ejaculate on her face as depicted in the majority of the pictures."

Under the continuing questioning, Mike began to admit that he and Jennifer had discussed that he might be "addicted" to pornography, but at the same time, he insisted that he'd been accessing it less and less in the months leading up to November.

The sheriffs told him they had evidence from his computer indicating he'd been looking at girlie pictures on the web right on the very evening of November 12, just hours before Jennifer vanished. Mike insisted that wasn't the case, that it had been days, possibly weeks, earlier when he'd last accessed an Internet porn site from his home computer.

The sheriffs walked him backward through their version of a simmering angry weekend: Jennifer's 'Keys to Peace' note taped to his mirror, the dispute over the orange juice that Abby had witnessed, a bigger fight on Friday that triggered all these events, the porn woven through everything. Jennifer had finally had it, they said, and on Monday night she'd told Mike she was finally leaving, so he'd preemptively killed her, hadn't he? The fight was over his insatiable appetite for computer pornography, which he had been downloading that very Monday evening.

No, no, no, Mike insisted. It was not about porn. There was no big fight on Friday—it was a pointless misunderstanding at worst. There'd been no ultimatum from Jennifer. He hadn't been downloading porn that night, he hadn't written the apology earlier that very day . . .

Sergeant Weyler, who'd been on the Blagg investigation from Day One, went for it. He leaned in and told Mike that he was convinced Mike had killed Jennifer—he just didn't know why.

Twilight had long since fallen outside the sheriff's office. Mike had been answering questions for over ten straight hours when he broke down. Tears welled in his eyes.

Mike began to literally cry on Weyler's shoulder.

Sergeant Weyler pressed the advantage. "Tell me the truth about what happened," Weyler urged Mike.

"I can't," Mike said, sobbing lightly as he repeated it over and over. "I can't. I can't. I can't tell you."

"At least tell me where Jennifer and Abby are at," Weyler pleaded.

Pulling himself together, Mike looked Weyler right in the eye and calmly replied, "I really don't know where they are at."

"Are they in the river?" Weyler pushed.

"I really don't know," Mike answered, his composure returning by the moment.

The detectives and agents had collectively held their breath through much of the exchange, letting Weyler have room to run. It had looked for a second like Mike might have been about to make a real admission. Now it looked like he was drifting back away from the edge of the precipice.

A short while later, for the first time that day, Mike began asking the questions.

What, he wondered, were the consequences when it came to various types of murder charges? For instance, what defined the difference between a premeditated killing and one committed in the heat of passion?

The men cautiously talked for a few moments about the different categories of murder under Colorado law, and soon Mike began sobbing again with his head slumped over and his lips quivering.

Weyler leaned forward again and insisted that after three months of stalling, the time had finally come. Mike needed to get rid of the guilt he was carrying around and explain to them the truth about what had happened that day in the Redlands.

Mike asked to pray, pausing for a moment before looking up and then asking tearfully, "May I have the opportunity to speak with a lawyer first? I'm asking because I don't want to mess anything up here."

"It's up to you," Weyler said. "You can have a lawyer."

"I can tell the truth with a lawyer," Blagg said.

"You won't, but it's up to you," Weyler responded.

Mike began to pray again and then buried his face in his hands.

"Now's the time," Weyler urged. "Let it out."

"I want to tell the truth," Mike sniffled, but, he added, "I want a lawyer to tell me what the truth is going to mean."

The lawmen gathered in the room silently bit their lips. It had looked for a half-second like they were so, so close, and yet Mike had just snatched victory right from their grasp. He'd come into the sheriff's office voluntarily, he'd sat there for nearly eleven hours, he'd been offered breaks, food, water . . . He wasn't in custody and all they needed him to do was admit to something concrete and tell them where Jennifer and Abby were.

Instead Mike had uttered the magic words.

Once he'd said "I want a lawyer," Mike could have turned around and confessed to every unsolved case in Mesa County and they wouldn't be able to use it against him in court. There was no way the sheriffs were going to get a lawyer to come in at this hour and, even if one had, there was no way a lawyer was going to let Mike finish the confession that, it had appeared to the investigators, he'd been right on the brink of making.

It was late and the detectives had no choice but to stop the questioning and prepare to send Mike back out into the night. If he didn't crack today, there was always a chance he'd crack tomorrow, and they wanted to keep up the head-splitting pressure they'd brought to bear on him.

To that end, they told him that before he left, he had a phone call they wanted him to take. Mike picked up the receiver. It was Wes Hardin, his supervisor at work. Hardin explained that AMETEK Dixson was aware of the thefts, that he'd written code numbers on the missing furniture, and effective immediately, Mike was suspended while the company conducted an internal investigation. Mike needn't bother coming in to work on Wednesday.

As his new jobless reality sunk in, Mike gathered up his jacket and began heading for the door and the clear, crisp night beyond. The sheriffs acidly suggested that if he planned to kill himself any time soon, he should leave them a note telling them where they could find his wife and daughter's bodies.

Like a reprise of the end of his first multi-hour questioning by police on the night of Jennifer and Abby's disappearance exactly twelve weeks beforehand, Michael once again left the station only to find Pastor Art Blankenship and a posse of church members waiting outside in the parking lot to offer hugs and take him to dinner.

Blankenship and the group tried to cheer Michael up, encouraging him, praying aloud for him to be strong, but it was clear, as he dejectedly explained, that police were now openly calling him a suspect right to his face. Mike was depressed and hurt, and the little support party sitting around the table at the Shake, Rattle & Roll Diner simply wasn't able to snap him out of it.

Pastor Blankenship would remember Mike's eyes that evening as "glazed over." Some in the group picked up on the fact that sometime during the hours of interrogation, Michael had removed the little handmade white cardboard "Hope" pin that he had worn continuously since the early frantic days of searching along the banks of the Colorado.

When the evening was finally over and the downcast gathering began to break up, some of Blagg's friends even wondered amongst themselves if Mike was sufficiently distraught that he might try to harm himself. The decision was made to keep a close eye on things, to check with him again first thing in the morning, and just keep working to bring his spirits up.

Late in the evening, after an exhausting day, Mike returned to his townhouse to find that it had been searched by police while he was being questioned. They'd left a copy of the warrant and taken the furniture and paper shredder that belonged to AMETEK as evidence.

The message light on his answering machine was blinking.

Unbeknownst to Mike, while he had been sitting in the conference room being interrogated in Grand Junction, Mesa County Sheriff's Detective Lissah Norcross had traveled clear down to Haltom City in Texas and sat down with Marilyn Conway.

Norcross was looking for Conway's help to finally crack the case. She explained that the sheriffs now felt that Mike was the suspect, and told her why, including the sheriffs' theory that Jennifer had been preparing to leave Mike over his interest in Internet pornography. Norcross asked Conway if she would be willing to help by calling Mike and asking him about the allegations. Conway agreed and Norcross set up recording equipment on her phone line, not realizing that Mike's appointment at the sheriff's office was going to drag on well into the evening.

When Mike listened to his answering machine that night, he had a series of six increasingly frantic messages from his distraught mother-in-law. "Mike, it's Mama. I would like it if you would pick up the telephone," Conway began. "I've seen information no mother should ever see from the sheriff's office."

"Mike, will you help me out with Jennifer and Abby?" began another. "I would appreciate it, Mike, if you would give me any information that you feel in your heart that you can possibly give me as to where my girls are. If you have any information in your heart about my girls, would you please relay it to me, Mike?" Conway begged.

It was a bad ending to a bad day.

Wednesday would be worse.

# 22

**INVESTIGATORS** were up first thing Wednesday morning and more determined than ever to put Mike straight back under pressure to see if he would break.

They knew that he had to be disoriented by the sudden turn of events. The police who'd been consoling him and consulting him and treating him with respectful sympathy for weeks had spun 180 degrees and were now raining accusations down on him. His company had slammed its door shut. Even his friends would now be harboring darker doubts.

He had already handed police the excuse they needed to come right back that morning and spend some more time interrogating him: the other white table and the small yellow plastic bins he'd admitted to taking from AMETEK.

Blagg had been through a horrible night, and from what the detectives had already told him, he knew that the police were poised to return. His answering machine was filling up with messages from his friends from church, who were determined to lift his spirits, but Mike didn't pick up the phone.

Clutching a copy of their updated search warrant, detectives pulled up at 10 A.M., and once again knocked on the red front door of Mike's tan stucco townhouse. This time they were met with silence. Blagg's car was parked nearby, and Investigator Dave Rowe had been watching the place all morning and hadn't seen Mike leave, so George Barley, Scott Ehlers, and other investigators who'd come, along with several Grand Junction police officers, knocked again and announced themselves. They took out a cell phone and gave Mike a call. Still no answer. Thinking that perhaps Mike was just being sulky, the officers knocked some more and tried talking through the closed door in an attempt to cajole him into opening up.

Nothing worked.

Now the officers began to get nervous. This just didn't feel right, and the minutes were steadily sliding away. The decision was made to go in and check on Mike's well-being. Search warrants allow police to enter whether or not the resident is home, so they had a legal right to let themselves inside. The manager of the apartment properties was summoned for a master key. Officers instinctively began to slide their firearms out of their holsters as the deadbolt clicked out of the way at 11 A.M.

"Mesa County Sheriffs! Mike? Michael? . . ." the investigators yelled out as they slipped into the apartment.

One deep breath and the officers knew something was definitely wrong. A thick odor of car exhaust hung in the now-claustrophobic air of the townhouse, and there were droplets of blood in the central hallway. Guns forward, the police pushed themselves deeper into the fetor, quickly scanning each room for any sign of Mike. Living area, kitchen, bedroom . . . all were empty—which left the bathroom at the back of the apartment.

Nothing quite exceeds the shock of suddenly being confronted by someone who has slashed their wrists slumped in a bathtub, their oddly pale naked body surrounded by the bright blood-red pool of water. That was the searing image Wayne Weyler, Steve King, and the others took in as they pushed open the bathroom door and finally found Michael Blagg hovering on the brink of death, with an open Bible and a photo of Jennifer and Abby propped up on the edge of the tub.

The townhouse exploded into action. Frantic calls for a rescue squad were shouted into police radios. Within moments the sounds of sirens could be heard coming as an ambulance and more cruisers began slamming through town toward the complex. Blagg seemed barely conscious as officers grabbed towels and tried to staunch the bleeding from the deep vertical slashes that he'd cut down his forearms.

Sheriff's Investigator Wayne Weyler seized the chance to end the case once and for all, getting down next to the groggy figure in the tub and telling him matter-of-factly, "You could die here. It doesn't look good.

"Where's Jennifer?" Weyler asked succinctly.

"I do not know," Blagg whispered back.

Weyler tried again. "Where is Abby?"

Again, Blagg softly replied, "I do not know."

Weyler tried one last time, asking Mike if he'd harmed

either Jennifer or Abby in any way. Blagg shook his head and arriving emergency medical technicians began working their way into the crowded bathroom and taking over the effort to try to stop Michael from bleeding to death.

As the EMTs bundled Michael out the door, trying to start several IV solutions running into his sliced arms as he lay close to death on their rescue gurney, the grim investigators realized that, even if Mike recovered from this, it was a near certainty that he had just concluded his last questioning by police.

Detectives didn't have any sort of useful "dying declaration" from Mike, but they did still have a valid search warrant. So, as the chaos began to subside, they took a look around and soon found a single handwritten page near the bloodied bathtub. As detectives picked up Mike's suicide note, there was another brief moment's hope that they might finally be holding the confession that would let them at last close the books on the Blagg case and put the mystery of Abby and Jennifer to rest. However, as they read rapidly through the brief missive, it became clear that there was still nothing that would implicate Mike in his family's disappearance.

In fact, far from confessing, Mike, in what might well have been his final communication, had once again steadfastly maintained his innocence:

> God love you all! I have tried to do the right thing throughout my life. I have made many mistakes along the way, and I am sorry for any of those mistakes that have harmed any of you out there now. The Sheriff's Department is going to say many things about me in the coming weeks. I am not perfect, but neither am I a murderer. I love my wife and daughter and I plan to see them in heaven some day. The investigators have led me to believe that Jennifer and Abby are dead. I cannot live on this

*earth without them. I am sorry for all of you but
without Jen and Abby I am incomplete. I love you
all! Michael. PS: My Lord of Hope and Peace is
now my Lord of Comfort.*

In keeping with their long-standing policy, the Grand
Junction Police Department didn't release the contents of
the note to the public, but in an effort to tamp down inevitable questions, they did explain to reporters that it did
not contain any kind of admission of involvement in Jennifer and Abby's disappearance.

Because of the substantial loss of blood that had occurred while he was in the tub, Mike's life was initially
on the line. As a result, he was admitted to St. Mary's
Hospital in critical condition. Overnight, as his situation
began to improve, he was upgraded to serious condition.

Mike's doctors ordered him placed on a "psychiatric
hold," which gave them a legal window lasting up to
seventy-two hours to keep him, involuntarily if necessary, in order to determine whether or not he was going
to be a continuing danger to himself or the public.

Blagg was content to stay put while he recovered. His
ministers, who had stood by him from the beginning, visited him in his hospital room that Thursday, and his
mother flew all the way in from Georgia, with his sister
from Louisiana, to see him.

In the hospital, Mike's visitors were limited to family
members and his close friends Pastor Art Blankenship
and Pastor Ray Shirley. Reporters weren't allowed in to
speak with him, and the police had made a deliberate decision not to try to interview him further, so it was up to
Blankenship and Shirley to pass on to the public what little information came out of the hospital. The pastors told
reporters that Mike had been saddened by the recent
developments and the sudden shift in the police's attitude
toward him, but added that in retrospect, he felt that

attempting to kill himself was the wrong thing to have done.

Blankenship was puzzled by the turn of events, saying it was completely out of character for someone who had been so giving of both his time and his money to suddenly turn around and steal from his own company.

Shirley spoke of the pressure his parishioner was under, and noted that Mike had been too sedated to speak, so it wasn't possible to really know yet what had been on his mind.

While the mood around Mike's bedside continued to be somber and supportive, outside the hospital, there was a sea change underway in public opinion.

The residents of Grand Junction had been terrorized all fall by the notion that someone was on the loose in their community prepared to snatch a respectable woman and her child right out of their own house in a safe neighborhood in broad daylight, leaving nothing but a bloodstain behind for a clue.

The public and the press had looked hard at Mike from the very first hours of the case, but again and again they'd been reassured by Mike's friends, and Mike himself, that anyone who was such a pious straight-arrow kind of guy was simply incapable of being mixed up in anything so heinous.

When word hit the newspapers that the police had caught Mike stealing from his employer, followed almost immediately by the news that he had nearly succeeded in killing himself just hours after being questioned about his possible role in his family's disappearance, the community took the juxtaposition of incidents as tantamount to an admission of double murder.

With the sheriff's spokeswoman openly saying that her department planned to file felony theft charges against Blagg for the five hundred dollars' worth of furniture and equipment that had been taken from AMETEK, it wasn't much of a surprise when it was announced that Blagg had finally retained a lawyer, Stephan Schweissing, to represent him in any upcoming court case.

Steve King told reporters that police were not planning to interview Blagg while he was hospitalized. In fact, they weren't planning to interview him after he was released either.

"If we speak again to Mr. Blagg in reference to this case, that will be up to him," King told reporters.

Michael Blagg was now unofficially the main suspect, and the sheriffs wanted him to realize that from now on out, he would be treated like it every minute of every day.

# 23

THE week following the suicide attempt was another rough one for Michael.

He walked out of the hospital on Monday, February 11, 2002, and returned to his townhouse, only to learn the next day from AMETEK Dixson's headquarters in Paoli, Pennsylvania, that he was officially fired.

The detectives who had been thinking and living this case day-in and day-out for three months knew that if there ever was to have been a time when Michael Blagg was going to confess, it would have been in those moments as he wrote his note before settling into the bathtub with his razor blade. The fact that he hadn't, the fact that he'd "lawyered up" from his hospital bed afterward, all suggested to detectives that whatever explanation was eventually going to be developed about the real events on November 13 wasn't going to come from Mike.

Without a solid scientific clue from the crime scene, and without a confession from their suspect, what police still needed most to crack the case was a body.

The searches in the late fall had been thorough, but

there was always the hope that as the weather continued to warm toward summer, Mesa County's 3,300 square miles of scenery would begin to pull in hikers, mountain bikers, and horseback riders, and lead to the chance discovery of a shallow grave.

As the detectives considered their next move, one seemingly minor point from the previous hectic weeks struck them as interesting . . . and the more they thought about it, the more interesting it got.

In the back of their minds the investigators had wondered if Mike really would have had the nerve to drive to his own workplace and put his dead wife and daughter into the company's Dumpster. Now they had watched firsthand as Mike stole furniture from AMETEK Dixson's secluded loading dock. The thefts, and Mike's use of the company pickup, were actually far less interesting than the fact that he had seemed so comfortable doing something criminal and complicated in the loading dock area after regular hours.

The factory's great big blue Dumpster was not the typical square bin with a hinged lid that sits out behind every donut shop and apartment complex. It was a larger industrial unit with a hexagonal cross-section and a built-in compactor that turned like a screw in order to push the trash tightly into the far side of the container.

Whoever used the Dumpster had to stand up on the metal walkway and drop the trash down into an opening. Then, using a control panel on the dock, which was activated by a key that was kept just inside the building, they would run the compacter through a cycle and the trash would disappear from view.

If Michael had used the Dumpster to dispose of the bodies, he would've had to load them in and then had the presence of mind to activate the control panel, but once he'd done so, those bodies would be out of sight and, unlike a regular Dumpster, anyone who added rubbish to it afterward wouldn't have had any way of seeing what was inside.

The average paper-pushing office worker might not be comfortable firing up a trash compacter the size of a large recreational vehicle, but Mike had been a Navy chopper pilot. The detectives knew that that meant he had not only been trained to operate all the small intricate systems on one of the world's most sophisticated aircraft, but must have had years of familiarity with all kinds of larger mechanical and electrical devices used on the military ships from which he'd operated.

Enthusiasm for the fascinating new theory taking shape at the Mesa County Sheriff's Office was tempered by the realization that it still wasn't backed up by anything concrete. Perpetrators get convicted all the time on circumstantial evidence, but not on evidence that is downright ethereal. At the end of the day, the sheriffs needed something they could put before a jury of twelve people, all of whom were going to require certainty beyond a reasonable doubt.

Mike's helping himself to some furniture and a paper shredder was a petty crime that was notable for its sheer banality rather than its sinisterness.

The more the investigators thought about where they were with the Blagg case, the more they realized that if they were ever going to have a chance at proving their suspicions about Mike's involvement, they would need to find Jennifer and Abby. If the Dumpster theory was correct, then the answers to this entire mystery were in just about the single most inaccessible place in all of Mesa County— in the vast landfill, under three month's worth of trash, which was literally getting deeper by the hour.

# 24

A dig at the landfill was going to be Mesa County's most difficult and costliest option—and frankly, it was also the option that was the least likely to succeed. Mesa County Sheriff Riecke Claussen knew that before he asked the county's administrators for permission and funding to carry out a landfill excavation, he would first have to exhaust every other alternative. That meant there needed to be one final definitive search of the wild landscapes surrounding Grand Junction.

The words *empty* and *rugged* don't begin to describe the extreme terrain that extends in all directions from the edges of Grand Junction out to hundreds of miles beyond Mesa County's borders. Looking randomly for something out there would be like trying to search the surface of the moon.

In order to have any serious chance, the sheriffs needed some way to narrow the scope of their search. To that end, they possessed one sliver of a clue. Their working theory was that Mike had used the mini-van he'd bought for Valentine's Day to drive the bodies somewhere. Detectives had checked the Blaggs' credit card receipts and found that the last time Jennifer had filled the van with gas was on November 9, just four days before she vanished.

Steve King and Sergeant Rusty Callow checked the van out of the sheriff's impound lot and drove it across the street to a gas station. Then, like a story problem in a junior high math class, they figured out a scheme to calculate how far the van had been driven since November 9. They topped off the tank while measuring the amount of gas it took to fill the van again. Then, using the odometer and the average mileage from the van's on-board computer system, they drove to every known place that Jennifer had gone during that four-day period. When they were done, King and Callow figured that, at most, the van could have traveled 125 miles since it had been filled that Friday, and they were able to account for at least 35 miles of that by retracing Jennifer's movements.

That left up to 90 miles unaccounted for.

Since the van had been returned to the Blaggs' garage, it stood to reason that the bodies must have been placed somewhere within 45 miles of the house.

A straight-line search of up to 45 miles was bad enough, but authorities had no idea which direction the van might have gone. When they swept that radius around in a circle, the target search area suddenly encompassed a massive 6,360 square miles of Colorado and Utah. There was simply no way that the region's professional search-and-rescue organizations could turn out the kind of manpower that would be required to cover every square yard of such a vast territory.

In the midst of all the turmoil that hit the Blagg case in February 2002, Sheriff Claussen had watched as another tragedy involving a missing 7-year-old girl unfolded clear across the country in San Diego.

Just as Abby Blagg's disappearance had made national news back in November, the abduction of Danielle van Dam right from her bedroom in California had now gripped February's headlines. Day after day, Danielle's parents pleaded for the safe return of their daughter, only to be devastated in less than a month's time when her naked body was recovered from a vacant lot 25 miles from her home.

What caught Sheriff Claussen's attention was the well-organized volunteer search for Danielle that ultimately led to her discovery, and to the prosecution of a man who'd lived two doors away from her. That search had been coordinated by a Texas non-profit group called the Laura Recovery Center Foundation, named in honor of abduction victim Laura Kate Smither, a 12-year-old Girl Scout from Friendswood, Texas, who was found strangled in 1997.

By the time Sheriff Claussen called, Laura's group had assisted in over 440 missing child cases nationwide, and pulled together thirty large-scale ground searches that had resulted in the recovery of six bodies and helped to rescue three kidnapped children.

Normally the Laura Recovery Center Foundation would have been summoned by a distraught family in the days immediately after a child had vanished, but after Sheriff Claussen described his dilemma and explained the deep wound that the disappearances, Abby's in particular, had inflicted on Grand Junction, the center agreed to send its experts to help set up a full-scale search effort timed to begin in mid-April.

This was the first time that the Laura Center had ever come at the request of police rather than family members. It was also rare for them to participate in a case that was months instead of days old, but after hearing what was at stake, a half-dozen of the Center's experts, including Laura's parents Bob and Gay Smither, made the trip to Colorado to get the ball rolling.

What they found was one of the most difficult swaths of terrain the Center had ever been asked to take on. In every direction they looked, the land around Grand Junction was a geologist's grab-bag that ranged from sage-covered arid desert to the tangled deep-river canyons and high alpine woodlands of the Colorado Monument, to the unscalable Bookcliff Range, and even the towering wonder of the Mesa with its otherworldly weather patterns. Punctuating the landscapes were abandoned coal mines and uranium digs. Cattle rustlers and even entire tribes of the Ute Indians had successfully hidden out in these same spots for decades—and now it was going to be up to the Rotary Club and several hundred other well-meaning residents to try to find even the smallest clues.

By the last week of March 2002 the pieces were in place and the sheriff's department unveiled plans for a sweep that would require at least 1,200 volunteers. They needed it all: hikers, bikers, horseback riders, technical rock climbers, pilots, and people who could just come in and answer the phones.

At the press conference, the sheriffs made clear their working assumption was that both mother and daughter were dead, and the best they expected to find would be the pair's bodies, either in a shallow grave or abandoned out in a remote ditch line somewhere beyond the town.

"Our job as law enforcement officers is to assume the worst has happened," acknowledged Mesa County Sheriff Riecke Claussen. Asked why he felt that way, Claussen explained, "Obviously, it's the whole situation—the blood at the house, other things we've investigated—so now we focus on recovering the bodies."

Something else was markedly different about the sheriff's department's tone—their new attitude toward Mike.

Sergeant Rusty Callow came right out and told the press that Michael was specifically being excluded from the new search effort because "We won't invite anyone who hasn't been eliminated as a suspect, and Michael Blagg has not been eliminated as a suspect."

Called at his home by a reporter, Blagg's only comment on the search was simply, "Anything to help find Jennifer and Abby is great."

Although the search area was theoretically everywhere within 45 miles of the Redlands, the reality was that police were looking for a secluded spot Mike could have reasonably driven to in the two-wheel-drive Ford Windstar van. Getting the mini-van and its inherent limitations as an off-road vehicle into the public's mind was important because, with its relatively long body and low bottom-to-ground clearance, it was not something that could have been driven into most remote canyons. Once Mike got out of the van, the sheriffs' expectation was that he would have carried the dead-weight of the bodies for at most a few dozen yards before either dumping them, hiding them in some cave or under some outcrop, or maybe even going to the arduous effort of burying them.

There were a lot of truly remote places within the arc of the search zone that for years probably hadn't seen anything bigger than a coyote wander through, but the sheriffs' expectation was that if Mike had taken the bodies to an outdoor location, then it was probably somewhere he'd been at least once before—which meant that its actual remoteness was probably something he'd overestimated.

On April 16, 2002, the sheriffs held a large public "town meeting" attended by 1,100 people to give out one final round of information before the first day of searching was set to begin.

Even though he would be in charge of the entire operation, George Barley characteristically chose to watch the meeting from a seat in the middle of the room with his wife, rather than sit on the stage.

Gay Smither, Laura's mother, traveled up from Texas to watch the meeting, as did Marilyn Conway, who spoke to the gathered volunteers, saying that the hope that answers might be found "is something we've prayed for, and I think our prayers are being answered. You are a very gracious community."

The organizers explained the basics of the search "grid" that was being laid down over the area, and how the individual teams would be dispatched from a command post in a construction trailer that had been rigged up in the parking lot of the Fellowship Church, the largest church in Mesa County.

Searchers were told that if they found anything suspicious, they were to mark it with fluorescent tape or a little neon survey flag and call it in to search leaders, who would relay the location to police for follow-up.

Some of the same searchers who had helped find Danielle van Dam's body in San Diego were coming out to help in Grand Junction, where whole church congregations and bridge clubs were signing up to participate en masse, and some businesses were letting employees off work, or even preparing to close down certain days, to send additional search volunteers. Horse-riding clubs and some of the West's mounted sheriffs' posses were planning to come help, and a camera crew from CBS' *48 Hours* news show was poised to follow the searchers into the field.

The National Park Service and the Bureau of Land Management, which together were responsible for much of the land in question, were already on board to help, as was a county map specialist.

The first day of the search focused on the Little Park Preserve, in large part because of a woman who'd placed an anonymous call months beforehand saying she'd seen "something suspicious" out there on the night of November 12.

Police had already checked the park where the Blaggs had taken Abby mountain-biking, but this time 175 volunteers made the trek through the juniper bushes. It took a while to get everybody divided into teams, and the buses were late in getting to the Fellowship Church, but by mid-morning the groups had arrived at their grids a dozen miles from the Blagg residence, and the out-of-towners were getting their first taste of just how daunting year-round "perfect" weather in the high desert could be. Wind gusts that hit 45 miles per hour were blasting clouds of reddish dust down from the hills into the Grand Valley.

Within hours, as the volunteers just began to get off the

beaten paths and into the more remote canyons and bluffs, reports started coming in about a dozen suspicious-looking mounds that might be potential burial sights.

Again and again, Barley and other investigators grabbed radios and sped out to the fringes of town to take a look. It quickly became apparent that memorials to pets were going to be a problem for the search. At least ten pet graves, some as simple as a disturbed patch of ground with a wooden cross made of sticks, some as elaborate as a cairn of rocks garlanded with artificial flowers, would eventually be disinterred by detectives with the help of an archeologist who double-checked to make sure they were indeed the sites of animal remains.

Despite the battering winds, the searchers pressed on into the early evening, coloring in over six square miles on the search maps before calling it a night.

The rhythm of the search quickly fell into a pattern: twelve-hour days at the command post, beginning with a couple hundred searchers signing in at a time, picking up the provisions and first-aid kits that had been put together by Grand Junction's Boy Scouts, and catching a briefing before clambering onto buses for the ride out to the day's designated search grids.

Jennifer's family members arrived before dawn each day with the police to help set up, some days joining the searches themselves and on others answering phones and helping to prepare meals for the returning search teams.

Jennifer's mother and brother, Marilyn Conway and David Loman, made a collage of photographs of Jennifer and Abby, which they put up inside the command trailer where everyone signing in to participate in the search could see it. Marilyn also made it a point to go out into the parking lot each morning to wave to the departing buses, in order to assure the searchers that she appreciated their willingness to keep giving their time.

"I think we have to realize that my Jennifer is gone," Conway said through tears during an interview with reporters from *People* magazine, "but I haven't been able to turn Abby loose. I can't say that she is dead."

Minister Ray Shirley captured the mood of much of the search when he told *The Denver Post* that there was an overwhelming desire toward "giving closure and bringing justice" for the family and the larger community. But at the same time, he noted, "This is very tough. I think a lot of people are fearful they'll be the ones to find them."

Others were drawn to the search out of their own sense of loss and obligation. Laura Smither's mother, Gay, came to help. The first Saturday of the search would be the fifth anniversary of the day Laura's body was found in Texas.

Paul and Ramona Blee, whose daughter had disappeared following a teenage dance party, helped search on what would have been their daughter's 38th birthday. "It's hard," Mona Blee told *The Denver Post*, "but I want to be able to give someone else some closure."

Ed McNevin flew in from Chicago a week early and immediately began his own search under bridges and along the riverbanks before joining the official search. McNevin had lost his daughter in a car accident twenty years earlier and had been praying for Jennifer and Abby Blagg from the first day their story had hit the news in Chicago.

By Friday evening, as searchers gathered inside the Fellowship Church for a candlelight vigil to conclude the week, the total number of volunteers involved in the first three days had reached 831. On Saturday morning a surge of new weekend searchers allowed organizers to put thirty-six separate teams into the field around Grand Junction.

On Sunday the winds finally died down enough to allow a medevac helicopter from St. Mary's Hospital to join the search, checking along the Price Ditch irrigation canal and other remote spots it had been difficult for the ground search to reach, as the total number of volunteers climbed to over 1,200, some having come from as far as Connecticut to help.

That Sunday was the Laura Recovery Center's last. Having stuck to their model of training the local community and getting the ball rolling, the half-dozen organizers who'd been working on the project turned it over to several Grand Junction residents and headed to the airport for a flight back to Texas.

As the week progressed, an average of 200 searchers a day continued to turn out, and enthusiasm continued despite the fact that more and more areas of interest were being ticked off the sheriff's maps in the command post with little to show in the way of real clues.

With the departure of the Texas founders, the organizers had renamed the local effort "the Jennifer and Abby Blagg Recovery Center," and as the second week of the search progressed, the decision was made to turn it into a permanent chapter of the Laura Foundation so that it could be reactivated to help with any similar searches in the future in the region.

Connie Flukey, a mother of eight who had turned out to help on the first day, said the establishment of the search operation had been a life-changing experience for her. "It's not a depressing situation," Flukey told *The Denver Post*. "You come back, you're tired, it doesn't matter. You go back out, you don't want to leave. You just want to help bring them home."

Marilyn Conway told reporters she was moved by the decision to form the new group in honor of her daughter and granddaughter. Her son David Loman had taken a tremendous amount of time off from managing a Wal-Mart in Oklahoma City to help with the search effort for his sister and niece. The motto of the new chapter was "Let It Shine," from Abby's favorite song, "This Little Light of Mine."

As a second week of searching drew to a close, it became clear that the search itself was approaching its final hours, and on April 27, 2002, searchers finished the last areas that had been designated by police as being of potential interest in their sweep of the Grand Valley.

It was a Saturday, and as such, it drew a larger than average turnout of volunteers, who concentrated on the few remaining target search grids out on the desert bordering Utah, and in a series of deep canyons at the southern edge of Mesa County.

After eleven days of hard work, emotions were running high, and there were still dozens of small neon flags logged down on the maps that needed to be double-checked by investigators, but the sense was that every point that could have been reached by a Ford Windstar had finally been checked.

It had been the largest search ever conducted in Mesa County, and it had used manpower, horsepower, all-terrain vehicles, rope belays, and helicopters. It had found animal bones, pieces of clothing, shell casings, strange markings on rocks, and a few rolls of carpet—but, in the end, nothing that contained any obvious link to the Blagg disappearances.

"It was hard to sit home and not be a part of it," Mike told *The Denver Post*. "I would have been glad to help. I sure do appreciate everything everybody did during the search."

For the 2,200 volunteers from across Colorado and nine other states who had trekked the backcountry looking for Jennifer and Abby, there was a clear sense of disappointment, but, despite the lack of any dramatic discoveries, the sheriffs themselves were quietly optimistic, because they knew the ground search had always been more of a prelude to what was coming next.

"While the search didn't find Abby and Jennifer, it has progressed the investigation forward," sheriff's spokeswoman Janet Prell told reporters, adding cryptically,

"And we probably would not have been able to move on to the next step—which I can't go into—without having done a search of this sort."

For the investigators, the final massive ground search of the county had from the start been a necessary means to go to another end—the landfill. Having accomplished the seemingly impossible goal of eliminating all of the "reasonable" 2,400 square miles thought to be accessible by mini-van from within the larger 6,360 square miles of the 45-mile search radius, the sheriffs were now about to take on a much, much more difficult task—even though this time the search area involved would be far less than a single square mile.

# 25

THE sheriffs went out to meet with the county officials and the private hauling companies that operated the Mesa County Landfill, explaining that, while they realized they were six months behind the curve, they wondered if it would be feasible to go back in and look for something.

Stunned laughter filled the room. The short answer was "No." It was impossible.

"Well," countered Lieutenant Dick Dillon, "we're sure we have to."

Slowly the mood began to change and the landfill personnel began to discuss ways that it could theoretically be done. But they were still certain that the sheriffs were crazy.

As the notion of digging into Grand Junction's landfill began to take serious hold among Mesa County officials in the first weeks of May, the phrase "like trying to find a needle in a haystack" inevitably surfaced in conversation after conversation. But even that time-worn cliché didn't begin to capture the real immensity of what was being contemplated.

A haystack is full of nice clean hay. What was lurking under the surface of Grand Junction's landfill was anything but nice, and anything but clean.

Sifting through the garbage in a municipal dump anywhere in the world would be just a god-awful punishing task, but there were two extra twists to the Grand Junction landfill that also gave investigators pause as they considered whether this was really going to be possible.

First, this was a landfill that accepted "sludge" from wastewater treatment plants—meaning that waste collected at the facilities was driven out to the landfill in tanker trucks and pumped directly down onto the layers of trash before it was closed over by a thin layer of dirt. Not something that anyone ever contemplated uncovering again, at least not in this century.

The other retch-worthy menace were the hundreds of elk carcasses that had been randomly dumped as the result of road kills and the recently concluded annual elk-hunting season.

Digging down to the mid-November layer was going to entail peeling back through five solid months' worth of things that were truly meant to be left undisturbed.

Not only would this be a dirty, unsanitary job, with the real possibility of exposure to injury and pathogenic substances, but it was a job that the sheriffs knew they would have to do themselves.

If an outside contractor were called in, there was a risk they would not be as thorough as police and, even if they did find something, a sharp defense attorney could be expected to raise all kinds of questions about potential evidence contamination, whether the contract workers had cut corners or overlooked other clues, and conjure up basic "chain-of-custody" issues for whatever was found.

The only way to defend against all of the possible things that could go wrong would be to have sworn law enforcement personnel do the digging instead.

Nobody had joined the force thinking they were going to have to stand ankle-deep in rotting elk guts day after day looking for clues, but the sheriffs had decided this was an effort worth making. If Abby or Jennifer were in the landfill, then a determined excavation would be the only shot at finding out—and of doing something to right a terrible wrong.

It would be a monumental gamble, and time was not on the investigators' side.

If the bodies were in the landfill, then they were being buried deeper every day as dozens of trash trucks continued to build the gigantic mound of garbage higher and higher on top of them. That meant any serious effort aimed at recovering evidence would have to start as soon as possible—right in May when spring temperatures in the high desert could easily soar to over a hundred degrees.

A random dig into the landfill looking for something that had been thrown out six months beforehand would have been a complete non-starter, but the sheriffs had one critical piece of information that tipped the scales in their favor—literally. Every trash truck that entered the landfill had to drive over a set of scales near the entrance in order to be weighed before it proceeded up the big hill to that day's open dumping site. Sure enough, on November 14, the landfill had a record of the truck that had made the run to AMETEK Dixson weighing in at the facility, stamped with the precise time of arrival.

One reason that 21$^{st}$ century landfill operators bristle at having their heavily regulated, multi-million-dollar facilities called "dumps" is that landfills really are carefully thought-out engineering projects now. Garbage trucks don't just trundle in willy-nilly and scatter trash on any available spot before scooting back out.

Building a landfill is probably the closest thing in the modern workday world to constructing one of the ancient pyramids. Each day the arriving garbage trucks drive up an access road onto the growing mound of trash, and are directed to a particular area that is being built up according to a long-term blueprint designed to allow the landfill to operate for decades.

That open section of the landfill where the trash is being dumped at the moment is called "the working face" and, as the trucks back up and empty their loads, the trash tends to scatter a bit more widely down over the slope, creating a "lift"—a three-dimensional field of debris shaped like a slice of pie.

Whether they are owned by a municipality or operated privately, landfills are essentially a business, and the product they are selling is space. The more trash that can be fit into each cubic yard of "airspace" inside the landfill, the longer the facility can operate, and the more money it can make operators—or save taxpayers. Every old coffee can that sits empty inside that growing pyramid is costing somebody money for a cubic foot of space that could have been better used; therefore, one of the primary goals of any modern landfill operation is to maximize compaction.

The ideal way to compact bulk solid waste would be to run it all through some kind of giant industrial tree chipper and just powder it before packing it back into the landfill as solid as sand on a beach. But doing something like that would be impractical for a host of reasons.

The realistic compacting solution, which most landfills have now used for decades, is a piece of heavy equipment called, appropriately enough, the compactor.

Landfill compactors are essentially a cross between a bulldozer and a wheeled front loader. Like a bulldozer, they have a fifteen-foot-wide plow blade on the front that spreads trash out across the lift, but what sets them apart from most other specialized construction-type vehicles are their unique "sheep's foot" metal wheels. Instead of tracks or tires, landfill compactors run around on huge five-foot-diameter solid steel drums that are each studded with up to fifty giant steel "teeth" the size of toasters.

As the trash is poured out over the day's lift, the 80,000-pound compactor ranges back and forth over the landfill "cell" that is being constructed, using an engine that cranks out nearly 400 horsepower as it shoves the debris field into shape. Each time the compactor moves, those steel teeth are punching down through every plastic garbage bag, mushy cantaloupe, and discarded computer monitor.

It only takes a few minutes for the compactor to turn everything into an unrecognizable gray tangle of shredded plastic, glass, metal, and putrid-smelling organic matter that is covered at the end of every day with a thin layer of dirt to cap it and keep it all from being blown out across town by the wind.

Watching from a distance, it seems like a lone compactor rolling around atop a giant landfill would miss a lot of spots. But the thousands of revolutions by those wheels each eight-hour shift mean that, before the dirt cover is finally spread on top, each day's trash lift has been stabbed by the steel teeth approximately one million times.

If Jennifer and Abby were in the landfill, then the investigators knew the odds were that their bodies had also been run over by the forty-ton compactor, not just once, but hour after hour after hour.

# 26

ANYWHERE else on the planet, the ridgeline occupied by the Mesa County Landfill would probably be considered prime real estate because of its sweeping views down into the rolling grassy hills that make up the Gunnison River Valley, bracketed by the Grand Mesa and the Rockies beyond; however, in an area with no shortage of gorgeous scenery, the trash still had to go somewhere, and this 270-acre property just off the southeastern corner of Grand Junction was it.

The question of precisely where to start digging fell to Mesa County Surveyor Frank Kochevar and Mesa County Landfill Manager Bob Edmiston.

The landfill was actually being built up layer-by-layer, day-by-day according to a design scheme listed on a series of blueprints so that someday, forty years out, when it was finally filled, it would be just another rolling hill at the head of the valley. Delving into the records at the landfill office, Edmiston and Kochevar determined that the trash arriving on November 14 could have been dumped into one of two cells that were being constructed that day.

In order to find those cells again in the featureless dirt of their giant man-made anthill, the men pored over a series of aerial photographs that had been taken each year in order to gauge the landfill's annual rise in elevation. The landfill was already sectioned off into an imaginary grid, and by using a GPS surveying system, the team was able to narrow the search area down to a 150-by-150–foot area.

The landfill staff had the weigh slip for the AMETEK Dixson Dumpster that had arrived on November 14, and it showed a 1.95-ton load of trash going in. The trick was going to be finding its contents among about 7,000 tons of other trash that had been packed into the same pair of cells that were open that particular day.

Normally the task of finding a body within a small piece of terrain could be accomplished with specially trained "corpse-sniffing" search dogs, but the use of cadaver canines was ruled out because there were too many bits of broken glass, nails, and other things that would be too dangerous for the dogs. Besides, there was simply no point. The rotten meat, animal carcasses, and vast amount of items contaminated with human scent ranging from tampons to discarded clothing would make it impossible for dogs to distinguish a body. However, there were two types of clues that investigators were counting on to help them stay on track.

The first was newspapers. Every day tens of thousands of newspapers were delivered to homes and businesses, and printed prominently on every single page was that day's date. Buried newspapers are an archeologist's dream, because they come out of landfills' oxygen-depleted depths in pristine condition. But investigators knew it wasn't quite as simple as digging down until they started hitting November 13. Papers can lie around for some time before they're gathered up and thrown out, so something that was dumped into the landfill on the thirteenth could be buried among newspapers that were days, even weeks, older.

The second telltale sign the diggers were hoping to locate was trash they could actually trace right back to AME-TEK Dixson. Things like cardboard packing boxes that had been delivered to the company were likely to be indistinguishable among the vast compacted mass, but during a visit to the factory, several of the workers showed the detectives an array of things, mostly plastic, that were unique to their manufacturing plant's waste stream.

On Monday, May 13, 2002, the sheriffs spent their first day digging in what they expected to be at most a three- or four-week project.

The dig itself would consist of one big yellow excavator equipped with a steel bucket, and six to twelve sheriff's investigators at a time, armed with shovels and rakes.

Leading the dive downward was the sheriff's lieutenant directly in charge of Mesa County's Investigative Division. Dick Dillon had served the Army in combat zones in Dominica and Korea before spending three decades in law enforcement, but this type of challenge was a completely new one for him.

In order to make the dig possible, Lieutenant Dillon

first had to squeeze the funding for it out of the sheriff's existing departmental budget. His solution was to keep everyone on the clock and not use any overtime hours to do the search. With only a dozen investigators and two sergeants in the department, Lieutenant Dillon planned to rotate at least half of his total staff, plus himself, out on the landfill each weekday, which would leave six or fewer detectives to pick up the normal policing duties for a county that was larger than the state of Rhode Island.

The litany of what could go wrong was extensive. There were even concerns about hitting pockets of methane gas, being exposed to virulent pathogens carried in medical waste, or getting stuck by used scalpels and hypodermic needles.

Dillon learned that police in San Diego had recently searched their own landfill for paperwork that proved critical to a case, so he contacted them to see what tips he could pick up. "They said their biggest issue was impales through the bottom of their footwear," Dillon related. "During the three days they were in there, they had four impales, so we went and lobbied with our administration to get footwear for everybody that had a steel shank."

"We had the fire department standing by in the early stages, just in case we did actually start the landfill on fire, because it would have probably burned for a million years, and it wouldn't have looked good on my résumé," Dillon explained, rolling his eyes.

Standing high above the surrounding valleys on the landfill that first morning, George Barley looked at the wide man-made plain of packed dirt that was as flat and feature-less as a tabletop and thought, "Oh my word! How are we going to do this?" But soon the first clues began to emerge.

The search began with an archeology technique known as "potholing." The big yellow excavator dug straight down in a quick series of small test holes that looped out in a large circle across the area that was thought to contain the two targeted cells.

Sure enough, within minutes they were getting newspapers from a range of dates that included November 14 out of the first hole. By the time the group had progressed around the circle, they were confident that they had indeed dug down into both of the cells they were hoping to find. They were also able to tell from the dates that the second cell in question hadn't actually been receiving any trash on November 14, which allowed them to quickly eliminate it from the search area.

The decision was made to begin at the first test pothole and just start working to the right around the circle and see what could be found.

The search procedure was simplicity itself. The excavator operator sank the big metal arm into the dirt-covered ground, pulled up a load of trash, and spread it out in a line about a foot thick on top of the flat landfill surface known as "the deck." After three bucketloads of debris had been laid out, the sheriffs would rush in and rake it, ripping open every garbage bag, and taking a good look at what had been found, before hustling back away from the stench to wait for the next several scoops.

"We didn't know how the Blaggs might have been killed, so we didn't know what kind of murder weapon to look for," recalled Lieutenant Dick Dillon. "But it made sense, if you are going to dispose of the bodies, to get rid of the weapon also, so we were looking for that while we were looking for products that came from AMETEK Dixson. Their waste is very distinct because of its circuit boards. Those are bright green, and on the landfill they stood out like a sore thumb. That's what we were using as a trail to follow."

The sheriffs might have been searching for AMETEK Dixson trash, but that was by no means all they were finding.

"Anything that is manufactured on this planet eventually winds up in a landfill," Dillon pointed out. "You'll have the odor from trash, but that almost becomes extinct because we acclimated to that to the point we didn't smell it. Decomp was another issue. Being in western Colorado with hunting season . . . Our rendering plant had closed, so now even all your farm animals that died and roadkill animals and processing places for wild game would bring all that meat and the carcasses out there, and that would start to decay," Dillon reminisced, chuckling. "It seemed like our excavator operator had a talent for serving us a rack of sun-baked ribs just before lunch, and it would gag a maggot. I know that was the worst thing."

The Colorado National Guard had pitched one of their big green military tents out on the landfill deck at the edge of the search area to serve as both a command post and a lunch room for the sheriffs, and by the end of the first full day of digging, when the crew had gone through nearly a hundred tons of garbage—along the way coming to realize just how many dirty diapers the average American city really throws out in a day's time—a sign appeared over the tent's entrance reading, "HEADQUARTERS OF BIG DADDY AND THE SOGGY BOTTOM GANG."

The members of the Soggy Bottom Gang (who soon had matching orange hardhats with their new moniker emblazoned on them) knew from the beginning that they were signing up for one unpleasant task. Just how unpleasant became apparent during the first few days.

The dig began each morning at 7 A.M. and ended around 2 P.M. in order to avoid the heat of the day, which in May of 2002 began setting records for spring temperatures—clear up to 104 degrees on one of the days. The wind was another factor. A steady 25-mile-per-hour breeze was a good day. The bad days were when it came in random gusts as high as 45 mph.

When the winds were really blowing, each scoop the

excavator pulled from below would appear almost as if it were on fire because of the smoke-like clouds of fine dust that would boil off it. As the load was dumped, the stinging clouds of dirt would be joined by a shotgun blast of plastic grocery bags, paper, old Kleenex, wrappers, and other light material that would race across the deck to the distant debris-containment fences that ringed the boundaries of the landfill.

One gust blew Dillon's hardhat off, and it sailed right past Steve King, who ended up chasing it like a tumbleweed across hundreds of yards of the deck, the whole time thinking, "This is what I went to investigative school for?" But King and the others were in awe of Dillon's decision to stay on for every single day of the dig, even though the rest of them were given occasional days off to recover. "He could have just as easily sat in the office and said, 'I'm the lieutenant and you guys are the investigators. Go out and do this,' but he led from the front and was out there digging like the rest of us," King recalled.

Mesa County District Attorney Frank Daniels came out one morning to check on the progress of the investigation and after spending just a half-hour amidst the heavy stench, he had to go home and mow his lawn just to get the smell out of his head.

As bad as it was, the gang developed an unspoken pact not to complain, but just to forge ahead. They knew that if they gave up, someone might literally get away with murder. "The only thing in your mind all day was, 'I can make it to lunch,'" Steve King recalled. "If you could make it to lunch, you could make it the rest of the way through the day."

One lunch break in particular would stand as the emblematic moment of both Dick Dillon's and the searchers' perseverance. The gang had just sat down and started to eat under the large National Guard tent when a huge gust of wind hit, lifting the canopy right off the posts that were holding it up. "Those big four-by-four posts came tumbling down over the table and a second later the tent comes down on top of it, so everybody dove underneath," King remembered. "There's this pause. Then Lieutenant Dillon says, 'Anybody hurt?' and everybody's like, 'No . . . Nope . . . No . . .' Then Dillon just goes, 'Okay . . . Where's my lunch?'"

# 27

**AS** soon as the investigators began to dig up the Mesa County Landfill, word reached them that their prime suspect was making plans to get out of Dodge.

Mike made a few attempts to find a new job around town after being fired from AMETEK Dixson, but he soon saw the writing on the cliff walls. With his public image in tatters, local reservoirs of sympathy nearly exhausted, and his legal and other bills mounting by the week, Michael Blagg had finally had enough of Grand Junction. Word leaked out that he'd been telling his friends he was preparing to move away. "I am looking for a job in every way I can," Blagg told reporters, adding, "I would rather not say where I am going."

Although he was now openly being called a murder suspect by the investigation, Michael hadn't been charged with anything—not even the alleged thefts from AMETEK—so legally he was free to go anywhere he wanted. Police weren't thrilled about him leaving their sight, but at the same time, they weren't overly concerned.

"You can be assured that we're going to want to know where he winds up," Lieutenant Stan Hilkey told the newspapers. "It'll be our job to make sure we know wherever he goes."

Two days after the landfill dig began, on Wednesday, May 15, 2002, the lease on Blagg's townhouse expired, and Mike appeared in line at Walker Field with a ticket out of town.

But as Mike's jet lifted off and headed out over the mesas in full view of the Soggy Bottom Gang, who were knee-deep in trash far below, the investigators had already figured out right where he was headed—about 100 miles south of Atlanta to stay at his mother's home in an upscale, lakeside section of Warner Robins, Georgia.

Tuesday, June 4, 2002, the sixteenth day of the landfill search, and two weeks after Mike's departure, began like every other day of the dig as the weary group took up their tools at 7 A.M. and trudged out in their steel-toed boots to stand beside the excavator. By 10:15 A.M., the usual rhythms of raking and sorting were well underway and a new bucket that had just been pulled up to the deck from about fifteen feet down in the open pit was about to be dumped when investigator Henry Stoffel suddenly waved everyone to a halt. The excavator operator, Michael Doyhenard, had already seen what Stoffel was staring at, and gone white as a sheet.

Dangling out over the edge of the metal bucket was an adult human leg ending in a withered foot.

Up until that moment, the arduous landfill excavation had been a time-consuming and expensive guess. Now it was officially a crime scene. The detectives knew they had to quickly regroup and make sure what happened next went by the book.

The investigators peering at the bucket could see that the leg was protruding from some sort of lumpy red cloth shroud like a tarp, or possibly a nylon bag of some kind.

The wind was blowing and the leg was rocking back and forth rather precariously in the gusts, but the investigators didn't want to touch anything or probe around inside the bucket for fear they could lose or contaminate any trace evidence that might still be present.

The combined FBI and CBI recovery team that had been on stand-by since the start of the search was still in Denver, and by the time they traveled the 250 miles with their equipment, it would be dark, so the decision was made to secure whatever was in the bucket just as it was, and wait until morning for the team to arrive.

As the group took pictures and tried to figure out how best to deal with the leg, which in only a few hours was going to be exposed to the hottest part of the day, Lieutenant Dillon had the excavator operator lower the bucket all the way down to the surface. As he was doing so, fate intervened and the wind finally twisted the leg loose. It fell with a sickening thump onto the deck.

At Sergeant Rusty Callow's suggestion, dry ice was quickly trucked out to the scene and packed around both the leg and the large bucket. The scoopful of material inside was left alone, the entire area was cordoned off with crime-scene tape, and a cruiser was posted to keep twenty-four-hour watch on everything until the recovery team could make the trip over the Rockies.

At the crack of dawn on Wednesday morning, the team was assembled, and by 8 A.M., forensic specialists wearing plastic coveralls to prevent exposure to pathogens had made their way over to take a closer look at what was in the bucket.

The centerpiece of the load was a red-and-black piece of oilcloth-like material that appeared to be wrapped around something. Investigators lifted it out and placed it on a tarp on the ground. A closer look revealed that the piece of colored cloth was actually a tent.

The investigators shook their heads in amazement. Designed specifically to keep out even wind-driven moisture, the weatherproof camping tent was a fiendishly clever thing to use to contain a bleeding body, and it went a long way in their minds toward explaining why there hadn't been more blood found in both the house and the van.

As they gingerly unwrapped the tent, the investigators knew they were finally approaching the moment of truth. Inside was the rest of a human body, most of it anyway, shrouded in a dirty gray cloth that on closer examination turned out to be an oversized T-shirt. The body's overall appearance was exactly what one would expect to see if they unwrapped a mummy, except that the facial features had been distorted into a goblin-like grimace, and the torso and limbs had been flattened and grotesquely bent.

It took only an hour on the scene to inspect the body, and Mesa County Medical Examiner Dr. Robert Kurtzman quickly determined that it was in fact an adult female. There was no way to tell just from looking at the dark brown leathery remains that the body was Jennifer's, but that was the working assumption as the investigators waited for a positive identification. A complete set of photographs was taken before the corpse was bagged and handed over to the Mesa County Coroner's Office for an immediate autopsy.

Dr. Kurtzman was joined downtown at the Mesa County morgue in Community Hospital by Dr. Dean Havlik, Mesa County's other medical examiner, who would lead this particular autopsy, and by Sheriff's Investigators Lissah Norcross and Jim Hebenstreit, CBI Agent Kevin Humphreys, and FBI Agent Arnold Bellmer.

The body lying on the steel autopsy table was the ultimate testament to the real horror that underlay all of the events of the preceding six months.

The landfill had not been at all kind to Jennifer.

The compactor had torn Jennifer's left leg completely off during the first few minutes or hours she had lain among the scattered debris on the surface, and as more and more trash had been dumped that afternoon, the repeated passes of the heavy machine had stretched and flattened her body. Top to bottom x-rays showed too many post-mortem fractures of bones to bother counting.

As Jennifer's remains had descended into the depths, they had then been further bent and twisted by the twin forces of tons of crushing weight and the stifling 130-degree temperatures that fermenting garbage caused to build up within the landfill.

Jennifer's head was intact, which would prove critical to the investigation, but the left half of her torso had largely vanished due to decomposition driven by the bacteria that had naturally been within her body at the time she died.

The same random factors that had placed the left half of her body in a position where nature had worked to disintegrate it, happened to have exposed her right half with its remaining leg to the slow drying effects of the landfill's internal heat. This had removed the moisture from the rest of her body and, in the process, mummified it, so that what remained of a 130-pound woman now weighed only 70 pounds.

About the only indignity the body had been spared as it lay entombed in the landfill was an attack by insects and animals. The same low-oxygen environment that slowed the pace of bacterial decay within the body had kept any insects from laying eggs on it, and thus having their larvae hatch and rapidly putrefy the corpse—something that would have happened within hours had it been dumped somewhere out in the canyons.

Jennifer's once-vibrant face had been distorted past the limits of humanity into an appalling scowl, but as the medical examiners gingerly looked it over inch-by-inch, they realized that despite someone's deliberate efforts—not only to kill her, but to hide her away where she would never be found—what still remained of Jennifer would be enough for her to finally tell the story of how she'd died.

One of the first orders of business was to take an x-ray

of her head, and it immediately told the investigators three important things. First, there was a single bullet lodged squarely inside her skull. Second, there was a dental appliance of some sort in her mouth. And third—using a dental x-ray taken back in 1990, when she was still Jennifer Loman, for comparison—Dr. Kurtzman was at last able to officially identify the body as that of Jennifer Blagg.

Sheriff's Investigator Hebenstreit was quickly dispatched to show both x-rays to Grand Junction dentist John Bull. Right at noon, Dr. Bull confirmed the match, and went on to identify the item in Jennifer's mouth as her custom-made lower retainer.

Back in the morgue, Dr. Havlik retrieved the bullet and several fragments from the brain, and took a look at the shattered piece of metal under a microscope. The bullet was a hollow-point, which was designed for just this kind of killing. It had entered through Jennifer's left eyelid and, in a split instant, had slowed and expanded, imparting a deadly paralyzing shock wave straight to her head. Even though the skin on her face had been altered by its ordeal in the landfill, Dr. Kurtzman could still clearly see that it was textured with a grainy pattern known in forensics as *stippling*. The embedded stippling indicated to him that the gun had been only a few inches from her head at the time it was fired, so her skin had been sprayed with still-burning grains of gunpowder.

Havlik passed the recovered bullet over to Agent Humphreys, who put it under a microscope for a preliminary look. Humphreys said it appeared to be something that would have been fired from a 9mm or similar-sized gun, but what was especially interesting to him was that the bullet had caught something in mid-flight and driven it right into Jennifer's head—a tiny strand of blue thread. The thread embedded in the bullet made sense if a pillow had been placed over the gun barrel in order to muffle the sound of the shot.

The autopsy was winding up, but investigators had a checklist of things they'd be looking for if they ever found Jennifer or Abby's remains, and one thing they still really needed was fingerprints. Neither Abby nor Jennifer had any fingerprints on file, and that had meant some unique prints around the house and in the van had to be recorded as "unknown." Now that they had Jennifer's body, investigators were hoping they could catalog all of her prints and eliminate them completely from the crime-scene analysis. In a grim bit of forensic efficiency, the coroners surgically removed both desiccated hands, packaged them, and had them shipped to the Colorado Bureau of Investigation office in Montrose to see if they could inject liquid into the withered fingertips and re-inflate them long enough to ink them and get prints.

At 12:20 P.M., the team finished the autopsy, and Dean Havlik typed up Jennifer Blagg's death certificate. The cause of death was a gunshot wound to the head. The manner of death was ruled a homicide. It was time to brief the rest of the investigators on what had been found.

# 28

AS far as the detectives were concerned, the fact that Jennifer was in her nightshirt, and still had her dental retainer in her mouth, clinched it.

Jennifer only put the retainer in when she was going to sleep for the night, and she took it right out when she got up in the morning. It seemed obvious from the beginning that she had been injured while she was lying on the bed, but now there was clear evidence that the shot had been fired before she got up in the morning.

There might have been some reasons to wait and weigh the evidence a bit further, perhaps waiting to see if Abby could be found, but the detectives who had worked the case for six months straight were adamant—they didn't want to give Mike another chance to take the easy way out by killing himself before they could put him on trial. They begged Mesa County District Attorney Frank Daniels to act and, having seen what they had been through at the landfill alone, he made the decision to go ahead and have Mike arrested with all possible haste.

After placing calls to Jennifer's family in Texas, Mesa County Sheriff Riecke Claussen held a press conference to announce what had happened.

"Obviously, we'd like to locate Abby if we can," Claussen noted, explaining that the sheriffs planned to push on with the grueling search until all the trash in the target area had been checked, a process that could require several additional weeks. Claussen continued, "A lot of people would like to have hope that Abby is alive somewhere, but our job is to assume the worst has happened and continue the investigation."

"We're not even talking about stopping," Sheriff's Lieutenant Stan Hilkey added.

New Hope Fellowship Pastor Art Blankenship spoke of his sadness at the press conference. "I love and care about this family, and we're praying for them," he said. "It's been a spiritual . . ." Blankenship's voice trailed off as he paused to wipe away a tear before adding, "Words fail me. I really have nothing more to say."

Stephan Schweissing, Mike's attorney in Grand Junction, made a brief statement saying that he'd passed the news of Jennifer's positive identification on to Mike, who was shocked and distraught when he heard. "It's something you brace for, it's your fear, but when it comes to fruition, it's still a terrible blow," Schweissing said, adding, "This has just been an extremely difficult six or seven months for him, and this has been a very emotional time for Mr. Blagg. He's doing his best to remain positive. It's certainly very important for him to find out what happened to his family. We're supportive of the continued investigation."

Reached at her home in Texas, Jennifer's mother Marilyn Conway told the *Fort Worth Star-Telegram*, "One of our prayers has been answered, because we found one of our girls. We need to find Abby." When asked what she made of the homicide, Conway replied, "I don't know why someone would do this. I don't know who would do such a thing."

In Pauls Valley, Oklahoma, Jennifer's uncle, Wayne Loman, echoed Conway. "I'm just glad she's been located. It's a little bit of closure. I just wish they'd go ahead and find the killer." Asked if he thought Mike could actually be that killer, Loman replied, "I haven't wanted to think so. I just don't know. I'm still real concerned about the little girl. I hope they find her alive somewhere."

Reporters who attempted to call Mike for further comment down at his mother's house in Georgia on Thursday were at first frustrated by the lack of a listed phone number. They soon found that there was another reason they couldn't get him on the phone—Mike was already under arrest.

The Colorado paperwork had been faxed over to Georgia Wednesday evening and at 11:45 P.M., several cruisers with Houston County sheriff's deputies pulled up in front of Mike's mother's house on Beaver Run Drive in Warner Robins. After the deputies knocked on the door and had a brief conversation inside, Mike walked out to the waiting cruisers without incident.

Mike had been attending the Christ United Methodist Church in Warner Robins and doing some construction work to earn money for his legal bills. Congregation members who hadn't known Mike's story were stunned by his arrest on a murder charge, saying that in the brief time he was in town he'd been a tremendous help with a church volunteer program that made home repairs for low-income elderly and disabled people.

In a television interview following his arrest, Mike's mother Elizabeth Blagg was asked by Susan Spencer, the anchor of the CBS News program *48 Hours*, if she had ever honestly asked herself whether the accusations about Mike could be true. Betsy replied, "Well, if we're talking about have I thought for a second he might have murdered his wife? Not one second." However, Blagg said she was concerned about whether Mike could get a fair trial after all of the negative speculation.

During the same program, Blagg's sister Clare Rochester also defended him, saying, "It is not true that he is cold or that he lacks expression. We're the kind of people who like to help other people. We're nice people. We're good guys. And it's pretty hard being one of the good guys and being seen as an absolute horror."

Because Colorado officials warned them about his previous suicide attempt in February, Mike was immediately placed on suicide watch at the Houston County jail in Perry, Georgia, and ordered held on $1,000,000 bond.

The discovery of Jennifer's body on Tuesday and the events that led up to Mike's arrest on Wednesday night had marked major turning points in the investigation, but on Thursday the searchers were right back out in the heat and dust on top of the Mesa County Landfill, continuing to look for Abby.

So far they had dug through about a third of the trash in the target area, and they were hoping against hope that Abby was somewhere within that circle.

"If Abby is in the landfill and was in that same load of refuse, the bulldozers spread it out over quite a large area. Abby could be quite far from her mother," sheriff's spokeswoman Janet Prell noted, adding, "I think that the investigators are not going to be able to complete that search until they have covered the whole area. The idea of leaving that child in there is abhorrent to them. They are doubly committed to finding her now."

The dig resumed again in earnest right after Jennifer's body was removed from the scene, but after another half-dozen bucket loads were raised to the deck, there was another sudden halt when the investigators spotted Jennifer's missing left leg. There wasn't any additional evidence with the severed leg, but it took only a few more scoops from the same area before the sheriffs once again began finding multiple plastic gauge punch outs from AMETEK Dixson.

That Friday the search was cut short by high winds, and on Monday when it resumed again, they were still gusting at 25 mph and had whipped up a 4,500-acre wildfire north of Grand Junction. But the sheriffs continued raking open every garbage bag, even as Mike made his way into his extradition hearing 1,600 miles away in Georgia.

With Jennifer accounted for, Mike in custody, and confirmation at long last that the murder weapon they were looking for was in fact a gun, there was a new sense of optimism among the Soggy Bottom Gang. If they could find Abby, if they could perhaps find a bundle with the pistol, the pillows, and the jewelry, then they could leave and draw the curtain down on the entire case.

Mike's appearance in the Houston County courtroom in Perry, Georgia, the next Monday morning was a bit of a shock. Instead of the business executive and former Navy lieutenant commander, what people saw was a figure in leg chains and wrist shackles who shuffled into court wearing sandals and a bright orange prison jumpsuit, not having had the benefit of a shave for several days because of the prohibition on giving razor blades to anyone on suicide watch.

Mike nodded to his mother, his brother, and his sister, all of whom had made the short trip over from Warner Robins, but the only two words he spoke during the ten-minute hearing were to retired Superior Court Judge L. A. "Buster" McConnell, who asked if he had any questions about the extradition proceedings.

"No, sir," Mike said softly.

Houston County Chief Assistant District Attorney Katie Lumsden had the deputies briefly unshackle Blagg's wrists so he could sign the papers acknowledging his desire to voluntarily return to Colorado.

On Friday, June 14, 2002, Mike, sporting an even thicker beard due to his continuing lack of access to razors, was flown back from Georgia to Grand Junction in the company of two Mesa County sheriff's investigators.

Touching down at 4 P.M. at Walker Field Airport at the base of the Bookcliffs, Mike was brought straight to the Mesa County Detention Facility, a modern but forbidding bunker-like structure with narrow horizontal slit windows that sits tucked in behind both the Justice Center and the sheriff's office. He was lodged there, in a building whose few windows nonetheless had a view out to the Redlands and the Colorado Monument beyond, to await his first hearing in Colorado on the following Monday.

The press was told of the interstate transfer only after it had been accomplished. "He's under very close supervision," said spokeswoman Janice Prell. "We're doing everything possible to ensure his safety in our jail."

# 29

DURING the first months after the disappearance of Abby and Jennifer, the sheriffs had turned to the FBI for help with several aspects of the investigation, and one of them was the task of interviewing several of Jennifer and Mike's friends in South Carolina. After Mike was charged, the information from some of those interviews was released to the public, and it managed to raise eyebrows almost immediately.

In February 2002 an agent had sat down with Edith Melson, Jennifer's best friend in Simpsonville. The investigation was trying to figure out if there had been any indication, even just in hindsight, that Mike was capable of harming his wife and daughter.

Remembering the two years she knew him, mostly through encounters at church, or calling the house to speak to Jennifer, Melson described her impression of Mike as "quiet, very private, and somewhat aloof."

The agent interviewing her wrote, "Melson said she felt uncomfortable around Mike but could not describe why she felt that way."

Melson remembered that Jennifer was nearly constantly beset by any number of health issues, ranging from the anorexia that she told her friends she had struggled with for most of her adult life, to her gall bladder surgery and subsequent reactions to medications, to an eventual diagnosis of chronic fatigue syndrome.

The fatigue would hit Jennifer so hard that she would drop out of sight for seven to ten days at a time while Mike would answer the phone and discourage Melson and other friends from visiting her.

The agent wondered if any of that could have been a cover story for physical abuse, but Melson said that, as wary as she was of Mike, especially of his physical size, which she thought he used to intimidate other people, she never saw any signs of domestic violence and never suspected it was happening. She took Jennifer at her word that much of the time she was just ill or too tired.

The very last time Melson had spoken to Jennifer on the phone was about ten days before she disappeared, and Melson told the investigator that ever since then, she'd been "haunted" by several things that Jennifer had said during the conversation.

The first thing was Jennifer's enigmatic request that Melson pray for her concerning "a problem" she was having. Jennifer said she also had something she wanted to tell Melson, but could not at that time, except to say that when she did, "it would be upsetting."

Next Jennifer made a comment to Edie that she was "praying for her sex life," and hoped Edie never had to go through what she had gone through. The FBI agent said that Melson took it to be a reference to the sexual molestation Jennifer had suffered as a teenager, but regardless, Melson said that she and Jennifer had never discussed their respective sex lives with each other during all the years they had been friends, and the remark had made her "very uncomfortable."

Finally, Jennifer told Melson that she was planning to bring Abby out to South Carolina soon for a visit and that they would be traveling there without Mike. The agent said that Melson described such a scenario as "highly unusual," to the point that "she [Melson] was scared at the implications behind the visit," and "feared that that this may be a sign of serious marital problems."

After newspaper reporters read the FBI's transcripts of Melson's statements, they wrote stories saying that before her disappearance, Jennifer had been unhappy and wanted to leave her husband and head to South Carolina. Melson immediately took issue with the accounts and even circulated a statement saying, "I was expecting Jennifer and Abby to arrange a trip soon to South Carolina for a visit—not to leave Mike. Jennifer missed her group of friends here, and wanted to come on a short vacation."

Months later, when it came time to testify in court, Melson would reverse herself again, and describe Jennifer's call in much the same terms as the FBI said she had during their interview.

At the end of June, friends of Jennifer's organized a church memorial service for her in Grand Junction, which was packed with hundreds of the volunteer searchers who had been out looking across Mesa County for her and Abby back in April.

Abby's classmates from the first grade at Bookcliff Christian School sang a selection of her favorite songs while slides projected on large monitors showed scenes of Jennifer and Abby's life together, ending the service with photos from the massive search that had tried so hard to find them.

Both Pastors Ray Shirley and Art Blankenship spoke during the service about Jennifer, as did her uncle. "Prayer was her life," Shirley told the gathering. "I believed God had gifted Jennifer with a spiritual insight."

Mike was still in jail at the edge of downtown, but his mother Betsy and his sister Clare attended, as did Marilyn and Harold Conway. A contingent of law enforcement personnel who had worked on the case also made it a point to come and pay their respects.

"It was very sad," Janet Prell, the spokeswoman for the Mesa County Sheriff's Office remarked afterward. "When you're in law enforcement, the focus is on the case and putting the pieces together. This was a moment to think about Jennifer and Abby, and what their lives were about."

The memorial service in Grand Junction was followed a few weeks later by similar services in South Carolina and Oklahoma.

At the First Baptist Church, Pastor Harling held out hope during the service that someday Abby's body might be found as well.

"It's a tragic thing, because I am sure the family would at least start putting some closure to it. Without actually finding any remains, it's just going to make it increasingly hard to do that," Harling said following the remembrance.

The CBI technicians had been partially successful in obtaining some fingerprints from Jennifer's hands, but those they weren't able to get left the investigation with lingering questions about certain latent print images. When the process was complete, the hands were returned so that the relatively intact body could be released to Jennifer's mother for burial. In Ardmore, an actual funeral service was held for Jennifer at Northwest Baptist, where she had spent so much time as a teenager, before she was buried there in her hometown.

Afterward, Karen Loman, Jennifer's sister-in-law, said that for the family, actually finding Jennifer's remains had been both a source of grief and of relief, "only from the aspect that something horrible was happening that you can't stop, and once it's over for her, it's over, and you don't have to worry about her."

# 30

TWO weeks after Mike was arrested in Georgia, he appeared for the first time in Grand Junction's district court for his formal advisement that a first-degree murder charge had been filed against him.

The Mesa County Jail had moved Mike from his initial suicide watch to a slightly less restrictive "behavior watch" status, which still kept him in a section where he was isolated from other prisoners for his own safety.

Mike gave his mother and sister a quick smile as he was brought in to the courtroom under heavy security. The court officers removed his handcuffs before he took a seat at the defense table. Mike listened intently, sitting forward in his chair, as Mesa District Judge David Bottger finally granted the deepest desires of the press corps by agreeing to unseal some of the key pages out of the 16,000 documents the investigation had generated.

Reporters who had been working for months on end with just a trickle of information suddenly found themselves in the midst of an outright deluge as they looked over the dozens of new details listed in the arrest report, the four search warrants, and Jennifer's autopsy.

The most startling new information contained in the investigative files that were released on June 17, 2002, would also prove to be the most damaging to whatever reputation for being an upright, God-fearing, business-man, devoted husband, and doting father that Michael Blagg might have had left.

The news stories that hit in the following hours were inevitable, given what was contained in the sheriffs' paperwork, because, unlike even the theft of the furniture from AMETEK and the subsequent suicide attempt, they finally purported to show, if not a motive, then at least a reason. Namely, they painted a picture of Mike as a man who had been living a double life. As *The Denver Post* summed it up in their succinct June 18 headline: "Details of Blagg case reveal family man not as he appears."

The two most damaging new allegations, both of which were printed in papers across the West by the next day, were that Blagg had been secretly using his lunch hours to leave work and get massages from topless women, and that just a few days before she'd disappeared, Jennifer had shown up with Abby at an agency that sheltered women from batterers, begging for help in order to get away from her abusive husband.

As with many high-profile murder cases, it would be nearly two more years before Mike's trial would actually get started in front of a jury of his peers, but, in the interim, the allegations that Mike had been secretly cavorting with loose women and beating his wife behind closed doors would be constantly woven into the news coverage. There was only one problem—extensive police investigations had already shown that neither allegation appeared to be true.

Right from the beginning, the sheriffs had been turning Grand Junction upside down looking for people both Mike and Jennifer might have known and places they might have gone. One of the things that had made the case so baffling was that neither of the Blaggs was particularly social, and they didn't frequent many places beyond work, school, church, and Jazzercise classes.

Yet, out of the blue one afternoon early on in the investigation, a woman had called the sheriff's tip line and left an anonymous message saying that Michael Blagg had actually been a big fan of the masseuses at an escort service that went by the name of Baby Dolls Adult Entertainment.

The sheriffs knew right away what the woman was talking about and, as a bonus, Grand Junction Police Detective Kevin Imbriaco had previously investigated the service in question, so he recognized the voice of the anonymous caller as none other than Baby Dolls' proprietress Julie House.

Detective Imbriaco paid House a house call. She told him that someone using the name "Steve" who looked like Mike had been visiting Baby Dolls two or three times a month, mostly over the lunch hour, during an interval from December 2000 to April 2001.

When Imbriaco showed her a photo lineup on December 7, 2001, House picked out Michael Blagg as being "Steve," and said he'd gotten back to her escort service within a week after Jennifer and Abby disappeared, demanding sexual services.

House painted a vivid picture of Michael Blagg, describing him as someone who was "shopping around" among the service's available women looking for more than just a topless massage during his $60 sessions. House said that Blagg was antsy about her policy of always having a member of the escort service's security staff present and that he was clearly trying to find women willing to masturbate him or even have sex with him during the forty-five-minute sessions, which took place at their homes and in hotel rooms around Grand Junction.

"He begged for sex," House was quoted as saying in the *Rocky Mountain News,* adding that she'd called and reported him after the disappearances because "I wanted to get the truth out about who he was."

House remembered some tantalizing details, like

"Steve" having spoken about a daughter, "with an old fashioned name that ended in a 'y' or 'ie,'" and she recalled that during one of his last visits he was upset because in her closet, he'd found a shoebox belonging to his wife that contained either letters or receipts and had disturbed him for some reason.

Initially House had said that Mike had requested a massage two or three times a month, always showing up in business attire sometime between 11 A.M. and 2 P.M., but in subsequent interviews her estimate rose to two and three visits per week. As sheriffs tried to narrow down specific dates and places, her story kept changing.

Detectives had repeatedly pressed Mike about House's allegations, but every single time, he'd denied them vehemently. None of Mike's credit card receipts showed any strange billing, and there was no indication he'd been seen at any of the locations House described. There hadn't been any trips for trysts afterward when, unbeknownst to him, he was being shadowed everywhere he went by a police surveillance team that would have certainly noticed if something that interesting were taking place.

Throughout history there have been plenty of supposedly upstanding people who've taken some pretty wild risks in the name of sexual adventurism, but there wasn't any evidence that Michael Blagg was one of them.

Grand Junction isn't that large, and it was hard to believe that Mike, who didn't even leave AMETEK Dixson for lunch most days, had been able to thread his way past everyone at work, and three to nine phone calls a day to and from Jennifer, whilst zipping in and out of hotels undetected during the downtown's busiest hours.

Once House began to waffle about the details, the Mesa County sheriffs effectively dropped that line of inquiry. In the end, the only people who really believed that Mike had been cruising the fringes of town looking for sex were members of the public at large who had seen it reported for two years running as though it were established fact.

Much the same thing happened with the report that Jennifer had shown up with Abby at the office of Colorado Legal Services on or about November 2, 2001, with "a hurt look in her eyes," seeking help filing for a divorce.

Luella Cross, a secretary who had worked at CLS for more than six years, told police in an interview on November 16, 2001, that a woman she later thought had been Jennifer Blagg had come in to her office just two or three weeks beforehand saying she was "scared to death," and determined to leave her husband, adding, "I can't take any more of this abuse."

Colorado Legal Services only handles divorce cases where there are allegations of domestic violence or sexual abuse, and Cross said she had explained this to the woman, who stayed in the office with her young daughter for over an hour.

Cross remembered a number of details about the session, including teasing Abby about her cute overalls.

She said it had ended with Jennifer becoming upset after being told she couldn't immediately see an attorney and would have to return the next day to get a restraining order from the court. Cross said that Jennifer took an application with her and left the office, and that was the last she saw of her until she noticed the pictures of Jennifer and Abby Blagg on a newsstand.

The thought of Cross' widely reported encounter with a distraught Jennifer Blagg trying to escape a dangerous relationship apparently just days before it finally killed both her and her child was certainly enough to make the public's hair stand on end when they read about it, but, like the equally sensational reports of Mike out trolling for hookers, the public wasn't immediately told that the details of the report weren't holding up under scrutiny.

For starters, Cross was not at all convincing when she said she recognized Jennifer Blagg as being the woman she'd just spoken with only fourteen to twenty-one days beforehand.

Cross had begun her interview with Sheriff's Investigator Jim Hebenstreit by saying, "I'm pretty sure it was her, because she said she was from South Carolina . . . I don't want to say for sure it was absolutely her." A little later, when Hebenstreit asked her how certain she really was that it was Jennifer and Abby, Cross replied, "I'm not positive at all that this is the person . . . I don't want to get somebody in trouble . . . I want to make sure you guys know that I kind of feel that that's the girl." Cross concluded the interview by adding, "If that was her. I'm not saying for sure it was her."

Cross seemed more confident of her identification of Abby than of her mother, but the Colorado Legal Services offices were only open on weekdays, and Cross distinctly remembered the woman leaving in disappointment because Cross had told her she'd have to come back the next day to get a court order.

Since the courts aren't open on the weekends, that meant such an encounter could only have occurred Monday through Thursday. Cross remembered the visit as taking place "late one morning," but Abby Blagg had a perfect attendance record for the year in her first-grade class at the Bookcliff school.

The woman Cross remembered said she hadn't been in Grand Junction that long, about six months, and although she said she was originally from South Carolina, Cross recalled her saying she had just moved to Colorado from California. It was possible, if it had been Jennifer, that maybe Cross had mixed up the information, but the facts as she remembered them didn't match Jennifer Blagg's history.

Whether Cross could recollect the woman's biography properly was far less important than three other facts she was convinced she remembered correctly: that the woman said she'd been abused to the point she "couldn't handle it anymore," that she was sick of all of her husband's "lady friends" and especially his "girlfriend," and that she was standing with her daughter in a state agency designed to help indigents looking to get help in order to leave him.

None of those three points really made any sense when compared with everything else the investigators knew about Jennifer Blagg. Even those friends who had thought they had detected a controlling streak in Mike said that when he wasn't around, Jennifer was outgoing and even gregarious. She wasn't cut off from her family, and she had friends both in Colorado and back in South Carolina, none of whom had ever reported anything like signs of abuse. Nor had Jennifer's doctors, who'd seen her frequently for a whole range of maladies, ever reported seeing any injuries or hearing any statements from her that would have led them to think Mike might be hurting her.

The sheriffs had literally been looking under rocks for months on end trying to find Jennifer and Abby, and they had appealed to the public to call in anything, no matter how insignificant. Aside from the over-the-top allegations of the Baby Dolls escort service, there hadn't been any indication that Mike was having an affair with any woman, let alone a posse of female friends that he was flaunting in front of Jennifer. Of all the tortured worries and doubts that threaded their way through Jennifer's diary entries to God, none of them had even hinted at a concern about Mike being unfaithful to her.

Finally, Jennifer Blagg, certainly by the standards of Grand Junction's legal system, was rich.

Mike was one of the highest-paid people in town. Jennifer had plenty of spending cash. She had credit cards, access to a joint savings account, a brand new mini-van, and even some blank checks her mother had given her over the years in case she ever needed emergency money. If Jennifer Blagg had truly reached a point in her life where she couldn't take it anymore, all she would have had to do was strap Abby into her car seat at 6 A.M. on any weekday and start driving to Texas before Mike's first phone call of the day landed on the answering machine. She could have been at her mother's house in Houston by the next evening and, if driving was too much trouble, they could have hopped a plane at Walker Field and been there by 2 P.M.

Jennifer Blagg—by all accounts, a competent modern woman living in an upper-middle-class neighborhood— would not have needed to stop and get the state's help in order to come up with enough money to get out of an abusive relationship. That fact alone should have been enough to raise red flags about Cross' identification. Instead, the story that Jennifer had tried to flee Mike in the days before she was killed would circulate in the press right up until the opening of the trial, when Judge Bottger finally ruled it too tenuous to even be considered as evidence.

# 31

WHILE the media spotlight had already shifted to the courtroom, the sheriffs were still out every weekday at the landfill standing in other people's trash trying to bring closure to those still grieving the loss of a little girl.

On July 24, 2002, the investigators tore apart the final bucket of trash that had been in the target cell. There was no sign of Abby.

One by one the investigators dropped their tools and silently went to collect their thoughts.

There was nothing left to do. The Soggy Bottom Gang had spent fifty-three days over the course of eleven weeks picking its way bag-by-bag through the county's trash. They had excavated an area that would cover half a city block, and they had done it clear down to a depth greater than most swimming pools.

If Abby was somewhere in the landfill other than the area that had been searched, it meant the compactor must have thrown her tiny body over into another cell—but in which direction? How far? How deep? During the weeks that they'd been searching, the sheriffs had all had a chance to see the compactor working off in the distance, and they knew the heavy machine was capable of throwing a seventy-pound object across the top of the open lifts like a puck on an air hockey table.

As they stared at the packed walls of trash facing into the empty cell, the sheriffs knew that at that moment Abby might be just inches away, but they'd reached a point where, if they carved back even one more foot into any of the exposed sides, they would end up having to pull over 11,000 square feet of additional material that would have to be hand-searched. And that number would just keep expanding exponentially if they continued to work outward into the adjoining cells.

Lieutenant Dillon, along with Sergeant Callow, had been there every single day, and he recalled the shared anguish of having to stop without an answer. "These walls are sixteen feet down. That's just a solid wall of trash, and it's two hundred and fifty feet long—I mean, is she here? Another foot? Another three feet? Over here? It was a monumental task," Dillon said. "We were just being stubborn wanting to be the voice for somebody that met a violent death because, if we don't do our job, they're silent. So there was a hell of a drive to find Jennifer and Abby, and hold somebody accountable for it. We came up with fifty percent. We were elated that we came up with Jennifer

Blagg, but really sorry that we couldn't find Abby. On the last day, when we didn't find her, people just kind of walked off and handled it in their own way, but they are able to live with it today. We are only human and we did the best that we could.

"What we physically raked through there was four thousand, six hundred and twenty-four tons. I'll never forget that figure as long as I live," Dillon said, shaking his head in amazement, "We physically raked through all of it."

After Frank Kochevar had a chance to input all the GPS data into his computer from the survey measurements he'd taken during the dig, the sheriffs got a final ironic surprise.

The very first test pothole had come within three feet of Jennifer.

If they had started by going left instead of right, they would have found her on Day One. "You wouldn't have known it at the time, but once these maps were put together, we said, 'Holy Cripes! That's right where she was!'" Dillon recalled.

When the sheriffs had finally left the landfill, and the trash trucks began lining up to rapidly close up the hole that they had so painstakingly created, there was one clever little twist that Frank Kochevar left behind in order to prevent their ever having to come back and go through something so arduous again. A GPS transmitter was bolted right on to the compactor that now pings its location into a computer in the landfill office every fifteen seconds as it moves around the landfill. As Lieutenant Dillon explained with great satisfaction, "If we ever have a missing person again with overtones that they may have gone to the landfill, we will have a damn close idea of where that compactor was and which direction it was moving as that truck was dumping."

# 32

**WITH** Mike in custody, the momentum of the case switched from the sheriffs to District Attorney Frank Daniels' office. Daniels had grown up on Long Island, but had come to love Colorado, staying on after graduating from colleges in Denver and Boulder. In addition to his career as an attorney, he was an accomplished nature photographer and geologist, setting up his own publishing company in Grand Junction, which produced his amazingly detailed photo books of the region's sweeping landscapes, as well as the tiniest pieces of the geology that made up the whole. Daniels had been the president of the Grand Junction Gem and Mineral Club and inducted into the National Rockhound & Lapidary Hall of Fame in recognition for his work on fossilized wood, cones, and ferns.

In September of 2002, Daniels finalized the specific charges that Michael Blagg would eventually be facing at his trial. To the charge of first-degree murder, he added the special circumstance of committing a crime of violence. The distinction, although somewhat redundant, took into account the use of a gun and, if a jury found it was true, then the state would be provided an opportunity to argue for a longer sentence.

The next charge was abuse of a corpse, which is defined by Colorado law as treating a dead person "in a way that would outrage normal family sensibilities."

When asked by a reporter to elaborate on the reasoning behind that particular charge, Daniels replied, "Just think about where they found the body."

The final charge was felony theft, and it involved two separate allegations against Mike—that he'd filed a false homeowner's insurance claim for $29,000 worth of jewelry items that weren't actually missing, and that he'd stolen furniture and office equipment from AMETEK Dixson.

All of the new charges were relatively minor when stacked against the bigger question that was still on everyone's mind: whether or not the state was eventually going to seek the death penalty against Mike.

Colorado had the death penalty on its books, but it had only carried out a single execution, by lethal injection, in the years since the 1976 U.S. Supreme Court decision that reinstated capital punishment—and that case had featured a serial rapist who'd made a swift confession to a rape and subsequent murder.

In order to be sentenced to death in Colorado, the same jury that found a defendant guilty would then have to find that at least one of seventeen additional aggravating factors had also taken place. They would then have to weigh whether or not those aggravating factors were offset by mitigating factors, such as the fact that Mike had been an exemplary citizen without any prior criminal history, and, in the event the jury still voted for death, the whole question would have to go on up to a special three-judge panel that would make the final decision.

As upset as the community undoubtedly was that Mike could have put a bullet in Jennifer's head as she slept, the truth was that the most outrage and revulsion around Grand Junction had to do with the fact that Mike appeared to have then gone upstairs and murdered his 6-year-old daughter, just because she'd suddenly become a technical inconvenience to his alibi.

One of the aggravating factors in Colorado's death penalty statute is the killing of two or more people at one time. Another is the murder of someone under the age of 12.

On their face, the circumstances under which everyone assumed that Abby had died appeared to meet those two aggravating criteria and, if provable beyond a reasonable doubt, they could have turned the Blagg homicides into a capital case; however, Daniels knew that without a confession and without Abby's body, it would be next to impossible to surmount the legal hurdles that would be necessary to make such a dread sentence stick.

Having seen the state's hand when it came to the charges, Mike's new defense team, Mesa County Public Defender David Eisner and his Deputy Public Defender Ken Singer, moved to get Mike's bail reduced so he could get out of jail for what they knew was going to be a lengthy run of months before the trial actually began.

In a motion filed with the court, the defense protested the "oppressive" million-dollar sum, arguing,

> *The case against Mr. Blagg is circumstantial. There are portions of the arrest warrant affidavit which contain incomplete, misleading or false information and were, in all probability, included in an effort by law enforcement to attack Mr. Blagg's character. The bulk of that information should, in all likelihood, be inadmissible against him at trial.*

Noting Mike's history of steady employment, his service in the Navy during Desert Storm, his status as a model inmate in the months he'd been imprisoned following his arrest, and the fact that he'd never been convicted of anything more serious than a traffic violation in 1996 and one in 2000, the defense argued that Mike was not a flight risk.

Hours before Christmas, on December 24, 2002, Mike appeared back in Mesa County District Judge Bottger's courtroom for a preliminary hearing in which both sides agreed, Eisner reluctantly, that there was enough circumstantial evidence to at least bring the case before a jury; however, moments after being formally bound over for trial, Mike broke in a broad smile as Bottger announced he was reducing the bail amount to $500,000 and, if it were posted, he would allow Mike to live in Georgia with his mother while the trial was pending.

It would take family members several days to arrange to put up the titles to several pieces of property in Georgia in order to meet the bond, and Mike's passport, which the court wanted surrendered as part of the bail reduction agreement, was still in Georgia, so it had to be collected and brought to the court. So it was not until a couple of weeks later, just before 10 P.M. on the night of January 7, 2003, that Mike was actually released.

Early the next morning, Mike was right back in the courtroom in Grand Junction for his formal arraignment—but this time, instead of being hustled through a back door in prison attire, he walked right through the front door in one of his own suits, smiling and talking with his attorneys.

The sheriffs were kind of amazed that Mike was being let out at all, but they were determined to let him know he wasn't out of their thoughts. Steve King sat in the back corner of the courtroom throughout the brief procedure, never once taking his gaze off of Blagg.

January 8 was an interesting day to choose for the arraignment. It would have been Jennifer's 36 birthday, but instead it was notable for Mike's entry of an innocent plea to her murder some fourteen months before. Mike had spent half of that intervening time in the Mesa County lockup, but he appeared relaxed throughout the brief proceeding, telling reporters as he left, "It feels good to be out."

Once again Mike's family and his friends from church had turned out in force to support him. His sister Clare Rochester held hands with him as they walked out of the Mesa County Justice Center. "We are very happy to have him out, and we are looking forward to the opportunity to show he is innocent in court," Rochester said to reporters as she and the others prepared to head to the airport for the flight back to Warner Robins, Georgia.

# 33

ONE of the main themes that kept cropping up throughout the Blagg investigation from its first moments was the basic question "If Mike didn't do it, then who did?"

The complete and utter lack of a sensible answer to that question inevitably caused the pendulum of suspicion to swing right back over to Mike.

The detectives, the press, and the public had all struggled with that conundrum, and it was clear that any jury would be put right back in the middle of the same question whenever it came to a trial.

In the spring of 2003 Eisner and the defense team finally hit on an answer that was truly worthy of being the shocking plot twist in a made-for-TV movie.

What if, they wondered, someone had set out that morning to harm the Blaggs' next-door neighbor, Deputy District Attorney Tammy Eret, but had gotten the wrong house?

Then, taking the alternate suspect theory one better, the defense put a face on their mystery killer in the form of one of Daniels' own male deputy district attorneys, whom the defense claimed had been investigated for allegedly stalking Eret "after his romantic overtures were rebuffed."

"This isn't something we made up out of thin air," Eisner told reporters. "It was based on their own investigation. There was evidence that the female deputy district attorney had come to work in the courthouse with a gun because she was afraid of this guy."

The colorful theory that it was really a crazed prosecutor who'd shown up on Pine Terrace Court just after Mike went to work and killed Jennifer, then Abby—and then, realizing his mistake, removed their bodies to the dump—effectively took what was already shaping up to be a contentious season of pre-trial wrangling and threw a grenade right into the henhouse.

When Eisner filed a motion requesting that he be allowed to present the male deputy DA as an alternate suspect during the trial, Judge Bottger shot it down, calling the defense theory "irrelevant, scandalous and impertinent." For good measure, he ordered that a 16-page investigative report, which the DA's office had prepared on the personnel issues that had arisen from the strained relations and complaints between the two deputy DAs involved, be sealed.

Frank Daniels was incensed, not only that the personal lives of members of his office had been dragged into the public spotlight, but that it had been done in the context of whether or not one of them might be a homicidal maniac.

Daniels said little about the substance of the stalking and threatening allegations, but he pointed out that the male deputy DA in question had witnesses who could place him in a courtroom in the Mesa County Courthouse at 8 A.M. on the morning of November 13. Daniels immediately filed a counter-motion asking that Bottger remove Eisner and Blagg's other public defenders, because he thought they had crossed the line into unethical conduct.

Eisner didn't flinch. He fired back a motion requesting that Bottger be removed as the judge for what he called excessively harsh comments during the rejection of his request, which he said amounted to a show of favoritism toward the prosecution's view of the case. To top it off, Eisner filed a request with the Colorado Supreme Court, asking the justices to reverse Bottger's order sealing the internal affairs investigation report.

In mid-April Bottger sent out another of what was becoming a rapidly growing stack of orders saying that he had taken care to be unbiased and would therefore be staying put on the case, and so would Daniels. At the end of May, the Colorado Supreme Court denied Eisner's request to unseal the filing Bottger had pulled from the public record, and the case essentially returned to the point where it had been in March before the controversy had erupted.

The next significant controversy Bottger had to sort out was a request to pick up the trial itself and move it entirely out of Mesa County to some other corner of Colorado that hadn't been saturated in the press coverage with its unsubstantiated theories about Mike's abuse of his family, obsession with porn, and visits to hookers.

"A fair trial cannot take place in Mesa County," Eisner began his motion.

> Not only has the media coverage of this case been massive and pervasive leading to a large percentage of prospective jurors having formed opinions of the guilt of Mr. Blagg; but the community has assumed an ownership role into the investigation and prosecution of this case that exceeds any similar case within the last 20 years.

Edward Nugent, a former public defender, added his support for the venue change in a letter to the court which read in part.

> The comments that I continually hear from people who are not associated with the legal system are . . . virtually 100 percent to the effect that Mr. Blagg is guilty of the crimes for which he is charged and that he deserves to die for committing these crimes.

Saying that news coverage had been even-handed, Judge Bottger denied the request to move the trial, and the battleground between the attorneys shifted to questions about which of the notes and diary entries written by Jennifer would be admissible in court.

Daniels knew that even now, with absolute proof that somebody had murdered Jennifer, he still had a strategic hurdle to clear when it came to the motive. All it would take was one juror out of twelve who couldn't envision the squeaky clean church-goer before them as a multiple killer, and Michael Blagg could walk free.

Daniels wanted to show the jury that behind the façade of the typical American family, something had been rotten on Pine Terrace Court. To that end, he fought vigorously to put every piece of evidence of an escalating conflict between Jennifer and Mike before the jury.

The key piece to Daniels' theory of the motive was the notation Jennifer had written—and dated—in the margin of the book she had been reading. In his motion, Daniels wrote:

*This is the crime victim's very own statement made on the day of her death. It was in her own handwriting, written in a religious book. Jennifer Blagg was an extremely religious woman. She would no sooner put a false statement into a religious book than she would burn a copy of the Bible. This evidence has extraordinary inherent trustworthiness. What Jennifer Blagg wrote is her statement, just as if she had spoken it to a friend. It is her statement of concern about a fight with Mike Blagg. She was murdered that very night."*

Bottger agreed to let it in, writing in his order:

*The statement "Fought w/ Mike on Fri." is relevant to the existence of marital discord immediately before the homicide and is therefore evidence of a*

*material fact. As the last written words of the victim
on the topic, it is more probative than any other evidence the People can procure.*

It was a significant win for Daniels, but at the same
time, Bottger excluded several other statements as being
too far into the realm of hearsay, including Abby's comment to her Sunday school teacher that her parents had
been bickering over who got the last of the orange juice
on Sunday morning before church.

Daniels also wanted Jennifer's note that was taped to the
bathroom mirror entered, saying it was evidence of a fight
between the couple over the course of the weekend that was
"long-lasting and continuous, until the day of her murder."

Arguing that Mike had used the Bible to control his
wife up until the point that she discovered he was downloading porn, Daniels wrote:

*Every couple has arguments but this was big. It seems
Michael Blagg was having an affair. Not with a co-
worker, not with a neighbor, but with his computer.*

Daniels felt the "Keys to Peace" note on the mirror was
a signal from Jennifer that she was preparing to leave Mike.
He felt Mike was so inherently narcissistic that he chose to
kill her and Abby rather than have to suffer the humiliation
of being publicly dumped for his character failings.

That the note was written on an "Urgent Prayer Request Form" led Daniels to argue that Jennifer must have
felt it was connected with "a severe family crisis," since
none of the other PrayerGram categories fit.

The text of the note was definitely connected to the
sermon on the videotape by Dr. Charles Stanley that Jennifer had watched, but beyond that, it was difficult to in-
terpret what it meant to her. Aside from the single word
"marriage" in the middle and the fact that it was taped to

the mirror in the bathroom, there was nothing that even indicated it was meant for Mike's edification.

In its entirety, the note read:

*Jesus has the keys to life and death. But, He's left me some keys also, health, marriage, material; and my will as to what I do with these keys. The Key to Jesus' peace is to give Him the key to my will. Trust Him with the keys He's left me. Give them back and trust Him w/ them. I'll have peace, because he says I will.*

Eisner and the defense team watched the videotape of Dr. Stanley's sermon and then responded with a motion that argued against admitting the note, saying:

*Dr. Stanley discusses seven categories of thinking that cause a person to lose peace. In addition to enslaved thinking, there are sinful, negative, erroneous, unrealistic, rebellious, and obsessive thoughts. The discussion of enslaved thinking included a brief reference to addictions whether they be alcohol, drugs, sexual, or work related. The note is not directed to Michael Blagg and mentions nothing about problems in their relationship. It mentions nothing about enslaved thinking. It was not posted in a conspicuous place; rather it was on the side of the bathroom mirror away from the sink. It does not even appear in videotapes or photographs taken of the bathroom; the only photograph of it is a close-up. To suggest that Jennifer was telling Michael Blagg she was leaving him due to his "perverse interests" borders on the absurd.*

*If Jennifer Blagg would have intended this to be an urgent request she would have followed the necessary procedures as outlined in the [Intercessional Prayer Ministry instruction] booklet. It was not written in the usual format that a prayer request would have been written and it was not taken to the prayer room at the church. The Blaggs kept a pile of blank request forms next to the phone, something that Jennifer Blagg most likely used to take notes while watching the sermon on television.*

To show that the Blaggs were capable of writing PrayerGrams that were clearly meant for each other, and as an example of PrayerGrams that were properly formatted, the defense included an undated one that Jennifer had apparently filled out during her time in the church's intercessionary prayer room and mailed to Mike back at the house. It read:

*My Dear Husband, the love of my life, there's no words to tell you how I feel about you! I adore you. God has grown you darlin'. And He's continuing to do so. Thru every trial & every mountain top. How He loves you. Psm. 15:13 May the God of Hope fill you w/ all joy and peace as you trust in him. So that you may overflow w/hope by the power of the Holy Spirit. Psm. 5:12 for surely, O Lord, you bless the righteous.*

On the back of the note Jennifer added:

*I'll continue to pray for you sweetheart! I'm enjoying your love for me and the Lord. I enjoy our time together. Not wasting it w/fights!*
*I pray God continues to answer us & bless our marriage as we <u>obey</u> Him who is faithful to us. I love you . . .*
    *Jennifer*

Jennifer then added a postscript that appeared to be related to Mike's week at work:

*I'll pray for the continued success of the inventory process.*

In a PrayerGram sent back to Jennifer, Mike wrote:

*I love you Jennifer! I have been praying for your healing. I will continue to do so. I know you have called out, "Heal me, O Lord, and I shall be healed." Jer 17:14 just as Jeremiah did. Jesus is the Great Physician, in Matt 4:24 He healed the great multitude who were afflicted with various torments and diseases. He will heal you too, in His time. Until that time, know that I love and support you. I pray that this new medication will work. I love you! Stay strong and trust in Christ.*
   *Love always,*
   *Michael.*

In May 2003, Judge Bottger ruled that both the "Key to Peace" note and the videotape that had inspired it were irrelevant and therefore inadmissible; however, after another protracted round of motions, Daniels won the day in October when Bottger reconsidered and reversed his earlier decision on just the note, saying that a jury could decide for itself whether Jennifer's use of the prayer form "on this occasion is evidence that she and the defendant were undergoing a severe family crisis. The relevance of this inference is obvious."

# 34

**DURING** the last week of February 2004, the process of pulling together a jury got underway as notices went out to 500 residents of Mesa County ordering them to appear at the Justice Center to begin filling out questionnaires asking them what they'd already heard about the case and what opinions they'd already formed.

Judge Bottger himself removed almost seventy potential jurors right off the bat because their questionnaires indicated they were convinced of Michael's guilt. Further removals by the attorneys looking over the answers whittled the numbers down sharply, so that when jury selection formally began on Monday, March 1, 2004, both sides knew it was going to be an uphill battle to find enough competent people who hadn't already been saturated in the lurid speculation surrounding the case.

With a remaining pool of 133 potential jurors, the results at the end of the first day were not encouraging. Of the twenty-four prospective jurors interviewed, twenty-one were let go by Judge Bottger after they listed their opinion of Michael's guilt as either "strong" or "fairly strong."

Michael watched silently from the defense table as a slow parade of Mesa County's citizens explained that either the news that Michael had been caught stealing furniture from AMETEK or the discovery of Jennifer's body in the landfill had led them to believe he was guilty. Several also said they had strong feelings about pornography being immoral, to the point that it could affect their ability to be impartial.

On Tuesday the batting average improved a bit when both sides were able to agree to keep six candidates and send another nineteen packing, including one man who went straight into the out box when it was discovered that, in response to whether he'd formed any sort of opinion about the case, he'd written on his questionnaire, "Guilty—hang 'em high."

The preliminary qualifications were still in their beginning phases when Eisner and Singer were startled by a transcript they found among the state's discovery materials that had been turned over to them. It detailed a couple of phone conversations in December 2002 that a sheriff's department investigator had placed to Mike's mother, Elizabeth Blagg, out in Warner Robins, Georgia. The attorneys quickly called Elizabeth to see what had happened, and she said she'd thought the caller had been a member of Mike's defense team looking for information that could help him.

Calling it "blatant misrepresentation," the defense attorneys filed a motion with the court asking that the prosecution be sanctioned, and accusing the investigation of going on a fishing expedition. "The district attorney is desperately trying to find a 9mm handgun that he can link to Mr. Blagg in connection with the death of his wife," the motion read.

After six-and-a-half days of vetting what seemed like half the county, a panel of twelve jurors and four alternates was finally sworn in on Tuesday, March 9, 2004. The youngest member of the relatively young jury was just 19 years old, while the oldest was 81. The teenage member was one of ten women on the final panel, which included a rancher, a librarian, a rental car agency manager, and a retired school administrator.

Taking advantage of the couple of years that had passed while the case was working its way toward the courtroom, the jury included several people who had moved to Grand Junction after the disappearances, and who had missed being exposed to the initial waves of reporting.

"It's surprising how many didn't know anything about this case," Judge Bottger said from the bench. "It gives me great hope and confidence we do at last have a fair jury."

Eisner also dropped his immediate efforts to have the trial moved, responding when asked if he was satisfied with the jury during an interview with Denver's KCNC television news station, "I'm not sure if *satisfied* is the right word. I mean, I'm still concerned, just given the nature of the publicity that we've had, and we'll just have to see how it works out."

# 35

IT had been nearly two and a half years since that fateful day when Michael Blagg had walked in on the remains of a tragedy in his own home and rushed to dial 911. Now, on Wednesday, March 10, 2004, he strode into Courtroom 9 of the Mesa County Justice Center confidently holding his mother's hand as his trial finally got underway with both sides' vastly different opening statements.

Blagg's hair was now graying, but at 41, he still had the self-assured bearing of a naval officer. His mother, siblings, and friends from church seated in the rows behind his defense table helped make him look every bit like a responsible member of the community, and the gold wedding ring still on his hand reminded everyone that Mike had always maintained that he too was a victim in this case.

As Mesa County's district attorney, Frank Daniels had spent a solid year preparing to bring Michael to justice on behalf of the thousands of residents who had been worried sick for months about a mother and her young child. He knew Michael was clever, that Eisner was smart, and that his case was entirely circumstantial, but he was also rock-solid certain that Mike had killed Jennifer and Abby, and was prepared to hit Mike hard with each and every piece of evidence the investigators had come across during their long slog to this day in court.

Daniels began by playing the tape of Blagg's 911 call, and took care to point out the moments when Mike had inquired about the dispatcher's name and thanked her for her help even before the first deputies had arrived on the scene. It was that ability of Mike's to keep track of all the little moving pieces, to feign concern on cue, to tug at the heartstrings of his friends and even investigators that Daniels said Blagg planned to use to deflect suspicion away from himself.

Daniels explained that Mike was a smart guy, nuclear-engineering-degree smart, but he said Mike's innate intelligence couldn't change the fact that he was mired in a rapidly crumbling marriage.

In 2001, Grand Junction's long dry summer had been, according to Daniels, "the summer of discontent for Michael Blagg," who was fighting more and more often with a deeply religious and proper wife who was tired of his controlling nature and who'd had enough of his addictions to pornography. Blagg had been whipsawed by his wife's health problems and by his own struggles with insomnia, depression, and anxiety—all of it taking place in the midst of a personal life that revolved almost entirely around a tight circle of friends from his churches and his extended family members, people whom he was going to be abjectly humiliated in front of when his wife walked out on him, taking his only child with her.

Daniels described Jennifer as "lovely" and Abby as "perky," but he pointed out that they lived in a home that Mike kept shuttered, and which few people seemed to visit.

Daniels projected slides up on a screen in front of the jurors showing them some of the particular horrors associated with that November night—Jennifer's grotesquely flattened corpse, the bullet retrieved from her skull, the bloodstained bed, and the overturned jewelry box—as he explained how Michael Blagg had chosen to solve all of his impending dilemmas, saying, "Michael got his gun. He loaded a round into the chamber and he shot Jennifer in the face."

As the members of Jennifer's family scattered around the packed courtroom averted their eyes from the slide show, Daniels described Mike walking upstairs and killing Abby and driving the bodies to AMETEK Dixson. "When the job was done, he went home. He parked the van back in the garage and attempted to stage the bedroom to make it look like there had been a burglary. But nuclear engineers don't know how to think like burglars. He did a poor job of staging the scene," Daniels said, adding that after sheriffs were able to collect and analyze all of the forensic and other evidence, "too much about his story did not fit."

When it was the defense's turn, Mesa County Assistant Public Defender Ken Singer took the opposite tack. He described the Blaggs as a happy couple in the midst of a decade-long marriage characterized by "love, affection, and devotion." He projected pictures of the Blaggs smiling together during an outing a month before the murder, and for additional emphasis he put up enlargements of several love letters Mike and Jennifer had sent each other.

Then Singer brought up the wide-open back door with the dead alarm batteries, saying the door was sufficiently flimsy that it could have been jimmied open with something as simple as a piece of cardboard. He noted that a neighbor had heard unknown male voices outside at 6 A.M. on the morning of the disappearance, that scuff marks had been found on the back yard fence, and a patch of grass on the Greenbelt Drive side of the fence had been flattened.

There was also an unknown fingerprint found on the lid of the jewelry box, another in the van, and, Singer revealed for the first time publicly, there were several hairs found on the bloody master bed that did not match any family members either.

"Let's take a closer look at the bed," Singer urged. "That mixture of that DNA on that underside of the comforter is not Michael Blagg. It is not Jennifer or Abby Blagg. It is the mixture of a stranger. Someone else was there. Someone else was on that bed."

Singer argued that when police ran out of leads without finding any viable suspects, they'd simply come back and rearranged the puzzle pieces, talking themselves into believing that the one person they had to work with fit the crime. "The evidence will show the prosecution's case is based on inferences, assumptions, and speculation, and you will find that it is. Everywhere you go, it is based on suspicious vision," Singer told the jurors.

Taking pains to emphasize the lack of witnesses, or an admissible confession, Singer noted that even on the brink of death, after Mike had started his car in a closed garage, taken pills, *and* slit his wrists—and for emphasis, Singer projected a hair-raising police photo of Mike lying in the blood-red water of the townhouse bathtub with a Bible and a picture of his family clearly visible on the ceramic rim—even then, Mike had whispered to the deputy who was trying to elicit a deathbed confession, "I did not kill my family and I don't know where they are," Singer pointed out.

During the course of his lengthy opening, Singer rolled out the theme that would form the core of the defense's strategy during the entire trial, which was to relentlessly try to undermine any perceived certainty about individual pieces of evidence and to try to show breaks in the chain of events the prosecution was trying to string together into a coherent whole.

Some of the defense's quibbles about the evidence seemed a bit of a reach, like Singer's suggestion that Jennifer's blood could have gotten into the van because someone might have put Jennifer's body inside, but then changed their mind and pulled it back out right there in the garage. But there were other points—like the fact that none of the Blaggs' closest friends nor family members had any inkling that their marriage might be in trouble—that had a stronger ring to them.

Even though the judge had already ruled against admitting any testimony about Blagg allegedly getting topless massages on his lunch hours, the defense knew that allegation had received extensive media coverage, and there was a good chance the jurors had heard it somewhere along the way. Singer attacked the most damaging theories as to a possible motive head-on, telling the jury that the amount of time Mike spent accessing Internet pornography had declined in the months before Jennifer's murder.

"Michael Blagg did not commit this crime," Singer, gathering speed, insisted to the jury. "Michael Blagg did not have an affair with a neighbor. Michael Blagg did not have an affair with a co-worker. Michael Blagg did not have an affair with a computer. But he most assuredly had an affair. He had a love affair with Jennifer."

The opening statements left the room drained, and Jennifer's mother in tears, but the real work of the trial would be the hundreds of details large and small that had to be filled in during the coming weeks of testimony.

Afterward Jennifer's mother and other family members stopped to chat with reporters in front of the Mesa County Justice Center. Conway was relieved that the trial was finally underway and said she would accept whatever verdict the jury reached.

Noting that David Loman had still continued his lonely search of remote stretches of Mesa County looking for Abby even after the sheriffs abandoned the landfill search, reporters asked Conway where she thought Abby was.

"I think Abby is with her mother," Conway replied. "I think she sits with God same as Jennifer does."

# 36

THE prosecution called Colorado Bureau of Investigation crime-scene analyst Matthew Saluto, who described a series of scuff marks that were found on the weather-beaten wood fence along the back of the Blaggs' property. Over the fence, on the Greenbelt Drive side, Saluto said there was also evidence that the grass and other vegetation had been trampled down and, intriguingly, he said there were also some fresh tire marks on the ground.

Saluto spent most of his day in court going over 140 pictures of fingerprints and individual bloodstains found around the house and the van, many just pinprick-sized droplets belonging to Jennifer that had been exposed with the help of forensic chemicals.

On Friday, the third day of testimony, thirty-five students from nearby Fruita Monument High School dropped in for a field trip to the Justice Center and ended up sitting in the courtroom just as the topic of Internet porn finally came up in earnest. Judge Bottger warned the courtroom that what they were about to discuss would be offensive, but he also noted that there wouldn't actually be any pictures.

The students and their teachers remained and watched as Sheriff's Investigator Michael Piechota described his search of the files on the Blaggs' computer, which turned up visits to religious websites as well as those that dealt with real estate, travel, and health—and 668 pornographic images that had been saved. When Piechota began reciting some of the especially graphic names of the 1,863 X-rated websites the images had been selected from, Judge Bottger stopped him, noting from the bench, "There's no point in the officer describing what is obvious."

The jury was shown two page-sized collages that Blagg himself had put together from some of the saved images, using PowerPoint software, and then printed out and kept in his desk. The "redacted" versions presented in court just showed slivers of various women's faces as they knelt in front of men who had their genitals blacked out. It didn't take a whole lot of imagination to figure out what was happening in the photos, nor what was probably happening during the times when Blagg took them out of the drawer and viewed them.

Blagg hung his head and stared at the defense table as

Piechota explained that of all the images Blagg had looked at on the net, the ones he'd actually bothered to save involved men ejaculating on women's faces.

As Daniels began to try, ever so delicately, to have Piechota expand on that point, Judge Bottger cut him off.

"Excuse me," he interrupted. "I don't think this is necessary. The ladies and gentlemen of the jury have the idea what these exhibits show."

The whole issue of the pornography created tremendous headaches for the defense. On the one hand, they thought it was obvious that it wasn't relevant and didn't prove anything, and thus they wanted as little discussion of it as possible in front of the jury. But they had also seen from the pre-trial juror selection process that even its mere existence had the potential to irrevocably taint opinions about Mike, so they weren't sure they could safely ignore it.

In his very first interview, long before he'd gotten to know the investigators on a first-name basis, Mike had said that he and Jennifer had had to do "other things" sexually because of her hysterectomy. He also consistently said that the only times Jennifer was actually upset about the porn was when she thought he was off viewing it without her. As Mike reported it, her objection wasn't to the imagery or the sex acts it depicted, but rather to her sense that he could be using it to replace or exclude her from his sex life.

Mike's description of Jennifer as really being okay with his computer porn was the kind of conveniently self-serving explanation that would be easy to dismiss in the middle of a murder trial where it was impossible to cross-examine the other party as to the truth. However, most murder prosecutions didn't have the benefit of a victim who'd kept two years of running diary entries imploring God to help directly with just about every single source of anxiety in her life, from the most profound issues of health to the most trivial of household setbacks.

Given the range of what else was recorded in excruciating detail in her diaries, it was hard to imagine that if Jennifer had any serious objection to Mike looking at sexual images, let alone if she was thinking of taking Abby and walking out on him as a result of them, that she wouldn't have put at least one clear hint in her writings.

There were a few times in the diary when Jennifer mentioned her dissatisfaction with a "lack of communication" with Mike, and her desire to have a better marriage—but better than what? She never actually said the marriage she had was bad. In fact, the only times she directly criticized their relationship with any specificity was when she said she wished *she* had been nicer to Mike on certain occasions because she felt she'd snapped at him when he hadn't really done anything to deserve her anger.

During the two years she'd kept a journal, Jennifer never once mentioned a concern about Internet pornography. She didn't express a single worry about Mike straying, becoming interested in other women, or being in any way unfaithful to her.

One could speculate that Jennifer left certain things out of her diary because she didn't want other people to read them, or perhaps because she was so afraid of Mike that she didn't dare write anything negative about him. But if those were real concerns, then why even take the risk of keeping a diary at all?

The kind of men who abuse their wives physically or emotionally are notorious for their ability to seize upon even the smallest nuance of their spouses' personalities and thoughts in order to twist them into something hurtful. Jennifer's running account of her deepest feelings and fears doesn't read as though she was the least bit concerned that Mike might come across it. In fact, since she kept it in plain sight on the TV stand at the main focal point of the living room, there's no reason to assume that Mike couldn't have flipped through it at some point if he'd wanted.

If Mike had shot Jennifer in the head and smothered his daughter thinking that the issues in the journal and the note taped to the mirror had any real significance in precipitating those acts, then there would have been no reason he couldn't have grabbed those items and heaved them right into the same trash bag the gun, the jewelry, and the pillows went into that night on their way to the Dumpster.

Why leave that kind of glaring clue to a murder? Unless, of course, it was nothing of the sort. The police had always viewed the fact that Mike had left the note in place as an oversight. But it's possible that Mike left it because he didn't have any reason to feel it was connected to what had happened.

Jennifer was known to think that refrigerator magnets with inspirational sayings written on them that she noticed while shopping at Safeway were signs from God meant specifically for her. The fact that she had some snippet from her latest revelation from God taped to the mirror for a day or two might not have been the least bit unusual as far as Mike was concerned.

Overall, Jennifer's diary appears to have been exactly what she said it was going to be on the day in 1999 when she opened it to the first page and began writing: an intensely personal and private exchange between her and her God on issues relating to *their* relationship—i.e., God and Jennifer.

Although most of what she wrote about her circle of family and friends was glowing and effusive, Jennifer nonetheless had occasional criticisms and complaints that she passed on to God about almost everyone she knew. She repeatedly complained directly to God about aspects of Abby's behavior—and wanted Him to change it—but the person who seemed to raise her ire the least was Mike.

Despite the dozens and dozens of fears that Jennifer poured out of her very soul between the covers of the spiral-bound notebook—from her health, to her friends' health, to having grown up without a father, to not being godly enough, to appearing too godly, to dying, to raising her child the wrong way, to being an ungrateful wife, to career plans, housing trauma, plane crashes, school shootings, even the rain and the color of her hair—Jennifer never once expressed even the slightest concern that Mike would harm or abuse either her or Abby. Rather remarkably for a seemingly insecure woman in the 21st century, when half of all marriages, Christian or otherwise, dissolve, she never expressed any concern whatsoever that Mike would divorce her or that she would someday have to decide whether or not to leave Mike.

Far from backing up the prosecution, the theories about Jennifer's impending departure, or the prospect of Mike abusing either her or Abby, or of a running four-day battle over Internet porn, would have all made better sense if Jennifer's diaries *hadn't* existed.

Eisner had fought during pre-trial hearings and motions to keep as much of the porn imagery out of the trial as possible, arguing it was inflammatory and off-topic, but Daniels had strenuously insisted that it was critical to understanding the motive and Michael's state of mind on the night of November 12. Part of that rationale was that early on in the investigation, Piechota had reported that his research into Blagg's computer hard drive showed that Mike had visited a porn website at 8:50 P.M. that Monday evening, just a few hours before the giant bloodstain had appeared on Jennifer's side of the bed.

If that were true, it might well have been a serious clue

to events that evening, but during the trial, Eisner brought in forensic computer examiner Chris Buechner from the FBI's Denver office, who testified that Piechota and others were reading the timing data on the computer incorrectly, and that the last time anyone in the Blagg household had used the computer to visit a porn site was on October 4, more than a month before the shooting. Further, Buechner said that his analysis found that Blagg's accessing of porn websites had been steadily declining prior to that date.

Buechner also shot holes in the theory that Mike might have printed out the "don't let the sun go down on our anger . . . sorry if I gave the devil a foothold" note at work on November 13 and then stuffed it in the overturned purse before calling police. Buechner said the note was actually written on November 9, which was the previous Friday that Jennifer was writing about when she noted in her Bible study workbook that the pair of them had argued.

# 37

GIVEN the lack of any hard evidence that there had been ongoing marital discord between Mike and Jennifer, the theory that Mike might have lashed out after Jennifer became angry at him looking at pornographic pictures was the best potential motive that the sheriffs and Daniels had.

Judge Bottger had already excluded most of the porn itself by limiting the prosecution to showing only a handful of redacted images. But, even though that seemed like a victory for their side, the defense knew that holding up a picture that had 90 percent of the image blacked out in the very same courtroom where unedited close-ups of Jennifer's mangled dead body and the surgical autopsy of her head were being shown sent a not-so-subtle message:

Even against such a backdrop, what Mike had collected on his computer was just too terrible to behold.

Put in perspective, the 668 photos that he had saved amounted to about the same number of sexually explicit images that could be found in a single copy of any of the dozens of shrink-wrapped adult magazine titles that are for sale behind the counters of gas stations across the continent, millions of which are sold every month to men who don't go home and murder their wives and daughters as a result.

The images Mike saved depicted a sex act that reputable surveys like those conducted by the National Opinion Research Center suggest is routinely engaged in by something close to 90 percent of all married couples in North America.

Set against that reality, the notion that a 41-year-old man was having to sit in court in 2004 and have redacted pictures of couples engaging in oral sex shown to a jury in order to assault his credentials as a Christian had a bit of an echo of the Spanish Inquistion to it.

The defense's problem wasn't what the pornography proved, but rather that it existed at all. Courtrooms are by their nature imposing, solemn, and dignified places. There was just no way that sexual images were going to look *anything* but bad in a court of law when the question of why a mother and a child had been killed was under consideration. Mike had trademarked himself from the first day of the disappearances as "a good Christian" and thus above suspicion—which meant that if he deviated in any way from anyone's personal opinion of what it meant to be the purest of Christians, he left himself wide open to the conclusion that he really wasn't one to begin with. And if he was merely posing as a Christian, then he was that much more likely to be a closet homicidal maniac. In for a penny, in for a pound.

Just looking at the relative amounts of the literature involved—two printed eight-and-a-half-by-eleven sheets of pornographic photos hidden in a desk drawer versus an entire house filled with Christian books, videos, Prayer-Grams, inspirational writings, religious magazines, manuals, journals, and Bible study workbooks—it's easy to see what was the bigger factor in the Blaggs' lives.

Rather than abuse of pornography causing marital problems, it appears from Jennifer's journals that the actual root cause of the simmering anxiety within the Blagg household was a kind of abuse of religion.

Christianity, an ancient faith stressing forgiveness and love for strangers, the humble, and the poor with a promise of posthumous rewards for righteousness, was being used like a Ouija board to try to determine things like the very best option among middle management staffing opportunities at truck dashboard sub-assembly manufacturing plants across the country.

For whatever deeply personal reasons, Jennifer Blagg was constantly beseeching God—or "Dad" as she called Him on occasion—to step in and help her. Friends recalled Jennifer and Mike as being some of the "holiest" people they'd met, largely because they were willing to stop and pray for guidance over every matter, large and small, in their lives.

Mike and Jennifer were performing for the Lord according to what they thought His instruction book was asking of them, but they were ending up with a marriage that consisted of three people rather than two. Jennifer was writing daily notes to God saying that she was willing to turn every single aspect of her adult life—large, small, important, trivial—over to "Him" and even hand off "the keys" to her ability to make independent judgments. And yet, for all their prayers and devotion to the cause, it seemed that it was ultimately every bit as difficult for the Blaggs to tell what to do about important and difficult decisions—Should they send their daughter to private or public school? Should they buy a larger house now or wait until later in life? Should they take the job with the company they knew in Indiana or strike out clear for Colorado? Stay in Grand Junction or uproot so soon and hop to another position north of Denver?—as it would be for any other middle-class couple in America.

Add to that the burden of trying to manipulate religion into a reward/punishment system capable of predicting God's intent—and therefore the "correct answer" to any situation that would be worrisome, confusing, or confounding in any other normal marriage—and suddenly "the perfect couple" was having a host of psychosomatic health problems and taking handfuls of mood-altering psychiatric drugs just to be able to go to sleep at night.

Mike was taking a half-dozen anti-depression, insomnia, and anxiety medications, and a powerful new one had just been added to the cocktail six days before the murders.

Three days into his new mix of prescriptions he'd had "a fight" with Jennifer that was over something so trivial he initially said he couldn't even remember what it was about, but for which he felt compelled to make an elaborate written apology hours later when he came around, because he felt it was so out of character. Five days into the new mix of drugs and Abby said she'd watched her parents argue over the last glass of orange juice, which was something so strange to her, she thought it worth mentioning to her Sunday school teacher. The first employee to encounter him at AMETEK Dixson the morning after Jennifer's death described Mike as "dazed and surprised."

If there was any smoking gun in the Blagg residence, it was in the medicine cabinet, full of his-and-hers psychopharmacologicals, and in the written notes taped to the mirrors, refrigerators, and cabinets, folded in the purse, and stacked on the TV console, which indicated that after a decade of giving God their full attention, the Blaggs were still struggling to make any sense out of religion and where it was taking their lives.

Even in communities that aren't considered deeply religious, it would be next to impossible to press a prosecution on the theory that someone with no previous history of criminality or mental illness had snapped because of excessive interest in Christianity, so Blagg ended up being tried on the much easier track of excessive interest in sex.

Out of the potential universe of mind-warpingly kinky, extremely fetishistic, and downright disturbing sexual things that have been posted on the Internet over the years, it was what Mike had collected on his computer that was being relentlessly described to the jury as too "perverted" and shameful to even discuss. While it certainly wasn't a topic for polite conversation, it was hard to picture the same courtroom being convened in 2004 to consider whether or not oral sex between a married couple in the wake of a painful hysterectomy would have met the definition of *perversion*—which is "deviating greatly from what is accepted as right, normal, or proper."

If Mike's computer had instead contained 668 pictures of couples having straightforward missionary-position sex, would it have been more reasonable to assume that Jennifer wouldn't have cared and wouldn't have been on the brink of divorcing Mike? For that matter, if it had just been 668 *Playboy*-centerfold-style nude shots of other women, should that have been better or worse as far as Jennifer was concerned? Like the "correct reaction" to coming home and finding a bloodstain in your bed and your wife and daughter gone, the nuances of what the sexual images on Mike's computer meant were ultimately private subjective judgments that, by their very nature, varied from person to person. Seating one member of a couple in the middle of a venue as decorous, clinical, and standardized as a courtroom, turning up the lights, and asking twelve people to examine that person's private sexual interests for any sign that he might not be normal, in order to divine whether or not he would thus be capable of murder was a perilous undertaking—but one which the defense had no choice except to ride out.

# 38

AS the trial wrapped up at the end of its first week, Clare Rochester leaned forward and hugged Michael before the family and attorneys filed out of the courtroom. Eisner had just cast serious doubts on key pieces of what had been discussed for over a year in the press as the "final straws" that had supposedly led Jennifer to head for a divorce, and thus Mike's murderous reaction. Asked by reporters what he thought of the trial so far, Blagg smiled and replied, "I think our guys are doing great."

The next block of testimony came from a group of seven of Mike's former co-workers at AMETEK Dixson and some of the police officers who'd taken turns running surveillance on him. There were basically only two times during Mike's eighteen months at AMETEK that mattered to the jury: the day of November 13 itself and the week in January when he took the bins, paper shredder, table, and desk back to his new townhouse using the company pickup truck.

Singer had asserted during his opening statement that as one of the Grand Junction factory's three main managers, Mike actually had permission to take some equipment to set up a home office. However, that argument seemed largely undercut by Mike's own confession during his final intense police interrogation that he had stolen the furniture, and by testimony from his co-workers, who remembered Mike getting up in front of a large group of employees and chiding "whoever" had stolen the paper shredder, urging "them" to "just turn it back in, no questions asked."

The prosecution's point about the theft of less than five hundred dollars' worth of office furnishings was really what it showed about Mike's mindset and inherent criminal capabilities. If Mike was comfortable swiping things off the loading dock in broad daylight, then he might well have been comfortable disposing of bodies in the company's Dumpster in the middle of the night.

Shooting his wife, most likely asphyxiating his daughter, clearing up the crime scene, staging a burglary, sneaking across town in a van with his murdered family in the back, and then clandestinely operating a mechanically powered Dumpster at his own workplace all would have made for the single longest and most stressful night in Michael Blagg's life. But when the sun finally came up, he would've had to report for a busy workday and act like nothing unusual had happened, knowing the whole time that when he did return home after nearly thirty-six continuous hours without sleep to "discover" something was amiss, he was going to have to call authorities and all hell would break loose. Given those circumstances, Daniels wanted to know if his co-workers had noticed anything about Mike's demeanor on that particular workday.

Six of the seven AMETEK employees who testified said they had noticed things that were uncharacteristic or out of place about Mike's actions that day.

"He seemed 'different,'" Claire Loos testified. "I wish I could put another word to it, but I can only say 'different.'"

Loos thought Blagg had looked unusually pale and ashy.

AMETEK Dixson Quality Control Inspector Joan Cordova recalled seeing Mike unusually early that Tuesday morning, around 5:35 A.M. "He looked shocked, dazed, as I was talking to him," Cordova recalled.

Cordova said she remembered the encounter because she'd arrived at work early that morning and was surprised and a bit alarmed to find several exterior doors to the factory unlocked. She'd gone looking for a supervisor when she bumped into Mike, who didn't appear concerned once she told him the building had probably not been secured properly overnight. "I said, 'Are you aware the doors were open, not locked?' No response. So I asked him again," Cordova recalled. "He said, 'I'll get back to you.'"

Eisner wanted to know why, if Cordova thought there was anything significant about her exchange with Mike, she hadn't come forward and mentioned anything about it in the days after Jennifer and Abby went missing, instead of waiting for months until investigators finally showed up and interviewed her at her home. "You keep quiet because your job could be in jeopardy," Cordova replied.

Cordova said that on most days she would typically only see Mike once or twice, if at all, but on November 13, she saw him near the loading dock more than twenty times. She recalled him staring nervously out at the truck that was being packed for Mexico each time he would stop. Other employees recalled that he'd spent a lot of time around the loading dock area, where he was busy taking loads of trash out to the Dumpster, something unusual to see a senior member of the management doing at all.

Shawn Wallace in particular remembered an incident that Tuesday morning when he noticed Blagg was pushing two large taped-up cardboard boxes down a hallway on a pallet jack toward the loading dock. Wallace said that when he moved to help, he was surprised by Blagg's abrupt rejection of his offer to assist. Wallace recalled Blagg saying, "Nope, just get away!" with a serious look on his face. Wallace said he'd helped Mike with similar things in the past, and never received the kind of stern reproval that he did on November 13.

AMETEK Dixson technical writer Clayton Yancey went one better and stunned the defense by testifying that he thought Mike had stolen a work computer off of Yancey's desk. It had vanished back in the summer of 2001, which wouldn't have been all that long after Blagg had taken the job in Grand Junction, and Yancey said that overall security at the factory had been stepped up in the wake of that particular theft.

After the jury left for lunch, Eisner asked Judge Bottger to declare a mistrial. "It's highly prejudicial, and we were certainly surprised," Eisner said of the new theft accusation.

Bottger declined to scrub the whole trial over the matter, but when the jury came back in, he instructed them to disregard that portion of Yancey's testimony. "Certainly you're not to consider it evidence that Mr. Blagg stole this computer. He is not charged with stealing it, and you're not to consider it as evidence that Mr. Blagg is some kind of thief," Bottger admonished.

Mike's behavior after his wife and child disappeared was another area where Daniels wanted the jury to pay close attention.

At Christmas time Michael had made a poignant point to place presents for both Abby and Jennifer under the tree. But six days later, on New Year's Eve, Mike was at Circuit City picking up expensive TV and stereo equipment.

Called to the witness stand, Circuit City Sales Associate Devon Tilly remembered Blagg calling earlier during that week to "wheel and deal," and then making a trip in to look at the merchandise before finally coming back about ten minutes before the store was set to close to make the purchase.

Blagg, whom Tilly recognized in part because he was wearing one of his "Hope—Jennifer and Abby" pins at the time, took advantage of a no-interest credit plan promotion that the store had been running.

Deputy District Attorney Brian Flynn asked Tilly about Blagg's demeanor as he arranged for the goods to be delivered to his new residence.

Tilly recalled Blagg joking, "Man, this country is great! You can walk away with a whole bunch of stuff and not pay anything."

Daniels wondered aloud what sort of man would go spend nearly $7,000 on toys for himself when his family had vanished less than six weeks beforehand.

The defense countered that Blagg was simply attempting to cope with the situation and he could certainly afford to buy himself a modern television, especially one that was available on a no-interest payment plan. Eisner noted that Blagg's father-in-law, Harold Conway, had accompanied him on one of his trips to Circuit City and he'd worn his "missing" pin the whole time. Eisner argued that, since Mike was hardly trying to hide his identity, he must not have thought he was doing anything particularly shameful.

# 39

STEVE King came in and showed the jury the video- and audiotapes of the lengthy first interview that the detectives had conducted with Mike at the sheriff's office in the hours immediately after Mike had reported the crime scene at his house.

The main thing the prosecution wanted to show the jury was how "flat" and unemotional Mike seemed throughout hour after hour of questioning.

When it finally came time for cross-examination, Eisner again led King back through written transcripts of the taped interview, and he used King to highlight times when Blagg described himself as not doing too well, or said that he was feeling "shaky," or the three times he declined offers of food because he said his "stomach was turning inside out."

The most contentious exchange during the first weeks of the trial erupted on a cross-examination between Eisner and retired Orlando, Florida, police officer Kevin King, who had spoken to Mike a day or so after Jennifer and Abby vanished, when King volunteered to help with the initial search of the Redlands.

Kevin King said that Mike had been "passionless" during their talk about the missing pair, showing no emotion at all when Jennifer was discussed, and putting his head down "like he was crying, but there were no tears," when he spoke about Abby. Eisner shot back that Blagg could simply "have a faith in the Lord that would help him through difficult times."

Edie Melson had traveled from South Carolina to Grand Junction to testify on Tuesday, March 16, 2004, about her late best friend.

Melson's testimony on the stand was much more damaging to Mike's position than either side would have anticipated, given the report she'd provided to the FBI agents two years beforehand when they interviewed her at her home in Simpsonville.

Melson testified that her friendship all along had really been with Jennifer and that she and her husband Kirk rarely socialized with Mike and Jennifer as couples.

Edie reiterated her feeling that Mike was a controlling, and maybe even emotionally abusive, presence in Jennifer's life, but she nonetheless characterized Jennifer as an adoring wife. She remembered that when Jennifer had lived in Simpsonville, she and Edie had talked three or four times each week on the phone, but always during the work day when Mike wasn't home. On the occasions when Mike did pick up the phone, he would often have some reason why Jennifer couldn't talk to her at the moment.

Describing their November 2, 2001, conversation, ten days before Jennifer disappeared, Melson used words like "very upset" and "afraid" when she described the cryptic phone call during which Jennifer had asked Edie to "pray for something like you've never prayed before."

"From her voice, I could tell she was not happy," Melson recounted, but she said Jennifer wouldn't tell her the reason, saying instead, "I have something to tell you. I pray I will get the courage to tell you."

Two years before the trial, when newspapers had taken Melson's comments to mean that Jennifer was on the brink of leaving Mike, Melson had asked reporters to clarify that when Jennifer mentioned a possible trip back to South Carolina without Mike, it had struck her as unusual because the two always traveled together. Melson stressed at that time that she hadn't taken the phone conversation to mean that Jennifer was actually planning to leave Mike for good. Now she said she believed that might have been the case.

During cross-examination, Eisner was quick to seize on the apparent hardening of Melson's feelings toward Mike in the years after the discovery of Jennifer's body. He picked up a newspaper clipping that quoted Melson as saying the Blaggs were "a wonderful family, very close-knit," and noted how her assessments of the Blaggs' relationship seemed to have evolved into something more dire between the time she'd first talked to FBI agents and when she finally was called to testify.

Melson conceded that she hadn't previously mentioned that she might have any reason to suspect that the Blaggs' marriage was unhealthy or that it might be dissolving; however, she said she regretted that she hadn't done so when she talked to the FBI and the Mesa County investigators.

Eisner asked if it was just during the formal investigation that Melson hadn't told of any such concerns, wondering if she'd said anything like that to her own husband, to Jennifer's mother, or perhaps to other concerned friends. "Like I said, I regret that, and no, I did not," Melson answered.

Melson was able to fit a key puzzle piece into Daniels'

prosecution when she testified that she'd seen a red-and-black tent in the Blaggs' garage back in South Carolina.

Jennifer's best friend from Simpsonville was followed by her new best friend from Grand Junction, and the contrast between Edie Melson and Dianna Shirley's assessments of Jennifer's final days was pronounced.

Dianna and Jennifer had both volunteered at the Bookcliff Christian School, where Shirley's son was in Abby's first-grade class. The two women had also taken a Jazzercise class together and spoken frequently on the phone.

Unlike Melson, Shirley said she had no sense of foreboding about either Jennifer or the Blaggs' relationship in the days leading up to November 13.

"I saw a happy marriage. When they dropped Abby off for a rehearsal at church Saturday, we made plans for Thanksgiving dinner," Shirley testified. "She was excited because she and Mike were going Christmas shopping. She was happy and she was smiling."

The last time she saw Jennifer was on Monday, November 12, 2001, and she remembered Jennifer as "kind of down. She didn't feel well, and there had been a plane crash in New York. Everybody was trying to figure out if terrorists were involved," Shirley recalled, referring to American Airlines Flight 587, which had crashed in Queens that morning just moments after taking off from JFK airport.

When it came time for the jury to hear from one of Mike's closest friends, New Hope Fellowship Church Pastor Art Blankenship said that he hadn't seen any hints that the Blaggs' marriage could've been on the rocks.

Blankenship said he was close to both Mike and Jennifer, and he would have expected each of them to have been comfortable coming to him if they were having marital problems. He said neither of them even confided anything to him that would have led him to question what he'd always felt from his own observations was a close, loving relationship.

Blankenship recalled that he had asked Mike to consider becoming a church elder in the weeks before the disappearances.

Blankenship said he remembered picking Mike up in the pre-dawn hours of November 14 after that first ten-hour-long interview with investigators. "They let him go at two-thirty A.M. On the way home, he was almost absolutely quiet. He didn't say what had happened," Blankenship testified. "His only comment was, 'Art, have you ever been involved in anything like this in your entire life?'"

The pastor hastened to add that Mike hadn't been completely emotionless during the weeks he'd stayed with him. He testified that there were occasions when Mike broke down and cried.

Daniels needed to show that while Grand Junction certainly wasn't immune to crime, there weren't any reports of wild gangs of roving meth tweakers, child-stealing gypsies, or devil-worshiping cult members skulking around the Redlands during the pre-dawn hours of November 12 and 13.

To do that, he summoned up a parade of the Blaggs' former neighbors from Pine Terrace Court. While none of them had seen anything suspicious that night, there were several little things that they'd reported to police in the days immediately following the disappearances that had struck them in hindsight.

The woman who lived directly across the street from the Blaggs remembered being awakened by some sort of noise about 1:30 A.M. Two other neighbors who lived to the west of the Blaggs, including Ray Scott, who lived on the next block, said their dogs had begun barking uncharacteristically about 2 A.M. that night. Neighbor Helen West said she had gone to walk her dog after dark when she heard two or three male voices behind the Blaggs' house. She couldn't hear what the men were discussing, but it was disconcerting enough that she'd decided to skip the rest of her walk and return home.

A neighbor testified that at some point between 6:15 and 6:30 A.M.—after he'd left for work, Michael had said—she'd heard several male voices talking in what sounded like a normal tone out on the Greenbelt Drive side of the Blaggs' fence. Singer had actually touched on that report during his opening statement, but Daniels brought in a newspaper delivery woman who said that when she'd stopped that morning on Greenbelt Drive to fold papers, she'd seen four joggers coming down the road at about 6:30 A.M.

# 40

ONE of the key points the defense had made during the trial's opening was that during his February 2002 suicide attempt, Mike had not only left a final written note saying he didn't kill Jennifer and Abby, but also denied it when Investigator Weyler tried to coax it out of him in a final "come to Jesus" confession right there in the bathtub.

It was a powerful tableau for the jury to consider. Michael in agonizing pain, his life rapidly ebbing away, accoutered with a photo of his missing wife and daughter and an open Bible as the water in his tub grew an angrier shade of red by the minute, never expecting to see another living human being, but knowing that when his lifeless body was eventually discovered, his last sacrosanct protestation of innocence would ring out from beyond the grave.

Following the preceding night's scathing police interrogation, it served as an outstandingly dramatic, almost religious, affirmation of Michael's assertion that, far from being the murderer, he was really the third victim in the case.

That is, it did *if* it really was a suicide attempt.

Daniels brought Investigator Steve King back into the courtroom with a completely different theory about what had actually happened in the townhouse that blood-soaked morning.

King didn't think Mike's suicide attempt on February 6, 2002, was sincere. "My belief is that he was faking it," King told the jury. "My belief is that he was attempting to gain sympathy from the community."

King pointed out that the investigators had actually made remarks goading Blagg as he walked out the door of the police station, saying that if he was going to kill himself, he should leave them a note saying where the bodies were. He also noted that Blagg already knew the whole posse would be coming back to his townhouse the next morning. The police had started knocking on his door a full hour before they were able to make entry, and Mike would have had plenty of time to set things up so as to inflict the injuries, knowing it was a fair bet that help would be on the way sooner rather than later.

King said that as he rode through town with Blagg in the ambulance to St. Mary's Hospital, he thought Mike was only pretending to be unconscious. "I am sure that if Michael Blagg would have laid there two days, he would have died there from those wounds," King said. "But when someone is committed to suicide, three stitches in one wrist and four in the other probably is not going to get the job done."

Eisner was infuriated by the tack King was taking. He put up slides of Mike lying in the blood-red bathtub, and grisly close-ups of his slashed wrists taken by the doctors in the emergency room. Why, Eisner wondered, had King not mentioned his suspicion that it was all a fake earlier, considering that three other investigators who had written reports said they thought Blagg was unconscious and near death when they wheeled him out to the ambulance on a gurney?

King acknowledged that he hadn't mentioned his impression that the suicide had been a put-up job angling for sympathy until sometime, "probably in the last three weeks," before the trial. But he said he'd felt that way since the day it happened.

There was no doubt Mike was under tremendous stress, and Steve King had initially tried to give him the benefit of the doubt, but as the case progressed, he'd concluded that Mike was feigning the role of the grieving husband and father.

Looking back over the weeks he'd spent with Mike, King thought that on balance, Mike was simply trying too hard to play a role. King played the jury the tape of the initial interview with Mike, but he also showed them the video that went with it. He emphasized how Mike had seemed flat, distant, not concerned enough about what police were or weren't doing to try to find his missing family.

Eisner countered that it was Mike's tremendous faith in God that had allowed him to stay in control that night when it was important to help the police work the case. As proof, Eisner pointed to the seven-minute period when the investigators stepped out of the interview room and left Mike there alone. The tape showed Mike burying his head in his hands and praying, and then praying with his hands clasped and his head bowed.

The difficulty with all of the points that King and others were making about nearly every aspect of Michael Blagg's personality, demeanor, behavior, and attitude after November 13 was that for each little snippet that could be viewed in a negative light, there was also at least one potentially benign explanation. So it was particularly interesting when one of Mike's AMETEK Dixson co-workers testified that during a dinner less than two months after

Jennifer and Abby had vanished, Mike had said something truly weird.

AMETEK Dixson Supervisor Rita Meryhew explained that she, Mike, and two other women who worked at the plant had all gone out to get dinner because the four of them had been working late.

Mesa County was still papered in "MISSING" posters for Jennifer when Mike opened his mouth and left his dining companions completely nonplused.

"He made the comment about how lucky he was to be a single guy out for dinner and drinks with three beautiful women," Meryhew testified.

"Do you know how he would have known he was single at that point?" Daniels asked.

"No, we thought it was really odd," Meryhew recalled.

Ken Singer picked up the cross-examination by asking Meryhew if Blagg had made any attempt to put the moves on the women or pick any of them up. Meryhew said he hadn't. Singer suggested the whole thing could have just been a clumsy attempt at being jovial.

The testimony infuriated Jennifer's brother. "It's amazing how flippantly someone can use the word 'single,'" David Loman told a reporter afterward.

# 41

TWO local doctors who'd treated the Blaggs over the years, Dr. Gregory Reicks and obstetrician Dr. Barry King, both testified that they'd never seen any indication Jennifer was abused, nor had she ever reported any kind of emotional or psychological strain stemming from her marriage.

Jennifer had sought treatment for a range of medical problems, including depression, chronic fatigue, a loss of interest in sex, dizziness, indigestion, heartburn, weight gain, and various aches and pains.

What interested the prosecution was that Jennifer's host of symptoms tended to fall into a gray area of maladies that—absent a better, more direct physical explanation—can be brought about by underlying mental stresses.

"For all these conditions, we always have some concern that psychological factors could be involved," Dr. Reicks acknowledged, adding that one such trigger factor could be psychological abuse. However, Dr. Reicks also hastened to add, "Jennifer never gave me the impression that she was afraid of her husband."

Dr. King said Jennifer was being prescribed four or five types of antidepressants, and Dr. Reicks added that Mike was also on prescription medication for lower back pain, as well as nighttime leg spasms and insomnia. Like Jennifer's symptoms, Dr. Reicks said that much of what Mike was seeking help for—including the insomnia, headaches, fatigue, anxiety, and lower back pain—could also "possibly be related to psychological factors."

Eisner countered that all those symptoms could also be from physical sources, which is how the doctors had viewed them at the time they'd treated them, and he specifically noted that ten years of flying a military helicopter might have had something to do with Mike's lower back pain.

Privately, Daniels had been surprised that the defense hadn't pursued the angle that Mike might have been driven over the edge of temporary insanity by the changes that had been made to his medications in the fall of 2001.

Daniels had records showing that in August of 2001, Mike had been prescribed several powerful drugs, and in follow-up visits to his doctors, others were added, including nortriptyline HCl, Xanax, Darvon, and Klonopin.

Daniels had filed pre-trial motions disclosing the medications that had been found in the Blagg home because he thought there was a chance the issue would rise to prominence during the trial.

That cocktail of meds, Daniels wrote in one of his motions, might explain

> why Michael Blagg, a man who by all outward appearances was a dedicated husband and father would commit such a crime. It stands to reason that one is more likely to commit an offense like this if he is suffering from anxiety or consuming narcotics and/or anti-depression, anti-anxiety medications.

When Mike's co-workers had testified, none of them remembered him saying anything in the run-up to the disappearances that would have indicated any family problems, but two of the managers who'd worked most closely with Mike said there had been a downturn in his usually upbeat and cheery personality, beginning two or three weeks beforehand.

Daniels figured that Mike's resistance toward the drug issue came from the fact that the use of a temporary insanity defense would have first required him to admit the killings, and then immediately put him in an uphill battle to convince a jury that the drugs' interactions had been so overwhelming that they'd compelled his actions that night, something no pharmaceutical manufacturer on Earth was ever going to give Mike any help in proving.

# 42

**WHILE** the main focus of the Blagg trial was clearly within the walls of Judge Bottger's courtroom, plenty was going on outside as it progressed.

It was because the furniture thefts had cost Mike his high-paying job that he suddenly found himself qualifying for Eisner's services through the Office of the Colorado State Public Defender, but, unlike most of the clients who found themselves relying on public assistance for legal help, Blagg was highly educated and able to follow the nuances of the law. As a consequence, he was able to do real work on his own case and he spent a great deal of time at Eisner's office pushing through research and paperwork. Each morning before heading in to the Justice Center for the trial, Mike would slip into church, attend a brief service, and pray.

Mike wasn't the only relative of Jennifer and Abby's who was putting in long hours. David Loman was not convinced that Abby was lost in the landfill, and most days after court and on the weekends, he was back out continuing his own lonely search for clues in the wilderness areas around Grand Junction. The Laura Recovery Center's volunteer search had scrutinized an immense swath of territory, but there were still tips that continued to come in, and the family and Loman felt compelled to make sure they were checked.

In addition to searching for a small grave in the wilderness, Loman also clung to a faint hope that by some merciful twist of fate, Abby might still be alive somewhere.

It was heart-wrenching for those who met Loman, seeing his absolute willingness, even in the face of insurmountable odds, to do whatever it took to make things whole again. It appeared Loman was the last to accept what others had so grudgingly reconciled themselves to about Abby's likely fate, simply because he had the hardest time believing it was possible for anyone, let alone Mike, to really be so incredibly cold and evil as to walk into Abby's happy little bedroom in the middle of the night and do her harm.

Mike's mother and sister were also holding out hope that Abby was still alive, especially since they were convinced that it wasn't Mike who was responsible for Jennifer being in the landfill. "The people in this town need to understand that all of this time and this money that the police and the DA have devoted towards accusing my brother has been wasted," Clare Rochester told CBS shortly after she arrived in Grand Junction for the trial, adding, "I think it should frighten this public that there is somebody out there who committed this crime."

With the encouragement of the Blaggs' relatives and friends, the National Center for Missing & Exploited Children posted a computer-aged image on their website of what an older Abby would look like, but despite a few tips and some vague sightings, no solid leads were developed.

Although there had been well-wishing, and even hugs, in the first days of the trial between both sides of Mike Blagg's extended family, there was a daily division as they split and sat on different sides of the aisle. Betsy Blagg and Clare Rochester sat directly behind Mike at the defense table, while Marilyn and Harold Conway, David and Karen Loman, and other members of Jennifer's family sat squarely behind Frank Daniels at the prosecution table.

Both sides told reporters they would simply be happy with the truth—but what that truth meant for each was a very different thing. "I do want to hug her and support her," Rochester told CBS, referring to her heartfelt sympathy for Marilyn's loss, but, she added, "I don't understand why Marilyn is not openly sitting on our side with her arm around Michael."

# 43

EVENTUALLY every murder trial reaches the point where the prosecution needs to pause and actually prove that a murder occurred, so Mesa County Chief Deputy Coroner Dr. Dean Havlik, the forensic pathologist who'd led Jennifer's autopsy with Dr. Rob Kurtzman's help, took the stand and explained to the jury in minute detail exactly how Jennifer had died.

Jennifer's mother and her aunt left the courtroom before the presentation, but Harold Conway and David Loman remained, steeling themselves for what was coming.

It was the first time Mike had seen any of the pictures of Jennifer's strangely misshapen remains being removed from the landfill, random bits and pieces of trash still stuck to her limbs, as crime-scene technicians laid her out on a tarp for an initial examination.

The jurors watched solemnly as Havlik traced the path the bullet had taken through Jennifer's eye and down into the back of her head. As x-ray after x-ray showing the catastrophic head wound was projected up on the screen, Havlik explained in calm clinical terms that although the tunnel that had been bored through her brain in a split second would have instantly deprived Jennifer of the ability to make any purposeful moves, that wasn't the same thing as saying she'd died instantly. She could have survived the initial impact of the bullet for several minutes and then died as the blood flowed out of her body, Havlik said to the grimly quiet audience seated before him.

Havlik said that because of the length of time that had passed, the damage inflicted by the burial in the landfill, and the advanced state of decomposition, he was unable to determine either the precise time of death or whether Jennifer had been sexually assaulted.

Mike rode through Havlik's testimony with his hands clenched tightly up near his mouth. He had a horrified look on his face at times, and at intervals he could be seen to tremble. When the slide show had finally ceased and Havlik was excused, Bottger called for a short break and Mike appeared to have trouble standing, as friends and a minister quickly moved forward to support him.

On the opposite side of the courtroom, Loman and Conway hugged each other.

The most damning pieces of evidence against Michael Blagg all had to do with Jennifer's body: She had a bullet in her head from close range, her retainer was still in her mouth, and she'd been found right in the exact spot at the landfill where the sheriffs had gone to look for her when they'd tried to zero in on the AMETEK Dixson Dumpster.

It would have taken one hell of a coincidence for somebody other than Mike to have randomly picked the very Dumpster that was sitting behind Mike's workplace in order to dispose of Jennifer's body. But that wasn't actually the nature of the coincidence that Eisner was entertaining. Instead, he wanted the jury to consider that it was at least plausible that someone other than Mike could have killed Jennifer and placed her in some other trash container around Grand Junction with the very same result—namely that she would have swiftly ended up in the Mesa County Landfill.

How, then, would that explain the sheriffs' discovery of her when they were specifically looking for the 1.95 tons of trash that had been weighed into the landfill in the AMETEK Dumpster load of November 14?

Eisner's answer was that if Jennifer's body was in the landfill at all, then there was no way it could have gotten there any earlier than November 13, so, in turn, it was really no surprise that it would be within a few yards of trash that arrived on November 14. There were hundreds of tons of trash arriving daily at the Mesa County Landfill, but it wasn't like it was Staten Island or some other big-city operation receiving trash around the clock, where the odds of finding anything next to anything else, even in the same date range, would be exponentially less likely.

Eisner pointed out that the primary clue the Soggy Bottom Gang had been using as their guide to the excavation wasn't actually the trash from AMETEK, but rather the dates provided by the thousands of newspapers that had been thrown out on or about November 14.

Lieutenant Dick Dillon showed the jury two hours' worth of the videotape he'd shot of the excavation, and gave them a sense—minus the smell—of the conditions the investigators were working under. "I've spent thirty years in law enforcement, and I'm a battle-tested combat veteran, and I've never put up with anything like that," Dillon told the jurors. "What we endured for fifty-one days would test the mettle of anyone."

Eisner complimented Lieutenant Dillon for having the fortitude to lead his team through the 4,624 tons of trash, but added, "I have to be the Grinch and start talking about, 'Does this really show that Michael Blagg put that body in the landfill?'

"Jennifer Blagg's remains were not found in a container that came from AMETEK Dixson, were they?" Eisner asked.

"No, they were not," Dillon concurred.

Eisner brought in the driver who'd actually hauled the Dumpster from Ametek to the landfill on November 14, 2001. Bill Scott was no longer working as a trash truck driver but, despite the passage of two and a half years' time, he was positive he remembered dumping out that particular load.

Scott said the Dumpster had only been about half full, and, as part of his job, he'd stepped out of his truck and walked around the load after he'd emptied it out. He hadn't seen any large objects wrapped in red cloth.

Daniels asked him on cross-examination how thoroughly he'd checked out the AMETEK Dixson trash. "I just kind of looked it over real quick. That was it," Scott said.

# 44

Mike watched with an approving smile and even chuckled at times as Eisner aggressively bore into witnesses during the cross-examinations. As the trial moved along,

Mike appeared increasingly at ease, mouthing "Good morning!" to some of the jurors as they arrived each day, chatting with supporters from his churches who turned out when they could take the time off, huddling with his sister and mother during breaks in the front benches of the courtroom, and even passing out candy to the public defender's staff and his gathered friends.

In a trial that was becoming notable just for the sheer volume of people who were making the trek to the witness stand to raise their right hands and swear to tell the truth, a pivotal figure in the case made her appearance during the sixth week of the trial.

Marilyn Conway was genuinely another victim who had lost so much in the Blagg case, but she was also someone who'd had unique access and insight into both Jennifer and Mike's lives together for fourteen years running.

In November and December of 2001, Conway had been Mike's staunchest defender, describing him at various intervals as someone she'd liked from the moment she met him, "a very compassionate" man, a great father, and a steadfast, loyal, and loving husband.

She would later admit that her feelings had changed in a matter of minutes when a sheriff's investigator merely told her about the pornography that had been found on Mike's computer.

This time, far from being supportive of Mike's cause, Conway's testimony would prove to be some of the most damaging of the entire trial.

Conway had watched the previous week as an insurance company investigator detailed the $29,000 claim Mike had filed for the items that were missing from Jennifer's overturned jewelry box. On the list were several loose sapphires and diamonds. Conway spoke up and told the court that she had found a plastic bag in the master bedroom several weeks after the disappearances containing those particular gems, and she had given them back to Mike.

The next bit of unexpected testimony from Conway was far more damaging. Daniels was querying Conway about the nature of Jennifer and Mike's relationship when he asked if there had been any previous indications of violence between them. It was really just a throwaway question to set up another point, because it had already been asked of Conway over and over again by investigators for years, literally from the very first day the case had begun. In every interview, regardless of the side asking the questions, Conway had always insisted that Mike cherished her daughter and had never done anything, nor would he do anything, to harm Jennifer. This time, in the eleventh hour of an incredibly long trial, Conway had a completely different answer.

"Michael hurt her in Corpus," Marilyn said, referring to Corpus Christi, Texas, which was one of the first places the Navy had moved Mike and Jennifer in the months just after their marriage.

"He hurt her in Corpus?" Daniels asked in amazement.

"He hurt her in Corpus. Yes, he did," Conway insisted.

"Mrs. Conway, you said that Michael hurt Jennifer in Corpus Christi, Texas?" Daniels repeated for emphasis, gathering his bearings as the weight of that statement continued to dawn on him.

"Yes, sir."

"What do remember about that?" Daniels asked, suddenly willing to overlook the adage that lawyers should never ask a question to which they don't know the answer.

"She called home one night and said that Mike had cornered her in the bedroom, and obviously he was drunk. She was upset and I understood that he had tried to choke her," Conway said.

Conway said Jennifer had put Mike on the phone, and he'd vowed he would never hurt her again.

"I offered to come down and get her. He said, 'No, I

love her and she loves me,' " Conway elaborated, adding that that was why she had sent Jennifer blank checks, so she could return home if she ever felt threatened. She said that even though that was the only incident of abuse, she had continued to replace the blank checks that Jennifer had over the years whenever she changed banks.

Eisner was livid. Conway's unexpected testimony had noticeably altered the atmosphere in the courtroom. Mike looked shattered, family members on both sides of the room were scowling, and the jurors were paying rapt attention to the first clear indication they'd gotten in six weeks that Mike might be a closet wife-beater.

"Have you reported this to any officer in this case sometime before today?" Eisner wondered in exasperation when it was his turn to ask questions.

"I'm sure that I did," Conway began before hesitantly admitting, "I may . . . I may not have."

Continuing his cross-examination, Eisner reminded Conway that on November 13, when Sheriff's Investigator Lissah Norcross has asked her what might be going on that would cause her daughter to suddenly vanish, Conway's first reaction was that it would be "absurd" to suggest that Mike might have hurt Jennifer. He added that in follow-up interviews, Conway had continued to insist that no history of domestic violence or other problems had ever existed between the couple.

David Loman would later tell the CBS News program 48 Hours, which had been covering the case intently with a camera inside the courtroom, that it was the first he had heard of the decade-old incident from either his mother or from Jennifer.

"It shocked me as much as it did anybody else in the courtroom," Loman told 48 Hours anchor Susan Spencer.

When it was her turn to be interviewed, Conway told Spencer that she just hadn't remembered the Corpus Christi incident before she had taken the stand that day, despite the numerous queries about just such instances from investigators over the preceding twenty-eight months.

"I wasn't even aware it was going to come out of my mouth. It just came out," Conway explained.

In the same program, which eventually aired as part of a *48 Hours* episode titled "Dark Side of the Mesa," Eisner charged that Conway's timing had simply been too good to be true.

"She got on the stand and lied. I think she saw the district attorney's case faltering, and I think she felt she would do whatever she could to help that case out," Eisner said.

"You think she lied outright?" Spencer asked.

"Yes," Eisner replied firmly.

"This assault never happened?"

"I don't believe it ever did."

"What, she just made it up?" Spencer challenged.

"She made it up."

The final piece of damning testimony that Mike's mother-in-law inflicted on him that day was her recollection that "In South Carolina there was a loaded gun in the night stand, and they kept one in Grand Junction."

Mike's mother, Elizabeth Blagg, testified later in the day and said that there had been many guns in her home in Warner Robins, Georgia, over the years, but they were always kept in a locked gun box.

"Are you hiding a murder weapon in your house?" Eisner asked.

"No, I am not," Betsy Blagg replied.

The question of who had owned what gun and when was an important one for both sides, because although three guns—a .22-caliber handgun, a .22-caliber rifle, and a Remington shotgun—had been found during the search of the Blagg residence, right where Mike had said they would be when he was first interviewed at the sheriff's office, none of them could have fired the bullet that was recovered from Jennifer's skull.

All of the guns that Mike had in the house had originally belonged to his father, and the sheriffs had found an insurance inventory that had been written back when Mike and Jennifer were living in Texas, which listed a 9mm Smith & Wesson handgun as well as the three firearms that were found in their Grand Junction home.

The sheriffs felt it was rather obvious that there had been a "fourth gun" all along that Mike had been in the habit of keeping in the bedside drawer, and that he must have used it to kill Jennifer and then thrown it out, probably in whatever bag or bundle had contained Abby's body.

The defense countered that as far as proof was concerned, this was nothing more than a wild theory and Michael had said that that gun had belonged to his father and had been returned to his mother's home in Georgia years earlier. Eisner argued that the gun that had been mentioned on the insurance forms was eventually found in storage in Georgia and had never been to Colorado.

Eisner called in CBI Agent Wayne Bryant, who testified that, while the bullet that had killed Jennifer could have been fired by a 9mm handgun, there were at least three other widely available types of handguns that could also have fired it—including .357s, .38s, or .380-calibers.

Eisner also called Mike's sister Clare Rochester to the stand to try to refute Conway's claim that Mike had committed insurance fraud. Rochester said she had gone in and removed everything from the bedroom at Pine Terrace Court while helping Mike move to his new townhouse. She said she had not seen the plastic bag of gems that Conway said she'd later found there.

Asked about the differing accounts by a reporter as she left the courthouse, Conway said, "I've told the truth. I can't change the truth."

# 45

**IN** the final days of the trial, Eisner summoned several character witnesses who extolled Mike's virtues as a husband and father.

AMETEK Dixson co-worker Wendy Holgate described Mike as a thoughtful and appreciative manager. She'd bumped into the Blaggs once while out shopping in Grand Junction and recalled that "Abby was just this little thing," who spoke right up, much to her father's delight.

Kathi Owens had traveled from Simpsonville to testify about her friendship with the Blaggs when they all lived in South Carolina. To Owens, Mike and Jennifer were a couple who were deeply in love, and represented "every picture of happiness you can imagine."

When Deputy District Attorney Brian Flynn asked Owens if she'd been aware that Mike was addicted to pornography, she said that she hadn't, but that the question reminded her that Jennifer had warned her about the dangers of Internet pornography back when her family had first hooked up their home computer to the Net. "Be careful, because anything can happen," Owens recalled Jennifer saying.

The final defense witness, Lee McElfresh, was another friend of the Blaggs who said he was "envious" of the Blaggs' marriage, and said he'd viewed Mike as "an immaculate representation of what a husband should be.

"Michael treated Jennifer like she was a gift that God has given him, a precious girl. They would sparkle with each other the entire time," McElfresh testified.

With no more defense witnesses on the schedule, Judge Bottger turned to the defense table and asked the day's big question.

"Is this an appropriate time, Mr. Eisner, to talk with your client about whether he'll testify?"

"Yes, it is, Judge."

"What is your decision?" Bottger asked Blagg.

"I will not be testifying," Mike replied.

After the judge officially declared an end to testimony in the trial and called a brief recess, Mike and his family joined in hugging the McElfreshes and members of the defense team, wiping away tears as they waited for the closing arguments to begin.

It had been an immense and costly investigation and it had taken seven weeks to present to the jurors all the myriad details that it had swept up as dozens of investigators had fanned out across five different states. But the time had finally come when everything—be it mundane, esoteric, extremely graphic, or horrifically gruesome—had been trotted out before the jury. It was time to sum it up into a coherent narrative.

Frank Daniels began his closing argument by pointing out what a completely "ordinary day in the neighborhood" November 13, 2001, had been on Pine Terrace Court. The neighbors were around, the postmen and the newspaper carriers went about their business, the landscaping crew across the street spent the day putting in a sprinkler system and shrubbery, and didn't notice anything the least bit unusual taking place within that little subdivision.

"There were no screams, no shots, no shouts, no alarms, no strangers," Daniels began. "The evil had been done in the dark of night."

To Daniels, the Blagg case was not about the surroundings and circumstances on Pine Terrace Court—the open door, mysterious voices, scuff marks on a fence—but rather about the interior workings of Michael Blagg's mind.

Daniels described Mike as someone who outwardly wore his pious identity as a born again Christian like a shield to keep people from realizing that he was really a deeply troubled control freak with a fascination for pornography depicting "perverted sex acts," all of which was causing his marriage to rapidly fall apart.

"I submit that this murder was a reaction to a situation that produced hurt pride, shame, and humiliation on the part of Michael Blagg," Daniels said to the jury.

He described Mike and Jennifer's constant need to seek treatment for anxiety, depression, and insomnia as "part of the whole picture" of sexual dysfunction and ongoing marital strain. "You can't separate them," Daniels argued.

The case against Mike was circumstantial, but to Daniels, it was devastatingly so. Someone had shot Jennifer within the most intimate space inside her home, and they'd done it by approaching within a foot of her bed and leaning down within mere inches of her face—as close as humanly possible—all without managing to awaken her. The nightshirt, the retainer, and her closed eyelid proved Jennifer was asleep when it had happened, and that would put only Mike within the reasonable time frame.

That it had apparently been necessary to kill Abby as well, that the bodies were removed from the house, and that a burglary and a back-door break-in had been faked were all things that suggested someone's biggest need was to cover their time-line, not just their tracks. The minute traces of Jennifer's blood on the outside of the van, and again on the inside, along with the fact that the van had been returned to the garage, and that Jennifer's broken body had turned up at exactly the one spot on Earth where the sheriffs went to look for it when they concluded that Mike must have disposed of it in AMETEK Dixson's Dumpster were, Daniels suggested, impossible to reconcile with some phantom perpetrator.

In a counter-argument that ended up spanning across two days, Eisner closed the defense case by attacking the prosecution's theories about both Michael Blagg and Jennifer's murder as just that—theories.

Taking a shot at Daniels, Eisner said, "It should be

painfully obvious the prosecutor is the one trying to do the fooling."

While he had concentrated on evidence of an unknown intruder during his opening arguments, Eisner spent the majority of his closing attacking the conclusions that were being drawn by Daniels from the pool of information that had been collected by the investigators, saying that, despite its vast scope, it "failed woefully" to prove that Mike had any reason to kill his wife.

Eisner said that Mike had been victimized three separate times, once by an unknown intruder and then by "overzealous law enforcement and an overzealous prosecution." In a mocking tone, Eisner characterized the official attitude as, " 'Well, we've looked everywhere else, we've uncovered every other stone and, if it wasn't him, who could it have been?' That's where they are with their case," Eisner suggested.

Eisner called the individual components of the prosecution's theories "as permanent as ice cubes on a summer day" and he argued that the case as a whole was "a shifting sand castle on a crumbling foundation."

Aiming straight at the most damning and direct testimony undermining Mike's image as a devoted husband and father, Eisner implied that Marilyn Conway had sensed the state's case was foundering due to a lack of specifics, and had helpfully stepped in and lied about suddenly remembering a previous incident of spousal abuse. "Maybe she felt like things weren't going well, and she needed to give the prosecution a boost," Eisner said pointedly.

Eisner noted that early mistakes in determining when the "give the devil a foothold" note had been written or when Mike had last been on the Internet looking at explicit pictures had led investigators to conclude early on that there was something Mike was hiding that revolved around sexual deviancy, and which they assumed must have been straining the relationship to a breaking point.

Eisner urged the jury to have the "courage" to reject the state's conclusion that Jennifer was on the brink of leaving Mike. Unless one took that theory as an article of faith, Eisner argued, there was nothing in Jennifer's notes, diaries, conversations with friends and relations, or behavior that would suggest that she was about to walk out the door on her marriage. If it hadn't been for Mike's admission to police that the topic had created some tension a few months back when Jennifer had walked in on him looking at porn by himself, then there wouldn't have been any proof whatsoever that Jennifer had even known Mike had ever looked at any of it. The fact was that there was not one action on Jennifer's part that looked like she was preparing to stomp out. She hadn't bought a plane ticket, packed a bag, mentioned anything to her mother, her brother, or her closest friends—in fact she had spent Sunday and Monday in the hours before she died trying to shore up a babysitter for her anniversary dinner on Friday with Mike.

Eisner rammed these points home to the jury with a final series of poster boards he placed in front of them, showing portions of recent letters Jennifer had written to Mike that were found in the house on November 13. On the courtroom's large video screen, Eisner put up a picture that had been taken less than two weeks before the disappearances, of Mike giving Abby a big kiss.

"This is actually in three parts," Eisner said as he began reading the first note from Jennifer.

*My dear husband, the love of my life, there's no words to tell you how I feel about you. I adore you . . .*

Moving to the next board, Eisner continued:

*Dear Mike,*
*I love you. I enjoy getting to spend my life with you.*

*We've had a good almost ten years of marriage together. I truly wouldn't have wanted to be with anyone else or with anyone else than with you. God just knew, that's all we can say. We didn't, but our Lord did. We don't know what the future holds for us, but I pray it's even better, however, we must live for Him! We must crucify ourselves, pick up our crosses daily, and truly rely on Him. Time and needs are earnest.*

*I desire to always be there for you, however, I won't be. But, He will, ALWAYS! But until He says otherwise, I'm your beloved wife who adores you. Thank you for being my husband and for loving me.*

And as Eisner progressed to the third, he read the opening lines:

*To Michael, my wonderful loving husband whom I treasure. I'll be waiting for you at home w/open arms and an open heart. May our love endure and keep growing each day. All my love, Jennifer (your bride).*

Turning to the jury, Eisner urged, "You look at these documents, you look at these pictures, and you decide. Is the Michael Blagg that's in this case—is he really the cold-blooded killer they want you to believe, or is this what he really is?" Eisner said, sweeping his arm toward the endearments and the giant photo. "You've got to decide."

As Eisner wrapped up his closing presentation, he concluded by telling the jury, "My last twenty-two months of carrying Michael Blagg's fate on my shoulders will now be over," before walking back to the defense table and embracing Mike, Assistant Public Defender Ken Singer, and defense investigator Pam Sharp in a group hug.

In his brief rebuttal, Daniels stood and said simply, "We never said Jennifer didn't love Michael. Mr. Eisner had some photographs and letters on large boards up here and, you know, that's the way it could have been, and that's the way it should have been. But that ended on November twelfth, 2001."

Daniels brought the final curtain down on the trial with a heartfelt appeal to the jurors following the years of solid work put in by his office, the Mesa County sheriffs, Grand Junction police, the CBI, FBI, and so many others who had worked on the pieces of this enormous puzzle.

"It's time for you to bring justice," Daniels implored, concluding, "And, in order to bring justice to the situation, you must convict Michael Blagg."

It was approaching noon on Thursday by the time both attorneys had returned to their respective tables, but this time, as Judge Bottger called both men up to the bench to discuss the instructions that he was about to give to the jury, he took a moment and asked Daniels and Eisner to shake each other's hands. The trial had taken a voluminous amount of work on each side, and it had been the longest case of each man's career.

# 46

THE Blagg case had been one for Mesa County's record books. It had taken more than two thousand volunteers searching the vast canyons and crags of the county itself, followed by a near-impossible excavation of the landfill, and then nearly two years of legal wrangling just to bring it to trial. By the time the jury commenced their deliberations late on Thursday afternoon, they'd heard 26 days of testimony from 114 witnesses who had shown them 350 exhibits.

It had been one of the longest cases in memory in western Colorado, and by that measure, the fact that the jury reached its unanimous verdict the next afternoon, shortly after 2 P.M. on Friday, April 16, 2004, after taking just ten hours to debate the evidence amongst themselves, said a lot.

In the taut atmosphere of the courtroom, all eyes were on Mike, who sat at the table between David Eisner and defense investigator Pam Sharp looking as though he were deep in prayer while the verdicts were handed from the foreperson to court clerk Joyce Lawrence and then up to Judge Bottger. Bottger opened them and then started reading the first of the four sheets to the hushed gathering. "As to count one," Bottger began, "we the jury find the defendant, Michael Blagg, guilty of first-degree murder . . ."

One by one, the verdicts were read—guilty as charged—of the murder, of abusing Jennifer's corpse, of stealing items from AMETEK Dixson, and of filing a false insurance claim.

Mike sunk forward as the verdicts were read, shutting his eyes and shaking his head as Judge Bottger promptly sentenced him to the mandatory term of life in prison without parole on the murder charge.

Bottger asked Mike if he had anything he wished to say.

"I can tell you, Your Honor, that I am innocent of these charges," Mike replied. "And I have nothing more to say. Thank you."

As the judge rose to leave, Mike turned back to his mother and sister, who were reaching out to embrace him, but deputies quickly interceded. Mike's family huddled in stunned silence and wiped away tears as he was handcuffed and led quickly toward the rear of the courtroom by the deputy sheriffs on his way back to the Mesa County Jail before being turned over to the larger state prison system.

"I love you, sweetheart," Elizabeth Blagg called out as Mike reached the rear door of the courtroom.

"I love you," Mike mouthed back in the instant before the door shut.

In the foyer of the Justice Center out in front of the

courtrooms, members of Mike and Jennifer's families took time to speak to the gathered reporters, as did four of the jurors who had made the decision on Mike's fate.

"Michael Blagg is innocent of all the crimes of which he has been convicted. He is not guilty," Elizabeth Blagg insisted.

Marilyn Conway thanked the jurors for doing "the best that they could do." Asked for her thoughts on the outcome, a tearful Conway said, "For years, Michael Blagg was a son-in-law to me. I loved him. My daughter loved him, and Abby dearly loved her father. God was with us through this whole thing, and I pray that He has been with the Blagg family. We've lost a son-in-law too, and I hope the Blagg family looks to the Lord." Her voice beginning to break, she added quietly, "There's just nothing else."

Jennifer's brother David Loman, who, out of duty and devotion to both his sister and his niece, had spent so many hours searching for any sign of them across miles and miles of the western Colorado sagebrush, said the verdict had brought him peace, and he hoped the Blagg family would be able to find it too somehow, concluding, "There are no winners in any of this."

"As far as I'm concerned, he's a narcissistic pig," Frank Daniels told reporters afterward, adding, "There is no way around it, Michael Blagg is guilty of these crimes."

Eisner, standing among defense team members who were wiping away tears, noted that, because of the mandatory life sentence involved under Colorado law, an appeal of the conviction would automatically commence at the Colorado Court of Appeals in Denver. "I'm very disappointed, obviously, but I think it was stacked against us from the start," Eisner said before adding, "A little bit of me is hurt, and I think I'll always carry it with me."

Even some of the detectives were rather amazed by the speed with which the jury had wrapped up such a complicated case, especially considering that the evidence had been measured out in weeks, not days, but, an hour after the verdict was read, the four Blagg jurors who came back into the courtroom and took questions gave the press a fascinating insight into what they had been thinking during their ten hours working together.

It turned out that very little of that time was spent on deciding whether Mike was guilty. From the start of their discussion, they were all confident that he had committed the murder.

Juror Todd Hoyt explained that the deliberations had begun with a prayer and the establishment of a "swear cup" in which they would put money whenever they slipped up and used a curse word. They were up to $25 by the time they were through, and they gave the money to the bailiff, who had been looking out for them over the weeks, along with a note thanking her.

Hoyt revealed that all of the jurors had cried at times during the emotional discussions, but in the end the unanimous decisions had been easy to make, based not so much on speculation as to motive, but rather on the circumstantial evidence that had piled up against Mike throughout the investigation.

The clincher was the fact that there were only two sets of keys to the van—one on Mike's keychain, which he'd handed to the deputies who arrived after he'd called 911, and one among the items from Jennifer's purse that had been dumped out on the carpeted floor of the bedroom.

"That was the smoking gun," said Hoyt.

The hard part of the jury's deliberation was deciding whether or not it had been first- or second-degree murder in Jennifer's case, which was really the only case at which they were supposed to be looking. Using Colorado's standard, which views premeditation as requiring enough time "for one thought to follow another," the jurors struggled with whether Mike had just pulled the gun from the nightstand drawer in a moment of rage and fired, or whether there was more to it.

The clue that they felt tipped the scales was the single blue thread embedded in the tip of the hollow-point bullet. If Mike had time to gather up a pillow and place it in front of the gun in order to muffle the sound of the shot, then as far as they were concerned, he'd had time to consider and reconsider what he was doing that night—and yet he'd pulled the trigger anyway.

"The landfill was not an issue," explained juror Andrea Taylor. "We focused on the blood in the van, the keys, and the blue fiber."

The jurors said that they hadn't been put off by Blagg's demeanor during his police interviews, when the officers thought he'd been flat and unemotional. "Everybody acts differently," Hoyt noted. Ironically, however, the jurors couldn't say the same for Mike's cloying mannerisms during the trial itself.

With the exception of Hoyt, all of the jurors who spoke to the press were women, and they said they'd noticed something interesting about Blagg's friendly beaming smiles, which he'd made a point of directing toward the jury box—they were only directed at the women. Hoyt said he too had noticed that Blagg was only making eye contact with the female jurors.

Juror Mary Gonzales said she would turn away whenever he seemed to be deliberately smiling at her.

"Looking at him, it was hard to believe him," said 19-year-old Melisa Lopez. "He tried too hard to come across as a sincere man."

Taylor agreed, saying, "I felt his sincerity was tested as soon as I made eye contact with him."

The fact that Mike's efforts to project an upbeat attitude to the jurors had backfired so massively was a tremendous blow, because, as he'd noted in one of his television interviews, doing so had been a deliberate strategy.

"While they hold incredible power, they're interested in seeing me as a person, too. And I think that it's important to make the eye contact when possible," Blagg told *48 Hours*.

Jurors also noticed that Blagg had a picture of Jennifer and Abby propped up on the defense table at a conspicuous angle where they would be sure to see it. That was one thing, but when he took the time to rub it wistfully and make eyes at the female jurors, they read his actions as smacking of desperation.

"The last week, he'd look at us with despair, pleading. He was hurting," Lopez recalled. "I think he'd convinced himself he didn't do it."

On the question of Blagg's motivation for the killing, the jurors agreed with Daniels' conclusion that Jennifer was on the brink of leaving Mike, although they were not sure why.

"He was controlling," Hoyt offered.

Taylor explained, "We all thought she was about to leave him. Her books, her journals, her notations were telling you the story of their life."

Gonzales agreed that the marriage was in trouble. "If you were able to read all of her writings, the relationship was clear," she said.

The jurors at the impromptu press conference said they'd taken the issue of Mike's collection of pornography more as something that was "about his character" than as the underlying motive for the murder.

"Me being a strong Christian, shame came across with that," the 25-year-old Taylor said, going so far as to add, "Being a Christian woman, I don't believe he was Christian."

Hoyt admitted to feeling pressure because of the

tremendous emotional investment that the Grand Junction community had in the case, but he and Lopez both said that while they would have liked to have heard Mike testify, they were convinced it wouldn't have changed the outcome. "Ultimately, we'll only need to deal with it ourselves," Lopez said of the verdict.

Reacting to Eisner's concerns that Marilyn Conway might have been giving a free throw to the prosecution when she said out of the blue that Mike had hurt Jennifer in Corpus Christi a decade earlier, the jurors said they'd found her testimony to be believable, "even though she had a vested interest."

Abby had technically been beyond the scope of the trial, but the reporters wondered what, if anything, the jurors had concluded about what happened to her. "We talked about it only after the verdict," Hoyt said, adding with a shake of his head, "There's about twelve different versions."

# 47

**WHEN** the Mesa County Sheriff's Office finally had a chance to step back and look at the Blagg investigation with real hindsight, they concluded that it was not only one of the largest, longest, and most difficult cases they'd ever investigated, but also one of the strangest.

Their murderer had been right in front of them from literally the second they learned of the case, but he'd done an exceptionally clever job of ensuring that he was just about impossible to suspect, let alone catch. Yet suspect him they did, and in the end, they'd caught him by doing the just-about-impossible themselves.

Pacing back and forth in the hallways of the sheriff's office in 2001, George Barley and his team had been acutely aware that they were up against an extremely intelligent and unflappable opponent. They knew Michael

Blagg had been trained by the military to think fast, pay incredible attention to detail, and even to resist interrogation. They knew he had sailed through an arduous interview and a polygraph exam, and then stood in front of television cameras on national news shows without flinching. But as they began to suspect Mike in earnest, the sheriffs developed a phrase that quickly became their behind-the-scenes mantra for the Blagg case: Mike may be smarter than any one of us some of the time, but he's not smarter than all of us all of the time.

Michael Blagg was consigned to the larger prisons of the state of Colorado, deep in the Rocky Mountains, where he was reportedly beaten by other inmates shortly after he arrived. Because of his educational background, he quickly got a position within the prison as a librarian, and to this day he maintains his innocence and is pursuing a variety of issues through the Court of Appeals in Denver.

The members of the Soggy Bottom Gang were all given commemorative plaques for their desks, complete with a sheriff's patch and a little yellow toy excavator, in recognition of a task so above and beyond what was expected of them that there really can be no other reward than the satisfaction of having successfully done it.

"The one thing about the case that haunts the investigators the most is the thought that Abby might be out there, and she just might never be recovered," Mesa County Sheriff Riecke Claussen said following the verdict.

But the investigators also knew that in finding Jennifer, they had in essence enabled justice to proceed for both mother and daughter.

"I think Grand Junction is a safer community without Michael Blagg," Steve King said afterward. "And Heaven is a better place with Jennifer and Abby."

Perhaps the one small mercy of the horror visited upon Pine Court Terrace, and really on the entire Grand Valley community, late that night is that Jennifer Blagg never saw the gun barrel hovering over her face, and never realized that her dreams of persevering for a better tomorrow were going to end with a bullet to the head.

The girl who'd grown up desperately missing a father figure, and who took it upon herself to craft a new one, had endured the countless tribulations of both her own health problems and Mike's career difficulties trying to maintain the faith that it was all somehow going to fit into God's larger schemes. Despite her own insecurities, she was willing to put in the time, make the sacrifices, and do so with a sense of warmth and friendship that others noticed wherever she went, all because in the end, she felt the signs had been clear: Colorado was the answer. God had told her He wanted her there, at least for a couple more years.

While it's too cruel to believe that a loving God had any particular plan in November of 2001 that required Jennifer and her 6-year-old daughter to have their lifeless bodies driven side-by-side through town in an industrial Dumpster and literally thrown out with the trash, it's also too silly to believe that some devil or demon thought the whole thing up and managed to pull it off at some hour of the night when God wasn't looking.

Grand reasons and supernatural plots would actually make for far more comforting answers than the simple but bewildering truth that it was a human being who chose to shoot Jennifer Blagg in her sleep before that same human being paused, made an unspeakable decision, and walked upstairs.

It would be easier to forgive God, the Devil, or any random stranger for what happened that night in an ordinary home on an ordinary side street. But the ultimate outrage of the Blagg case was that when and where they expected to be the safest, a vulnerable woman and an innocent little girl were betrayed and murdered by the one person who they'd every right to trust would do anything to protect them from harm.